Augustus H. Strong
and the Dilemma of Historical Consciousness

Augustus H. Strong and the Dilemma of Historical Consciousness

BR
115
.H5
W33
1985

by

GRANT WACKER

MERCER
UNIVERSITY PRESS

ISBN 0-86554-169-8

Library of Congress Cataloging in Publication Data
Wacker, Grant, 1945–
Augustus H. Strong and the dilemma
of historical consciousness.

Bibliography: p. 179.
Includes index.
1. History (Theology)—History of doctrines—19th
century. 2. History (Theology)—History of doctrines—
20th century. 3. Strong, Augustus Hopkins, 1836–1921.
4. Baptists—Doctrines—History—19th century.
5. Baptists—Doctrines—History—20th century.
6. Theology, Doctrinal—United States—History—19th
century. 7. Theology, Doctrinal—United States—
History—20th century. I. Title.
BR115.H5W33   1985   230'.6131'0924 [B]   85-13744
ISBN 0-86554-169-8 (alk. paper)

Contents

for KBW—
guardian angel

Historicism arises as
a decomposition product
of Christianity.

—*Mircea Eliade*

Abbreviations

Annual Report "Report of the President," *Annual Report of the New York Baptist Union for Ministerial Education*

AB *Autobiography of Augustus Hopkins Strong*, by AHS, 1896, 1906, 1908, 1917

AHS Augustus Hopkins Strong

CCEM *Christ in Creation and Ethical Monism*, by AHS, 1899

MISC *Miscellanies*, 2 vols., by AHS, 1912

OHCT *One Hundred Chapel-Talks to Theological Students*, by AHS, 1913

PAR *Philosophy and Religion*, by AHS, 1888

PL *Popular Lectures on the Books of the New Testament*, by AHS, 1914

RTS Rochester Theological Seminary

ST *Systematic Theology*, by AHS, 1886

ST (1907) *Systematic Theology*, 8th ed., by AHS, 1907-1909

Tour *A Tour of the Missions*, by AHS, 1918

WE *Watchman-Examiner*

WSIB *What Shall I Believe?*, by AHS, 1922

Augustus Hopkins Strong

3 August 1836—29 November 1921

Education: A.B., Yale University (1857); graduate, Rochester Theological Seminary (1859).
Honorary degrees: D.D., Brown University (1870), Yale University (1890), Princeton University (1896); LL.D., Bucknell University (1891), Alfred University (1894); Litt.D., University of Rochester (1912).
Ordained: Baptist (1861).
Pastor: First Baptist Church, Haverhill MA (1861-1865); First Baptist Church, Cleveland OH (1865-1872).
President and Davies Professor of Biblical Theology: Rochester Theological Seminary (1872-1912).
President: American Baptist Foreign Mission Society (1892-1895), General Convention of Baptists of North America (1905-1910), Rochester Historical Society (1890).
Trustee: New York Baptist Union for Ministerial Education (1903-1921); Vassar College (1884-1918), Board Chairman (1906-1911).
Married: Harriet Savage (1861-1914), Marguerite Jones (1915-1921).
Children: Charles, Mary, John, Cora, Kate, Laura.

Preface

SOMEONE ONCE SAID that all good books are about one thing. For better or worse, this book is about two things: Augustus H. Strong and the dilemma of historical consciousness. In one sense it is easy to justify a study of Strong, for he was one of the most influential conservative Protestant thinkers in the United States in the late nineteenth century, and he played an important role in the fundamentalist controversy of the 1920s. In another sense, however, Strong does not deserve so much attention. Like many theologians of that era, he is now something of a dinosaur: immensely learned, immensely irrelevant.

This brings me to the second and deeper concern of the book, the dilemma of historical consciousness. As Strong grew older he became increasingly uneasy about the relation between the cardinal doctrines of Christianity and the radically historical assumptions of modern social thought. Eventually his deepening ambivalence about these matters rendered his work problematic within his lifetime and shrouded his personal and professional career in disappointment. Thus Strong's principal significance for American religious history is representative: his struggle to hold together ancient faith and modern epistemology symbolized a rupture in the religious sensibilities of the age. Strong felt the tension more acutely than most believers, but the problem itself was widespread. It bedeviled conservative religious thinkers of all kinds, including Roman Catholics, Orthodox Catholics, and Orthodox Jews. Nor was it limited to the Victorian era. In the twilight of the twentieth century the dragon of historical consciousness still roams the theological landscape, and although conservative theologians have learned to live with the beast, they are no closer to taming it—as far as I can see— than Strong was a century ago.

In some ways the author of a book is least qualified to explain why it was written. Even so, I think it is only fair to acknowledge that I was first attracted to Strong because the questions that troubled him are pretty much the same questions that trouble me. At the same time, the answers Strong eventually settled on, imperfect as they may be, are pretty much the answers that I, too, have come to accept. Not everyone will be able to appreciate this. Many readers will grasp the intellectual significance of the conflict described in this book, yet never feel any measure of personal identification with it. Those who have been un-touched—or, at least, unmoved—by the cultural pluralism of the twentieth century are not likely to see why the profound historical con-sciousness born in the nineteenth century can or should pose much of a dilemma for their faith. On the other hand, those who have given their hearts wholly to the modern world (not to mention the "postmodern" world of the semioticians) are equally unlikely to understand why any-one should feel anxiety about the issue; for them a continually evolv-ing, endlessly plastic world is the only one imaginable. But I suspect that readers like myself, who believe that the Christian faith has a mes-sage to proclaim as well as a story to tell, will find Augustus Strong's effort to reconcile the faith of the fathers with the governing assump-tions of modern culture to be both reassuringly and uncomfortably close to home.

There is a sense in which all serious books are written more by teachers and colleagues than by authors. That is particularly true of this book. My first and greatest debt is to William R. Hutchison, mentor and enduring friend. Nathan O. Hatch, Samuel S. Hill, Winthrop S. Hudson, Peter Iver Kaufman, George M. Marsden, Martin E. Marty, James H. Moorhead, Mark A. Noll, Timothy L. Smith, C. Conrad Wright, and the late Ernest R. Sandeen offered thoughtful criticism and generous encouragement. Beyond that, each has been a role model, exemplifying the kind of personal and professional integrity that I hope friends and students also see in me. Conrad E. Ostwalt tracked down countless obscure citations; Jeanne C. Chamberlin patiently typed and retyped impenetrably scrawled pages. Part of chapter nine first appeared in my article "The Holy Spirit and the Spirit of the Age in American Protestantism, 1880–1910," in *Journal of American History* 72 (June 1985). The Research Council of the University of North Carolina provided travel and publication assistance. My mother and daughters provided support of a different sort, and so did my wife, to whom this book is dedicated with deep affection. To all, I am grateful.

27 March 1985   *Grant Wacker*

The Riddle
of Augustus Strong

I N THE SPRING OF 1917 the Yale Class of 1857 held its six-
tieth annual reunion. Augustus Hopkins Strong, who had
taken to describing himself as an "octogeranium," judged the
banquet dinner of lobster and champagne superb. "We ate as if it were
our last meal on earth," he grinned, "and since we were all over eighty
years of age, it was wonderful that any of us were able to attend the
alumni dinner next day." That was fortunate, for Strong had never been
inclined to deprive himself of very many of the amenities that well-fixed
denizens of the Gilded Age commonly enjoyed. But there were limits.
Early in life he had resolved that he would never drink beer or hard li-
quor—as long as he was in the United States. "I had to draw the line
somewhere," he told his friends (the grin, presumably, growing), "and
I drew mine in the middle of the Atlantic Ocean."[1]

The six hundred pages of Strong's meticulously handwritten *Autobiography* sparkle with self-depreciating drollery of this sort. It was an

---

[1]*Tour*, 38. *AB*, 365, 207.

irrepressible feature of his personality, and probably one of the reasons that he won the devotion of colleagues and students for so many years. When Strong's long life finally came to an end in 1921, tributes poured in from around the country. The *Baptist,* official newspaper of the Northern Baptist Convention, judged him "one of the great and influential teachers of his day." George W. Taft, the powerful former editor of the Baptist *Standard,* ranked him as the preeminent theological teacher of his generation, while the *Baptist Observer,* newspaper of the Indiana State Convention, extolled his "insight into the profound depths of religious truth." For years the pillars of Princeton orthodoxy had opposed Strong's influence, but in the end they too seemed genuinely touched with grief. Speaking for the group, Caspar Wistar Hodge allowed that Strong had done a "great work." At one point hard feelings had alienated Strong and Clarence A. Barbour, his successor as president of Rochester Theological Seminary. Yet Barbour readily acknowledged that the Seminary could "never repay its debt to him." One Rochester paper surmised that his "reputation as an educator [had been] almost equalled by his fame as an author." Another predicted that Strong's work would abide when "scores of modernisms have fallen into ruin." He was, said a spokesman for the Rochester Historical Society, "one of those rare beings who can think, and of the rarer few who can see." A faculty colleague remembered Strong's "unassumed affability" and his "urbane and spontaneous graciousness of manner." The *Watchman-Examiner,* largest and most influential Baptist newspaper in the North, undoubtedly summed up the views of many when it noted, simply, that Strong had been "tenderly loved and highly honored."[2]

---

[2]Arthur W. Cleaves[?], "A Great Leader Has Passed," *Baptist* (10 December 1921): 1422; George W. Taft, "Augustus H. Strong," *Baptist* (10 December 1921): 1420; "Immortality of Influence," *Baptist Observer* (22 December 1921): 2; Caspar Wistar Hodge, review of *WSIB, Princeton Theological Review* 20 (1922): 681; Clarence A. Barbour, *RTS Bulletin* [71] (November 1921): frontispiece; "Dr. Augustus H. Strong," *Democrat and Chronicle* (Rochester NY), 30 November 1921; *Post Express* (Rochester NY), quoted in "Dr. Strong's Last Work," *WE* (8 December 1921): 1551; "An Appreciation Presented before . . . the Rochester Historical Society," *RTS Bulletin* [72] (supplement, May 1922): 47; John P. Silvernail, "Dr. Strong in Relation to His Fellow Faculty Members," *RTS Bulletin* [72] (supplement, May 1922): 15; "Dr. Augustus H. Strong," *WE* (8 December 1921): 1549. See also "Dr. Strong Called Home,"

But there was another side to Augustus Strong. He admitted that he resented the "infelicity" of old friends who continued to call him Gus after he became president of Rochester Theological Seminary. Even as a young pastor he had, he remembered, deplored "women who, either from imperfect training or too great warmth of temperament, were prone to demonstrate their liking for [me] in unpleasant ways. More than once the grasp of the hand seemed too affectionate, and I was compelled to draw back with a dignity which had in it something of a rebuke." Since childhood, Strong added, he had felt an "instinctive repugnance"—we can almost see the arched eyebrow—for the "freedoms which to polite and educated people seem only rude and vulgar."[3]

Measured reflections such as these rightly hint that there was considerable flint in Strong's personality. Contemporaries repeatedly described him with terms such as courtly, grave, and aristocratic. One lifelong friend remembered that Strong almost never had been seen in shirt sleeves. Another spoke of Strong's lethal wit, yet added that he never had been known to indulge in "unrestrained laughter." Relentless work habits and cast-iron willfulness filled the memories of those who had known him. "Ceaseless and tireless toil," was the cornerstone of Strong's life, said Clarence Barbour. He held himself with "stern and resistless determination to the accomplishment of the exacting tasks which he prescribed for himself." Others were more pointed—sometimes much more pointed. William Arnold Stevens, another lifelong friend and colleague, wryly remembered that Strong did not tire and could not sympathize with "ordinary mortals who did." In the eyes of one chronicler of the seminary's history, his "regnant will" had been the "controlling influence" throughout.[4] Although Strong prided himself

---

Baptist Banner (15 December 1921): 6; John B. Calvert, "Dr. Strong, the Scholar and Friend," *WE* (22 December 1921): 1623; Augustine S. Carman, "The Legacy of a Life," *Baptist* (10 December 1921): 1420; S. Fraser Langford, "The Gospel of Augustus H. Strong and Walter Rauschenbusch," *Chronicle* 14 (1951): 9.

[3] *AB*, 240, 200. See also the measured words of Strong's grandson, Richard B. Sewall, an English professor at Yale, in a foreword to the *AB* (19).

[4] J. Heinrichs, "Dr. Strong and Foreign Missions," *WE* (8 December 1921): 1622; Langford, "Gospel of Augustus Strong," 9; Clarence A. Barbour, "An Address," *RTS Bulletin* [72] (supplement May 1922): 8. Stevens is quoted in George W. Taft, "Two Remarkable Men and Their Books," *Standard* (18 January 1913): 578. See also Augustine S. Carman, "A Great Theological Quintet," *RTS Record* 7 (May 1912): 26-27.

on openness of mind and on an ability to cultivate freewheeling inquiry in the classroom, not everyone saw him that way. George Taft remembered Strong's classroom style as imposing and aggressive. "Doctor Strong sees the other man," Taft recalled, "but does not give him a fighting chance . . . He dominates most of his pupils while they are with him and sometimes for years after they have left his class-room." As president of the seminary, Taft added, Strong was "autocratic and absolute . . . dogmatic in manner and positive in statement." There is, perhaps, more than meets the eye in the remark of the seminary dean, some years after Strong's death, that he might well have burst out: " 'The Seminary! I am the Seminary!' . . . and all who knew would have approved."[5]

Lovable and autocratic, affable and grave—all of these labels fit. Augustus Strong's personality was not simple, nor was any other aspect of his life. His faculty appointments, his denominational alliances, even the friends he chose, defy categorization. Strong hired liberals such as Conrad Henry Moehlman, Cornelius Woelfkin, and Walter Rauschenbusch, yet he also hired rockribbed conservatives such as Howard Osgood and Albert Henry Newman.[6] He vigorously defended Rauschenbusch's right to assail the capitalist system yet just as vigorously solicited endowments from John D. Rockefeller and other robber barons.[7] He was a devout churchman who attended church three times

---

[5]However, Taft elsewhere qualified these statements and indicated that on balance Strong had been well-liked ("Two Remarkable Men," 577-78). Stewart, "More Recent Days, 1912-1925," *RTS Bulletin* [75] (May 1925): 45. The influence of Strong's will on the seminary hardly can be overstated. When he retired in 1912 the *Watchman* editorialized: "He has selected the faculty, shaped the courses of study, and his relatives and friends have built the seminary buildings. It is, therefore, no extreme use of language . . . to say that what Rochester Theological Seminary is today is chiefly the result of Dr. Strong's labors." "Rochester Theological Seminary," *Watchman* (May 1912): 9.

[6]The theological diversity at RTS is described by LeRoy Moore, Jr., "The Rise of American Religious Liberalism at Rochester Theological Seminary, 1872-1928" (Ph.D. dissertation, Claremont Graduate School, 1966) 41-45 and chap. 3.

[7]"Report of the Presidents," *Annual Report of the New York Baptist Union for Ministerial Education* (1907) 33. Letter from Walter Rauschenbusch to George Cross, 5 June 1912, quoted in LeRoy Moore, Jr., "Academic Freedom," *Foundations* 10 (1967): 71. Conrad Henry Moehlman, "Walter Rauschenbusch and His Interpreters," *Crozer Quarterly* 23 (1946): 39. Frederick Grant Lewis, "The Presidency of Dr. Augustus Hopkins Strong," *RTS Bulletin* [75] (May 1925): 31-32.

a week, taught Sunday school class, and conducted a daily devotional at the seminary for the better part of forty years. He was also a shrewd man of the world who amassed a modest personal fortune and an enviable track record as fundraiser for the seminary.[8] Strong consistently championed home missions among the poor—once declining a call from New York's prestigious Madison Avenue Church because of its reluctance to establish an inner city mission—and advocated progressive reforms such as ordination, suffrage, and graduate education for women. At the same time, he was an uncompromising elitist. He derided the socialist schemes of "longhaired men and shorthaired women," and he seems never to have felt a twinge of guilt over his own conspicuously comfortable lifestyle.[9] Strong counted New Theologians such as Elisha Mulford and Theodore Munger among his closest friends, yet cherished his ties with conservative scholars such as Alvah Hovey and holiness leaders such as A. J. Gordon.[10] George Burman Foster, the most radical Baptist theologian of the day, always considered himself one of Strong's "boys." J. Whitcomb Brougher, a major force in the fundamentalist explosion that rocked the last years of Strong's life, was also one of his "boys." In 1917 Rauschenbusch lovingly dedicated his *Theology for the Social Gospel* to Strong. Shortly afterward Ernest Gordon, in a bruising attack on theological liberalism, raised Strong's work as a standard of orthodoxy that individuals like Rauschenbusch had grievously betrayed.[11]

Perhaps the greatest incongruity of Strong's life is, however, the contrast between the influence he once enjoyed and the obscurity that now shrouds his work. At the turn of the century he was one of the most visible churchmen in the United States. In addition to reigning over Rochester Theological Seminary for four decades, he was at one time or another president of the American Baptist Foreign Mission Union,

---

[8]*AB,* 118. AHS 1918 diary. *MISC* 1:152-59.

[9]*AB,* 201-203. AHS, "The Baptist Social Union," November 1892, and "Alumni Reception for Pres. Hill," 27 January 1890, unpublished addresses, American Baptist Historical Society.

[10]*AB, passim,* but especially 124-26. *CCEM,* 181-83, 298.

[11]Walter Rauschenbusch, *A Theology for the Social Gospel* (New York: Macmillan, 1917) v; Ernest Gordon, *The Leaven of the Sadducees* (Chicago: Bible Institute Colportage Association, 1926) 189.

American Baptist Education Society, General Convention of Baptists of North America, and chairman of the Board of Trustees of Vassar College. The University of Rochester and Alfred, Brown, Bucknell, Princeton, and Yale Universities awarded him honorary doctorates. Yet these achievements pale beside his *Systematic Theology,* which saw eight editions and may well have been the most widely read theology textbook in the major Protestant seminaries. In sum, among scholars of American religious history, both then and now, there has never been any doubt that Strong was one of the preeminent conservative Protestant theologians of the period.[12] Today, however, he rarely rates a footnote. The works of rivals to the left, such as William Newton Clarke and William Porcher DuBose, and rivals to the right, such as Charles Porterfield Krauth and Benjamin B. Warfield, continue to draw loyal readers who find them historically interesting and theologically perceptive. But by and large, the musty pages of Strong's books now lie quietly entombed in the basements of seminary libraries. That recent liberal and radical theologians would ignore Strong is hardly surprising; that recent conservative—indeed, conservative Baptist—theologians would ignore him is a measure of the obscurity into which he has fallen.[13]

---

[12]For Strong's influence see Sydney E. Ahlstrom, ed., *Theology in America* (Indianapolis: Bobbs-Merrill, 1967) 15; Leo Crismon, "The Literature of the Baptists," *Religion in Life* 25 (1955-1956): 130; Carl F. H. Henry, *Personal Idealism and Strong's Theology* (Wheaton IL: Van Kampen Press, 1951) preface, 11, 13, 228; Winthrop S. Hudson, *Baptists in Transition* (Valley Forge PA: Judson Press, 1979) 127-37, and *Religion in America* 3d ed., rev. (New York: Scribner's, 1981) 279, 370; George M. Marsden, *Fundamentalism and American Culture* (New York: Oxford University Press, 1980) 107; Mark A. Noll, "Evangelical Theology and the Life of the Mind," in John D. Woodbridge, et al., *The Gospel in America* (Grand Rapids MI: Zondervan, 1979) 68; Henry Burke Robins, "The Literary Contribution of Rochester Alumni," *RTS Bulletin* [75] (May 1925): 156; Gerald Birney Smith, "Theological Thinking in America," in Smith, ed., *Religious Thought in the Last Quarter-Century* (Chicago: University of Chicago Press, 1927) 97.

[13]Strong receives, for example, only a nod in Bruce A. Demarest, *General Revelation* (Grand Rapids MI: Zondervan, 1982) 229, 234, 249, and no mention at all in Bernard Ramm, *After Fundamentalism: The Future of Evangelical Theology* (San Francisco: Harper and Row, 1983).

There is little wonder, then, that Strong has puzzled his interpreters—or perhaps it would be more precise to say that his interpreters have persistently differed among themselves about where and how he should be pegged on the theological map. Current opinion tends to place him in one of four categories. One view is that he was an early fundamentalist, albeit irenic and consistently open-minded, but nonetheless a fundamentalist.[14] A second view is that he was a conservative in the true sense of the term: a man of catholic interests who sought to preserve the essentials of the Reformed theological heritage in the modern world.[15] A third view is that he is best understood as a mediator between liberalism and orthodoxy. These interpreters see him as one who tried to reconcile modernists and fundamentalists by urging a judicious accommodation with modern science and by insisting on the authority but not necessarily the inerrancy of Scripture.[16] The fourth view is that

---

[14]Kenneth S. Kantzer, for example, groups Strong with very conservative Reformed thinkers such as Cornelius Van Til and Carl F. H. Henry ("Unity and Diversity in Evangelical Faith," in David F. Wells and John D. Woodbridge, eds., *The Evangelicals* [Nashville TN: Abingdon Press, 1975] 47-48). See also Alan Gragg, *George Burman Foster* (Danville VA: Baptist Professors of Religion, 1978) 38-45, and Richard J. Storr, *Harper's University: The Beginnings* (Chicago: University of Chicago Press, 1966) 19.

[15]LeRoy Moore takes this position. He admits that Strong entered a reactionary phase late in life, and that his progressiveness was always obscured by a "rigid, scholastic framework." On balance, however, Moore sees in Strong the best of historic orthodoxy. Moore also suggests that fundamentalists eventually claimed Strong, not because they really understood or shared his concerns, but because his eminence conferred respectability ("Religious Liberalism," iv, 52, 62, 157, 263). Frank Hugh Foster gives a similar evaluation of Strong in *The Modern Movement in American Theology: Sketches in the History of American Protestant Thought from the Civil War to the World War* (Freeport NY: Books for Libraries Press, 1969 [1939]) 196.

[16]This third view is most common. Winthrop S. Hudson, George M. Marsden, and Mark A. Noll, for example, emphasize Strong's openness to contemporary philosophy and science but also note that by the turn of the century he had become alarmed by the increasingly naturalistic assumptions of Protestant liberals. Crerar Douglas, following Hudson's suggestion that Strong played a mediatorial role in the United States similar to P. T. Forsyth's role in Britain, likens Strong not to great "party leaders" such as Luther and Calvin, but to "great mediators" such as Erasmus and Melancthon. Norman Maring and Donald Tinder likewise picture Strong's work as an

Strong really was, ultimately, a closet liberal hiding behind the garments of apparent orthodoxy. These last interpreters suggest that his growing affinity for modern philosophical trends, and particularly evolutionary models of explanation, shows that Rochester really was more than halfway to Chicago.[17]

One reason why Strong's readers have argued so much about him is because he seems to have wandered a good deal on the theological landscape. Many believed that he took a step to the left in the 1890s, followed by two steps to the right in 1920s. Later we shall see that the major centers of review criticism, ranging from Baylor and Princeton at one end to Union and Chicago at the other, were again and again perplexed by the apparent quirks in his thinking. After Strong's death Conrad Moehlman observed that, although Strong had always been "very

---

effort to preserve historic orthodoxy with the methods and language of modern scholarship. See Hudson, *Baptists,* 131-37, and *Religion,* 279; Noll, "Evangelical Theology," 68-69, 119; Marsden, *Fundamentalism,* 107-108, 165; Douglas, "The Cost of Mediation," *Congregational Quarterly* 3 (1978): 28-35, and "The Hermeneutics of Augustus Hopkins Strong," *Foundations* 21 (1978): 74-75; Maring, "Baptists and Changing Views of the Bible," *Foundations* 1 (July 1958): 39-40; Tinder, "Fundamentalist Baptists in the Northern and Western United States" (Ph.D. dissertation, Yale University, 1969) 106-107. Briefer or less helpful studies that also cast Strong as mediator include Roland Tenus Nelson, "Fundamentalism in the Northern Baptist Convention" (Ph.D. dissertation, University of Chicago, 1964) 312-13; Irwin Reist, "Augustus Hopkins Strong and William Newton Clarke," *Foundations* 13 (1970): 28-35; Kenneth Cauthen, *The Impact of American Religious Liberalism* (New York: Harper and Row, 1962) 31.

[17]Carl F. H. Henry concludes, for example, that Strong's theology was weakened by "halfness and hesitancy" because he tried to build traditional doctrinal positions on post-Kantian premises. Henry Warner Bowden characterizes Strong as a "vigorous, independent mind" whose main effort was to emphasize the immanence of Christ. Herbert W. Schneider and Francis P. Weisenburger label him, without qualification, as a liberal. Fundamentalist historian George W. Dollar not surprisingly charges that Strong, despite good intentions, consorted with the liberal enemy and "thereby prepared the way for the downfall of his seminary." See Henry, *Personal Idealism,* 229; Bowden, *Dictionary of American Religious Biography,* s.v. "Strong, Augustus Hopkins"; Schneider, *Religion in Twentieth Century America* (Cambridge MA: Harvard University Press, 1952) 117-18; Weisenburger, *Ordeal of Faith: The Crisis of Church-Going America 1865-1900* (New York: Philosophical Library, 1959) 100, 152; Dollar, *History of Fundamentalism in America* (Greenville SC: Bob Jones University Press, 1973) 364, 146.

positive," the expansive posture of the 1890s was sandwiched between periods of—as Moehlman euphemistically put it—"thought conservatism." Other serious students of Strong's work, such as Carl F. H. Henry and LeRoy Moore, Jr., have similarly argued that there were distinct stages in his development—but, not surprisingly, Henry and Moore draw lines entirely differently.[18]

Each of these interpretations has merit. Yet when they are taken together Strong begins to resemble the Giant Pooka in Mary Chase's *Harvey,* appearing "here and there, now and then, to this one and that one at his own caprice." This elusiveness is the tip-off that the real reason that Strong is difficult to assess is not because his creedal formulations were inconsistent but because his epistemic assumptions were. The stress is not in his massive doctrinal system, but beneath the system, in the shadowy underworld of suppositions about the origin and nature of religious knowledge itself.

II

Until long after the Civil War most Americans seem to have assumed, if they thought about it at all, that the really important truths about God and mankind and society had been directly revealed by God himself. Perhaps some eternal verities had been discovered through reflection or careful induction, but certainly none had simply been invented by human beings in the course of history. In the minds of many well-educated Protestants, the distinction between immutable truth and historical flux was hardened by a cluster of assumptions and ideas that might be called "orthodox rationalism." There was no substantial doctrinal difference between sixteenth-century evangelical Protestantism and nineteenth-century orthodox rationalism, but the latter was, as we shall see, more smug in its attitudes, more apologetic in its purposes, and more self-conscious about its epistemic premises. Orthodox rationalism formed the core of mainstream—and especially Reformed—Protestant thought in the United States throughout most of the nineteenth

---

[18]Conrad Henry Moehlman, "Dr. Strong as Teacher," *RTS Bulletin* [72] (supplement May 1922): 19; Henry, *Personal Idealism,* 13, 15-16; Moore, "Religious Liberalism," 46-154. See also William Carey Morey, "Reminiscences of 'The Club' in Morey, ed., *The Club: 1854-1937* (Rochester NY: n.p., 1938) 24-25.

century, and flourished with particular vigor in the old line colleges and seminaries. What is most important about this tradition in the context of this study is that it powerfully sanctioned the commonsense supposition that all sane people perceive and think about the external world in pretty much the same way—which meant that there was little reason to believe that the processes of history had significantly differed from time to time or from place to place.[19]

In the 1880s and 1890s, however, an intellectual earthquake rumbled through the foundations of Western social thought. One by one the most advanced thinkers in each of the social disciplines became acutely conscious of the historical origin of culture. This is to say that they came to see that all creations of the human mind and heart are products of the historical process that fashioned them; that all ideas, values, institutions, and behavior patterns known to human beings are produced by human beings, and therefore bear the imprint of the historical setting in which they emerge. The starkness of this new, or at least new degree of, historical consciousness was captured by Justice Oliver Wendell Holmes's dictum that the law, which for centuries had been thought to embody timeless principles of justice, is, in fact only a shrewd prediction of what a judge will do next. The same unflinching relativism was expressed in sociology by Max Weber, in philosophy by John Dewey, in history by James Harvey Robinson, in political science by Charles Beard, in anthropology by Franz Boas. A few scholars of eminence, such as William James, were reluctant to take the notion to its logical limits, and some who did, such as Ernst Troeltsch, seemingly left the back gate ajar for the reentry of ideal values. But the trend was

---

[19]The literature on the development and influence of Protestant orthodox rationalism in the United States in the nineteenth century is recent, but it is sturdy and continues to grow. Especially important studies include Theodore Dwight Bozeman, *Protestants in an Age of Science* (Chapel Hill: University of North Carolina Press, 1977); Elizabeth Flower and Murray G. Murphy, *A History of Philosophy in America* (New York: G. P. Putnam's Sons, 1977) I, chap. 4; J. David Hoeveler, Jr., *James McCosh and the Scottish Intellectual Tradition* (Princeton NJ: Princeton University Press, 1981) esp. chaps. 4-5; E. Brooks Holifield, *The Gentlemen Theologians* (Durham NC: Duke University Press, 1978); Marsden, *Fundamentalism,* chaps. 6, 13, 24; D. H. Meyer, *The Instructed Conscience* (Philadelphia: University of Pennsylvania Press, 1972); and Conrad Wright, *The Liberal Christians* (Boston: Beacon Press, 1970) chap. 1.

inexorable. By 1921, when Augustus Strong died, the assumption that all knowledge, including all forms of religious knowledge, is fashioned wholly from the materials of human history, had come to be the hallmark of the modern mind.[20]

It is difficult to overestimate the impact of historical consciousness on religious thought in the West. It could be argued that late nineteenth-century Protestant liberalism was defined by its sympathetic response to the historical understanding of society and culture. Liberals made their peace with modernity in various ways, but in the end they all insisted that God's self-revelation is mediated through the flow of history. For Protestant conservatives, on the other hand, the story was quite different. Since the Reformation, most people had quietly, and probably quite unself-consciously, assumed that the core of God's self-revelation had somehow bypassed the process of history. Ironically, perhaps, assumptions that had been merely implicit in the sixteenth century became quite explicit in the nineteenth century, especially in the United States. Here conservative Protestant thinkers sculpted the cornerstone of orthodox rationalism by insisting that saving knowledge of divine things had been given to human beings directly, unmediated and uncontaminated by the historical context in which it was received. This presupposed of course, that the biblical writers had been essentially ahistorical figures, enabled by the Holy Spirit to transcend their social and cultural settings in order to articulate truths of timeless and universal validity. This meant that revelation was subject to clarification but not real development. Indeed, the conviction that God's self-revelation has not been significantly shaped by the particularities of time

---

[20]The literature is vast. Some of the more useful studies include H. Stuart Hughes, *Consciousness and Society* (New York: Random House, 1958); Georg G. Iggers, *The German Conception of History* (Middletown CT: Wesleyan University Press, 1968); Maurice Mandelbaum, *History, Man, and Reason* (Baltimore: Johns Hopkins University Press, 1971); Henry F. May, *The End of American Innocence* (Chicago: Quadrangle Paperbacks, 1964 [1959]); Edward A. Purcell, Jr., *The Crisis of Democratic Theory* (Lexington: University Press of Kentucky, 1973); Hayden White, *Tropics of Discourse* (Baltimore: Johns Hopkins University Press, 1978) esp. chap. 4; Morton White, *Social Thought in America* (Boston: Beacon Press, 1957 [1947]); Robert H. Wiebe, *The Search for Order* (New York: Hill and Wang, 1967) chap. 6.

and place has been one of the most prominent features of conservative Protestant ideology from the 1920s to the present.[21]

The picture is, however, more complicated than this. Many thoughtful men and women were torn between the ahistorical world of orthodox rationalism and the historically informed world of Protestant liberalism. They steadfastly refused to give up the quiet certitudes of the old time religion, but at the same time they knew that they could not ignore the powerful critique that the growing historical consciousness of the age had mounted against all formal, historically disembodied systems of thought. In the end this ambivalence about the ground rules of religious belief left these figures reaching for modernity, but never quite willing to embrace it.

Viewed from this perspective, the quirks in Augustus Strong's thinking begin to make sense. In this study I contend that Strong is best understood as a tragic figure, forced to choose between incompatible yet, in his judgement, equally cogent conceptual worlds. On one side he never trimmed, much less denied, the cardinal doctrines of evangelical theology. Although he veered a bit from the received tradition when he amplified the meaning of certain points (notably the

---

[21]For Protestant liberalism see Sydney E. Ahlstrom, *A Religious History of the American People* (New Haven CT: Yale University Press, 1972) 772-74; Langdon Gilkey, "Social and Intellectual Sources of Contemporary Protestant Theology," in William G. McLoughlin and Robert N. Bellah, eds., *Religion in America* (Boston: Beacon Press, 1968) esp. 139-40; William R. Hutchison, *The Modernist Impulse in American Protestantism* (Cambridge MA: Harvard University Press, 1976) esp. 2; Claude Welch, *Protestant Thought in the Nineteenth Century* (New Haven: Yale University Press) chap. 7. For Protestant conservatism see Marsden, *Fundamentalism,* 110-14, 225-27; Richard J. Coleman, *Issues of Theological Warfare* (Grand Rapids MI: Eerdmans, 1972) 22, 34, 52-56, 73, 87; Willis B. Glover, *Evangelical Nonconformists and Higher Criticism in the Nineteenth Century* (London: Independent Press, 1954) 80, 106; Jack B. Rogers and Donald K. McKim, *The Authority and Interpretation of the Bible* (New York: Harper and Row, 1979) chaps. 5-6; Ernest R. Sandeen, *The Roots of Fundamentalism* (Chicago: University of Chicago Press, 1970) 268. I do not mean to suggest that during this period (roughly 1870-1920) American Protestantism could be cleanly bifurcated between liberals and conservatives. Aside from the fact that neither of these groups was theologically homogeneous, it should be stressed that some of the largest Protestant families—Lutherans, Anabaptists, blacks, Pentecostals, some Wesleyans, and various immigrant groups—were not fractured at all, or were fractured along different lines and over totally different issues than the traditionally Reformed bodies.

atonement), no one has ever questioned Strong's essential traditional-ism on issues such as the deity, incarnation, virgin birth, miracles, vi-carious atonement, resurrection, and personal return of Jesus Christ. Moreover, for Strong, like most orthodox rationalists of the nineteenth century, the timeless and universal validity of these doctrines was but-tressed by the assumption that the biblical writers, like all sane per-sons, had conformed their minds to fit the plain deliverances of their senses, rather than the reverse. There was, in other words, no plausible reason to doubt the testimony of the senses. The problem is that some-where along the way Strong discovered that history, as Kenneth Clark has said, "is ourselves." At first only dimly conscious of the historicity of culture, he gradually came to see that creeds, like all human artifacts, are products of history. Thus, in the end, the doctrinal superstructure of Strong's thought was left precariously suspended in midair as the cor-nerstone—his conception of the origin of religious knowledge, and more exactly, his growing awareness of the role of historical conditioning in the formation of such knowledge—shifted ground.[22]

It would be an overstatement to say that Strong's perception of the link between religious knowledge and historical process constantly deepened as he grew older. At almost any point in his life we can isolate assumptions about these matters that were unclear at best and simplis-tic at worst. Still, in the long run, his thinking did acquire a degree of historical awareness rarely seen in conservative scholars. For a time he seems not to have discerned how a system originally forged in the ahis-torical world of orthodox rationalism would be imperiled by acceptance of historical assumptions and methods. But with the passage of years the dimensions of the dilemma became painfully clear. To the end he clung to the conviction that the faith once delivered unto the fathers somehow stands above the vicissitudes of history, even as he became in-creasingly conscious that all things human are fragile creations of time and place.

The immediate aim of this study is, then, simply to tell the story of Augustus Strong. It is, I think, a story of enduring interest. For many thoughtful men and women, both then and now, to discover the real

---

[22]The doctrinal superstructure of Strong's theology is meticulously described in Henry, *Personal Idealism*.

meaning of historical process remains a profoundly disquieting experience.

Beyond this, the larger aims of this study are threefold. The first is to suggest that Strong's dilemma was not unique. A generation of Protestant ministers were nurtured in his classroom and cut their theological teeth on his textbook. These ministers left few records of their thoughts, yet available evidence leaves little doubt that each Sunday they passed along the same intellectual perplexities that troubled Strong. Moreover, the principal casualties of the modernist-fundamentalist controversy of the 1920s were not, as is often assumed, the moderates who sought a peaceful compromise. The real victims were intellectually deracinated figures like Strong, who determined to preach the old-fashioned gospel even though they were increasingly certain that knowledge of divine things is not given from above but forged from below.

The second of the larger aims is to show, or help to show, that the conflict between orthodox rationalism and the modern world was not basically a dispute about doctrine, but a dispute about underlying epistemic assumptions. George Marsden has demonstrated that the wrangling between modernists and fundamentalists was, in the final analysis, a confrontation between rival epistemologies. I hope to amplify Marsden's analysis by showing that orthodox rationalism was and is intrinsically ahistorical. While various historians of Protestant thought have emphasized the plasticity of the Protestant tradition, this study, like Marsden's, stresses the essential incompatibility between the dominant nineteenth-century form of that tradition and the deepest assumptions of modern culture.[23]

The third of the larger aims is to illumine the glacial confrontation between orthodox rationalism and historical consciousness in American

---

[23]George M. Marsden has argued this point in several publications, most forcefully in "J. Gresham Machen, History, and Truth," *Westminster Theological Journal*, 42 (1979): 157-75; "Everyone One's Own Interpreter?" in Nathan O. Hatch and Mark A. Noll, eds., *The Bible in America* (New York: Oxford University Press, 1982) 79-100; and "The Collapse of American Evangelical Academia," in Alvin Plantinga and Nicholas Wolterstorff, eds., *Faith and Rationality* (Notre Dame IN: University of Notre Dame Press, 1983) 219-64. The plasticity of Protestant thought is emphasized in Hutchison, *Modernist Impulse,* and B. A. Gerrish, *Tradition and the Modern World* (Chicago: University of Chicago Press, 1978).

culture. In the last decade at least a dozen monographs have described the pervasiveness of orthodox rationalism in nineteenth-century civilization. And of course numerous works have charted the surge of historical awareness that overtook all branches of social thought between 1880 and 1930. However, none of these studies has systematically traced the tremors that resulted from the collision of those alien worlds. I have not attempted a systematic description either, but I have tried to address these questions in a more selective fashion by placing one man's inner war in a larger cultural context.

Perry Miller once remarked that the edifice of notions I have called orthodox rationalism "crumbled rapidly after 1870, and by 1890 had disappeared—except as it might survive in the dogmatic assurances of politicians and preachers."[24] The persistence of orthodox rationalism among thoughtful and well-educated Protestants in the 1980s—not to mention the vitality of its sociological cousin, evangelicalism, among ordinary church folk—is evidence enough that Miller was less than precise. But the more important point his comment obscures is that for individuals such as Strong the confrontation with modernity was both exhilarating and frightening—and never satisfactorily resolved. It is quite true that Strong ultimately patched together a workable accommodation between inherited doctrine and the modern world. But it was just that: an accommodation, a forced marriage unsoftened by the romance of genuine attraction. In the final analysis his work is, I think, best described as an uneasy and, in the exact meaning of the term, tragic effort to hold incompatible worlds together. Still, this is precisely why Strong may be more relevant than many of the better-known figures of that era who headed straight left, or straight right, and never looked back. Uncertain pilgrims are sometimes more useful than clear-eyed prophets.

III

"When I make a word work a lot," Humpty Dumpty remarked to Alice, "I always pay it extra." It may be prudent to take Humpty Dumpty's advice to heart and offer working definitions for several of the terms that figure prominently in this study. All have been used in other

---

[24]Perry Miller, ed., *American Thought* (San Francisco: Rinehart Press, 1954) xi.

ways, so I stress that in this book they mean only what they are here defined to mean.

Historical consciousness and *historical awareness* are used interchangeably to suggest substantial or complete acceptance of a philosophical orientation technically known as historicism. Historicism denotes, in turn, three closely related assumptions about the relation between history and knowledge. The first is that everything people know, including all they understand or think they understand about God's dealings with human beings, is forged in a particular historical setting and bears the unique imprint of that setting. The second assumption is that all cultural forms can be adequately explained by reference to the historical context in which they emerge. The third assumption is that all creations of the human spirit are swept along in a process of ceaseless change, governed by functional laws of social development, but not by any sort of preordained destiny.[25]

It is important to add that in this study historical consciousness (or awareness) does not necessarily imply interest in the past, much less a desire to read about the past in history books. Conversely, one might be keenly interested in the past, and conceivably know a great deal about certain events in the past, such as the American Civil War, and yet have little or no awareness of the radically contextual origin of all human phenomena.

Another important distinction is the difference between lack of historical consciousness (or ahistoricism) on one hand, and historylessness, which Sidney E. Mead and others have written about. Lack of historical

---

[25]The literature on the concept of historicism is extensive. The most helpful synthesis is in the *Dictionary of the History of Ideas*, s.v. "Historicism," by Georg G. Iggers. This article includes a handy bibliography of primary and secondary materials. Other concise and useful treatments include *Dictionary of the History of Ideas*, s.v. "Determinism in History," by Alan Donagan; *The Encyclopedia of Philosophy*, s.v. "Historicism," by Maurice Mandelbaum; Dwight E. Lee and Robert N. Beck, "The Meaning of 'Historicism,' " *American Historical Review* 59 (1954): 568-77; Iggers, *German Conception of History*, 4-13, 287-90; Hans Meyerhoff, ed., *The Philosophy of History in Our Time* (Garden City: Doubleday, 1959) 9-18. The German term *Historismus* is correctly rendered in English as historism, and that is how it generally appeared until the 1930s, when it was displaced by historicism. The latter apparently entered English usage as a translation not of *Historismus* but of Croce's *storicismo;* see Lee and Beck, "Meaning of Historicism," 568n.

consciousness and historylessness often turn up together, but they are analytically distinct. The former is an epistemic category that suggests a disinclination to acknowledge the historical origin of human phenomena. Historylessness, on the other hand, is a normative category that suggests that knowledge of the past, however it may have been derived, is simply irrelevant to the present. In (supposedly) historyless movements like the Churches of Christ and the Latter-day Saints, the main aim is not to sever the epistemic link between history and knowledge but to deny the authority of the past—or at least most of the past—over the life of the church today and tomorrow.[26]

Finally I should note that in this study the word history generally does not refer to the written record of the past, nor to the academic discipline devoted to learning about the past. Rather it denotes the fluid social process that produces culture. More precisely, history is understood as the continuous stream of social and cultural forms that historical consciousness presupposes and, in a very real sense, calls into existence.

A second, quite different set of terms that require working definitions are *evangelicalism, orthodox rationalism,* and *fundamentalism.* Evangelicalism denotes the conviction, rooted in the Protestant Reformation of the sixteenth century, and characteristic of most Protestants until the twentieth century, that the sole authority in religion is the Bible and the sole means of salvation is a life-transforming experience wrought by the Holy Spirit through faith in Jesus Christ. Orthodox rationalism is used in a more restricted fashion. It refers, first and most obviously, to the body of Reformed doctrine summarized for Episcopalians, for example, in the Thirty-Nine Articles, for Presbyterians in the Westminster Confession, for Congregationalists in the Saybrook Platform, and for Baptists in the New Hampshire Confession. Beyond that it refers to a cluster of epistemic assumptions and ideas that were peculiarly characteristic of Victorian Protestants, especially in the United States. I have already indicated the nature of some of these assumptions and ideas, and more will be said about them in the following chapters. At

---

[26]For the concept of historylessness see Sidney E. Mead, *The Lively Experiment* (New York: Harper and Row, 1963) 108-113, and Samuel S. Hill, "A Typology of American Restitutionism," *Journal of the American Academy of Religion* 44 (1976): 65-76.

this point it is necessary only to add that in this study the adjective orthodox and the noun orthodoxy denote these cornerstones of nineteenth
century Protestant thought. Fundamentalism is used in a still more restricted fashion to designate the militant emphasis on the inerrancy of
the Bible and the deity and miracles of Jesus Christ that emerged in the
early twentieth century in opposition to theological modernism. While
evangelicalism, orthodox rationalism, and fundamentalism have been
used quite precisely, I have employed the labels "conservative" and
"liberal" much more loosely to designate comparative proximity to
evangelical, orthodox, or fundamentalist versions of the Protestant tradition at a given point in history.

Overall, I should emphasize that throughout this book all of these
terms are used descriptively rather than normatively. This is to say that
they designate beliefs, attitudes, and behavior patterns that were, in a
particular time and place, commonly considered evangelical, orthodox,
fundamentalist, conservative, or liberal. In another setting the labels
might well be different.

Finally, it may be appropriate to say a few words about method.
Several years ago I would have readily described this study as foray into
the history of religious ideas in America. In the meantime methodol-
ogies drawn from cultural anthropology and the history of religions have
made the boundaries of intellectual and religious history difficult to pin
down. Nonetheless, I still think that a work of this sort is best described as a study of the career of two recurring clusters of thought—
what Arthur O. Lovejoy aptly called "unit-ideas." More precisely, this
book is an examination of the way that one unit-idea—namely, the
ahistorical origin of religious knowledge—was inexorably, but never
wholly, displaced by another unit-idea—namely, the radically historical origin of religious knowledge. Sometimes these unit-ideas were so
deeply embedded that they functioned as unrecognized presuppositions. Sometimes they were so obtrusive that they functioned as ideological banners. Most often, however, they had an intermediate status
that might be called working assumptions or operative principles. The
clash between these two unit-ideas is evident in many kinds of religious
materials of the period—hymns, autobiographies, novels, philosophical treatises, works of popular piety, even, perhaps, church architec-
ture. But because these notions collided in an exceptionally clear and

poignant way in the mind and heart of Augustus Strong, I have chosen to tell the story through the twists and turns of his theological journey.[27]

---

[27]Arthur O. Lovejoy, *The Great Chain of Being* (New York: Harper and Row, 1960 [1936]) 3-7.

Chapter One

Made in the Image of History:
The Epistemic Revolution
of the Late Nineteenth Century

IN 1936 PROFESSOR JOHN GRESHAM MACHEN of Westminster Theological Seminary published a series of radio lectures on the role of Christian faith in the modern world. Although Machen disliked the label, he was regarded by many as the leading scholarly spokesman for fundamentalism in America. The sermonettes Machen prepared for the occasion dealt with subjects of popular theological interest, such as the nature of revelation and the nature of God. But one address, significantly titled "Life Founded upon Truth," shed considerable light on the presuppositions underlying all the others. It dealt with the nature of truth. [1]

The argument of the address was that truth is timeless and immutable, independent of historical conditioning. This, said Machen, is what separates the "Christian view" of truth from the modern view. The

---

[1] J. Gresham Machen, *The Christian Faith in the Modern World* (Grand Rapids MI: Eerdmans, 1965 [1936]).

central error of the latter is that it "denies that there is any possibility of attaining to a truth which will always be true." It assumes that truth is relative to time and place, "truth . . . for this generation and truth for that generation, but no truth for all generations." Moreover the modern view imagines that there are different truths for the "different races co-existing today." Thus there is "an Oriental mind or an Occidental mind," a "truth for this race and truth for that race, but no truth for all races." Indeed, the modern view supposes that human understanding is so tied to particular circumstances that even the meanings of words wobble from century to century and from culture to culture. The flaw in this outlook, said Machen, is transparent: "Truth is not relative but absolute." His position was unequivocal: There is no such thing as an "ancient mind or a medieval mind or a modern mind." Indeed, such notions come "very near being nonsense." Scripture is unambiguous about the matter, for it "makes truth the foundation of conduct and doctrine the foundation of life." Christian doctrine is not a managed currency subject to human experience, but a gold standard that stands above the flux of history, independent of the passing generations and varying cultures of mankind. Truth does not grow out of human experience but precedes it. "Truth before conduct," he insisted, "doctrine before life."[2]

Machen's essay tells us a great deal about his general philosophy of history, for it is clear that in his mind history is irrelevant to the things that really matter in life. This is not to say that he lacked a "sense of history," if by that we mean a keen interest in the events of the past, especially the events recorded in Scripture. The point rather is that for Machen the meaning of historical events is not forged within history but ascribed from outside, anterior to and independent of the process. In his mind the past is simply the passage of time, a succession of temporal segments having no organic relation to the formation of society and culture. Machen's world was filled with people and issues drawn from the past, but ultimately, it was a "world without history."[3]

---

[2]Ibid., 75-93.

[3]It is significant that Machen considered his own specialty, study of the New Testament, derivative from and logically subordinate to systematic theology; Machen,

Machen was a superbly trained classicist and, by common agreement, a man of intimidating intelligence. Walter Lippmann warned fellow humanists as well as theological liberals that they should pay him closer attention. Even so, there was a bit of perversity in Lippmann's admonition, for in Henry May's words Lippmann himself had long been "cheerfully laying dynamite in the hidden cracks . . . of nineteenth-century America."[4]

The premises of Lippmann's contrasting view of the world were classically articulated in *A Preface to Morals,* published the year of the Great Crash. In this influential essay Lippmann forthrightly declared that the older feelings of certainty had crumbled for every one "who comes within the orbit of modernity." The thoughtful person of today looks to science for the explanation of existence, but science does not pretend to know a "fixed point called 'the truth.'" Indeed, for modern science truth is nothing but "the opinion which is fated to be ultimately agreed to by all those who investigate." In Lippmann's mind even the great philosophies of life that were based on science, such as positivism, had proved to be perilously time-bound—"nothing but provisional dramatizations." In this light norms and values are only "preferences," lacking a "sure foundation." Lippmann urged his readers to recognize, without equivocation, that in the end they must find the "tests of righteousness wholly within human experience."[5]

Undoubtedly there were many differences between Machen and Lippmann, but the critical difference, the difference that lay at the root of all the others, was that Machen, unlike Lippmann, doubted the power of history to condition human understanding. Machen was a Phi Beta Kappa graduate of Johns Hopkins; Lippmann a Phi Beta Kappa graduate of Harvard. That men of comparable intelligence and training could

---

"Christianity in Conflict," in Vergilius Ferm, ed., *Contemporary American Theology* (New York: Round Table Press, 1932-1933) 1:253. See also George M. Marsden "J. Gresham Machen, History, and Truth," *Westminister Theological Journal* 42 (1979): 157-75. "World without history," is the title of chapter 1 of David W. Noble's *The Paradox of Progressive Thought* (Minneapolis: University of Minnesota Press, 1958).

[4]Walter Lippmann, *A Preface to Morals* (Boston: Beacon Press, 1960 [1929]) 32-34. May's remark referred to Lippman's intellectual generation; May, *The End of American Innocence* (Chicago: Quadrangle Paperbacks, 1964 [1959]) ix.

[5]Lippmann, *Preface,* 19, 129, 131, 3-4, 137.

differ on matters of taste or political allegiance is hardly surprising; that they could differ so fundamentally in world view gives pause. How did these nearly opposite ways of seeing reality come about?[6]

II

In a general sense Machen's views about the relation between history and knowledge were rooted in the classical foundationalism of Greek philosophy, but the more proximate origins of his outlook can be traced to the apologetic writings of late seventeenth- and early eighteenth-century Christian rationalists such as John Locke and Joseph Butler. A. C. McGiffert once called this cluster of notions "supernatural rationalism," and though the label is clumsy, it is descriptively useful.[7] Like contemporary deists, supernatural rationalists were confident that careful observation of history and nature can lead to reliable knowledge of God's existence and attributes. Like pietists (and unlike deists), however, supernatural rationalists also believed that this natural knowledge of God is inadequate. For some, the special revelation given in Scripture was deemed to be effectively although not absolutely necessary for salvation. In the pink-cheeked words of John Wise of Ipswich, "Revelation is Nature's law in a fairer and brighter Edition." Others were less sanguine about human abilities. Honest analysis of the self, they held, exposes the limitations of reason and thus the need for special revelation given in Scripture. This does not mean that the content of Scripture is contrary to reason, but that it is above or beyond reason's ordinary range of discernment. But for all supernatural rationalists the governing assumption was that the human mind is able to perceive the divine truth as it is disclosed in history and nature as well as in Scripture.[8]

---

[6]C. Allyn Russell, *Voices of American Fundamentalism* (Philadelphia: Westminster Press, 1976). chap. 6, esp. 136; Ronald Steel, *Walter Lippmann and the American Century* (New York: Random House, 1980) 29.

[7]For classical foundationalism see the essays in Alvin Plantinga and Nicholas Wolterstorff, eds., *Faith and Rationality* (Notre Dame IN: University of Notre Dame Press, 1983) *passim*. For the historiography of "supernatural rationalism" see Conrad Wright, *The Liberal Christians* (Boston: Beacon Press, 1970) 6.

[8]Wright, *Liberal Christians,* 8-11; George M. Marsden, "The Collapse of American Evangelical Academia," in Plantinga and Wolterstorff, eds., *Faith and Ration-*

Particularly important in the present context is the epistemology of supernatural rationalism. Men such as Locke and Butler were certain that knowledge of divine matters, like knowledge of all matters, is derived from sensation and reflection upon sensation. In their minds this meant that Christianity stood or fell with the persuasiveness of the sensible evidence. Two arguments were common. First, Christ fulfilled prophecies and performed miracles that were seen and heard by numerous observers. Second, there is no reason to doubt the probity of the men and women who witnessed and attested to these events. Especially noteworthy here is the ahistorical nature of the assumptions underlying this outlook. To begin with, these supernatural rationalists thought that the formal and material functions of reason can be neatly separated. Though they did not put it that way, they believed that reason could prescribe the (formal) credentials but not the (material) content of authentic revelation. In the words of one adherent, reason is "a sentinel at the entrance of the human mind, to determine what is true and what is false, what is to be admitted and what is to be kept out." Underlying this notion was another assumption, buried so deep it might be better described as a presupposition. Supernatural rationalists assumed that Christian truth can be established with essentially a priori methods. Reason alone, shorn of contextual, developmental, or interpretive considerations, can determine the issue once and for all.[9]

In the later years of the eighteenth century the epistemic scaffolding of supernatural rationalism was increasingly buttressed by the rise of Scottish commonsense realism. The chief architect of this tradition was Thomas Reid (1710-1796), a Moderate Presbyterian clergyman who taught philosophy at Aberdeen and later at Glasgow. Reid was trou-

---

ality, 228-30; E. Brooks Holifield, The Gentlemen Theologians (Durham NC: Duke University Press, 1978) chap. 4; Claude Welch, Protestant Thought in the Nineteenth Century (New Haven CT: Yale University Press, 1972) 34-39; Basil Willey, The Eighteenth Century Background (Boston: Beacon Press, 1961 [1940]) 76-82; John Wise, A Vindication of the Government of New England Churches (1717) 32, quoted in Wright, Liberal Christians, 17.

[9]Wright, Liberal Christians, 12-15; Holifield, Gentlemen Theologians, 77-95; Willey, Eighteenth Century, 81-82. The "sentinel" remark is from G. W. Burnap, "Unitarian Christianity Expounded and Defended," in Samuel Gilman et al., The Old and the New (1854) 126-28, quoted in Holifield, Gentlemen Theologians, 63.

bled by the problem of the reliability of our knowledge of the external world. The problem was ancient, but it had been raised anew in the 1690s by John Locke, who had argued that sensory impressions imprint ideas on the mind, and these ideas are the source of all knowledge. But if this is the case, David Hume responded, how can we be certain that any element of reality that is not directly and sensibly experienced, such as causality or a substantial self, truly exists? Indeed, how can we be certain that any idea truly corresponds to the external world? To Reid, the flaw in this whole line of thinking was the assumption that sensations create ideas that then serve as mirrors of reality. To the contrary, said Reid, rigorous examination of consciousness reveals the continuous and unmediated presence of the external world, not a layer of ideas somehow sandwiched between consciousness and the external world. This is to say that ideas are mental acts, not mental objects, and these mental acts are direct perceptions (or memories of direct perceptions) of the environment. [10]

Reid's conviction that perception is trustworthy was based on the belief that consciousness embraces an array of forms that correspond to the intelligible forms of social and physical reality. He called them "first principles" or "direct intuitions." In his estimation, the first principles that inform consciousness include axioms of logic and mathematics and numerous assumptions such as the belief that I am the same person today that I was yesterday, that clear and distinct memories are reliable, that right is different from wrong, and that perception is perception of the real world. Thus Archibald Alexander, one of Reid's closest followers and probably the most influential teacher of theology in antebellum America, told the first class of students at Princeton Theological Seminary in 1812 that there are scores of "self-evident truths," which, "from the constitution of our nature, we are under the necessity of believing as soon as they are presented to the mind"—truths "which immediately on being proposed are perceived to be true without any process of reasoning in the case." The pertinent point here is that first principles can-

---

[10]Holifield, *Gentlemen Theologians,* chap. 5, esp. 115; Marsden, "Collapse," 224-28; *The Encyclopedia of Philosophy,* s.v. "Reid, Thomas," by S. A. Grave; J. David Hoeveler, Jr., *James McCosh and the Scottish Intellectual Tradition* (Princeton: Princeton University Press, 1981) chap. 4; D. H. Meyer, *The Instructed Conscience* (Philadelphia: University of Pennsylvania Press, 1972) chap. 4.

not be proved true. If they could, they would be derivative. Nor can they be disproved, for they are employed in all reasoning, and to refute them would require using them. First principles are, in short, prerational intuitions embedded in the very structure of consciousness. Neither innate nor learned, they are the forms that organize thought and make experience meaningful. They are the *common* sense of mankind, the arsenal of judgments everyone (including philosophers and other fools) presupposes in the daily routines of life.[11]

Taken together, then, supernatural rationalism and Scottish realism provided an epistemology that seemed to promise rational and reliable knowledge of social and material reality, including the divine truths woven into the fabric of reality. More precisely, this British-Scottish tradition shaped orthodox rationalism in the United States in the nineteenth century in at least three ways. First, it nurtured the conviction that persons have certain knowledge of the moral and natural realms because there is a perfect fit between these realms and the perceiving mind. There is, said Francis Wayland in 1835, "a world without us and a world within us, which exactly correspond to each other." By divine contrivance there is "light without, and the eye within; beauty without , and taste within; moral qualities without, and conscience [within]." Or as another writer phrased it in 1860, the perceiving mind is like a "clear mirror, which, when brought face to face with an external object . . . sees it *just as it is.*" Second, it bolstered the view that the truths that can be discerned internally (in consciousness and conscience), the truths that can be discerned externally (in history, society, and nature), and the truths that can be discerned in the specially revealed realm of the Bible are congruent. And the reason is plain: God is one, truth is one, and the perceptual mechanism for knowing truth in each of these realms is, ultimately, one. Another way of putting it is to say that the psychological, physical, and moral laws that govern, respectively, the objective facts of consciousness, nature, and Scripture are essentially alike. Finally, the British-Scottish influence strengthened the belief that the proper method for acquiring religious knowl-

---

[11]Holifield, Marsden, Grave, Hoeveler, and Meyer, as cited in note 10; Archibald Alexander, "Nature and Evidence of Truth" (1812), reprinted in Mark A. Noll, ed., *The Princeton Theology* (Grand Rapids MI: Baker Book House) 63, 67.

edge is identical to the proper method for acquiring scientific knowledge. In both cases the inquirer looks at the data, determines the facts, classifies them, then draws prudent generalizations.[12]

In this last respect the popularity of Francis Bacon and the "Baconian method" of pure inductive inquiry is difficult to overstate. At the outset of his 1872 *Systematic Theology,* Charles Hodge averred that "the Bible is to the theologian what nature is to the man of science. It is his store-house of facts; and his method of ascertaining what the Bible teaches is the same as that which the natural philosopher adopts to ascertain what nature teaches." Since the acquisition of religious knowledge was believed to be a quantitative rather than qualitative problem, a taxonomic rather than creative endeavor, it is not surprising that these conservatives came to see themselves, as Dwight Bozeman has said, as "theological scientist[s] . . . patiently and inductively coaxing the chaotic raw materials of revelation into scientific order."[13]

In short, orthodox rationalism embodied a distinctive epistemology and, more significantly, this epistemology afforded the priceless

---

[12]For the epistemology and methodology of orthodox rationalism, see Holifield, *Gentlemen Theologians,* chaps. 5-6; Marsden, "Collapse," 230-41; Meyer, *Instructed Conscience,* 23-24; and especially Theodore Dwight Bozeman, *Protestants in an Age of Science* (Chapel Hill: University of North Carolina Press, 1977) chaps. 3, 5. Francis Wayland, *Elements of Moral Science* (1835) 367-70, is quoted in Meyer, *Instructed Conscience,* 45. *"Just as it is"* is from Francis Andrew March, "Sir William Hamilton's Theory of Perception," *Biblical Repertory and Princeton Review* (1860): 292, as quoted in Bozeman, *Protestants,* 55.

[13]Charles Hodge, "Introduction to *Systematic Theology"* (1872) reprinted in Noll, ed., *Princeton Theology,* 125. Bozeman's remark is in *Protestants,* 153. I have chosen to call this tradition orthodox rationalism rather than Scottish realism or Baconianism. Although the latter two labels are frequently used in the secondary literature, they imply that the philosophical assumptions of conservative Protestant thought were uniformly drawn from Thomas Reid or, through him, from Francis Bacon. A more generic label, such as orthodox rationalism, is preferable because it better suggests the internal diversity (such as the powerful and distinctive influence of William Hamilton) that marked this tradition. See Henry F. May, *The Enlightenment in America* (New York: Oxford University Press, 1976) 344-45; Donald H. Meyer, *The Democratic Enlightenment* (New York: G. P. Putnam's Sons, 1976) 195; Herbert W. Schneider, *A History of American Philosophy,* 2d ed. (New York: Columbia University Press, 1963) 211; Garry Wills, *Inventing America* (New York: Random House, 1979 [1978]) chaps. 12-18.

comforts of an ahistorical universe. Its partisans were certain that the timeless and universal continuities of human consciousness provide a kind of seer stone through which the equally timeless and universal verities of society and nature can be discerned. When they thought about special revelation, this meant, first of all, that the events recorded in Scripture happened in just the way that the writers of Scripture said they happened. More crucially, it meant that the meaning of those events is fixed. The Bible is to be understood, not interpreted. Conservatives were dismayed by the growing idea that the meaning of scriptural events is open to a variety of interpretations. Learned biblical scholars such as Moses Stuart tended to regard even normative constructions, such as the doctrine of original sin or the doctrine of the atonement, as "hard" facts similar to the "hard" facts that the natural scientist discovers in the material world. And when these conservatives thought about God's general revelation in the social and natural order, the same assumptions again were operative. Everywhere they looked, social processes seemed to be governed by a single set of "fundamental laws." Beneath the legal codes enjoined by the courts, beneath the prescriptions of custom, beneath the Constitution of the United States itself, was the bedrock of fundamental law whose authority was absolute and immutable. Looking back from the perspective of the 1940s, Ralph Henry Gabriel judged that throughout most of the nineteenth century this cluster of beliefs, which he called "cosmic constitutionalism," formed the primary article of the American democratic faith. It gave Americans, said Gabriel, "that mental peace and that sense of security which comes to the man who feels that he has planted his feet upon the eternal rock."[14]

At this point I should acknowledge that even in its most imposing mid-nineteenth-century form, the epistemology of orthodox rationalism was not wholly ahistorical. Some of the most eminent and seemingly procrustean representatives of the tradition, such as Princeton's

---

[14]For the orthodox rationalist understanding of Scripture see Holifield, *Gentlemen Theologians,* 96-100; Bozeman, *Protestants,* 142-43; George M. Marsden, "Everyone One's Own Interpreter?" in Nathan O. Hatch and Mark A. Noll, eds., *The Bible in America* (New York: Oxford University Press, 1982) 79-100. For the view of society and nature see Holifield, *Gentlemen Theologians,* chap. 6; Bozeman, *Protestants,* chap. 4; Meyer, *Instructed Conscience,* 138-40, 144. Ralph Henry Gabriel, *The Course of American Democratic Thought* (New York: Ronald Press, 1940) 14, 18-19.

president James McCosh, sought to harmonize progressive creation with older notions of natural design and providence. And then there was the brief but extraordinary influence of Sir William Hamilton, the Edinburgh philosopher who seemed for a time to have synthesized the epistemic views of Thomas Reid and Immanuel Kant. Hamilton taught a generation of conservative divines (including Augustus Strong's Yale mentor, Noah Porter) to see that the first principles of consciousness, which make knowledge possible, also make it relative to the knowing mind. Hamilton insisted, moreover, that we know only phenomena; the noumenal substance "behind" phenomena can be logically inferred but never truly known. This means that reason, which deals with the phenomenal, is able to discern the outer evidences of revelation, but the inner life of the divine is forever beyond reason's grasp. Thus Hamilton would say, in what became a well-turned phrase of nineteenth-century theology, that a "learned ignorance is . . . the end of philosophy, as it is the beginning of theology."[15] These qualifications notwithstanding, Victorian Protestant orthodoxy was basically ahistorical. Indeed, it is significant that even William Hamilton, who had stressed the participatory and fractional nature of all knowledge, would eventually be praised by one Princeton reviewer as a thinker who was "in no degree under the influence of what is called the historical development of human intelligence."[16]

In summary, then, the epistemic ingredients of supernatural rationalism, fortified with a stiff jolt of Scottish realism, long satisfied the dialectical appetite of conservative Protestant thinkers in the United States (and many in Britain and Germany as well). The tradition was first discernible among latter-day Puritans such as Increase and Cotton Mather, and it persists in much the same form in the 1980s in the work

---

[15]For progressive creationism see Hoeveler, *McCosh*, chap. 6; James R. Moore, *The Post-Darwinian Controversies* (Cambridge: Cambridge University Press, 1979) chaps. 10-11; Cynthia Eagle Russett, *Darwin in America* (San Francisco: W. H. Freeman, 1976) 27-43. For Hamilton see *Encyclopedia of Philosophy*, s.v. "Hamilton, William," by Thomas J. Duggan; Bruce Kuklick, *The Rise of American Philosophy* (New Haven: Yale University Press, 1977) 16-21; George M. Marsden, *Fundamentalism and American Culture* (New York: Oxford University Press, 1980) 111. Hamilton's phrase is in *Lectures on Metaphysics* (1859) 2:530, quoted in Holifield, *Gentlemen Theologians, 118*.

[16]Samuel Tyler, "Sir William Hamilton and His Philosophy," *Princeton Review* (1855): 564, as quoted in Marsden, *Fundamentalism,* 111.

of evangelical thinkers such as Carl F. H. Henry and Ronald H. Nash. Nor was it restricted to Reformed writers. The ahistorical assumptions of orthodox rationalism influenced frontier Restorationists such as Thomas and Alexander Campbell, Wesleyans such as Nathan Bangs and John Miley, and even Unitarians such as Andrews Norton and William Ellery Channing. One of the charming twists of American intellectual history is that Ralph Waldo Emerson's Harvard senior thesis, written in 1821, was a defense of orthodox rationalism against the encroachments of German idealism. Orthodox rationalism "is a thing of the past, now," Conrad Wright has written, and it "has no power to stir us. Yet it once was the starting point of every young theological student's studies of divinity." Perry Miller's often-quoted remark that the "Scottish method" once constituted the "official metaphysic of America" may be an overstatement. Nonetheless, recent scholarship has made clear that a majority of nineteenth-century Protestant thinkers acquired their epistemic assumptions not from the figures some scholars now find most interesting—Emerson, Bushnell, Nevin—but from pious, sincere, and eminently rational apologists trained up in the ways of supernatural rationalism and Scottish realism.[17]

III

The epistemic revolution that overthrew orthodox rationalism was one of several fundamental changes that overtook American life during

---

[17]For the pervasiveness of orthodox rationalism in both the North and the South and on both sides of the Atlantic see, in addition to the works by Bozeman, Hoeveler, Holifield, Marsden, Meyer, and Wright already cited, Sydney E. Ahlstrom, "The Scottish Philosophy and American Theology," *Church History* 24 (1955): 257-72; Josef L. Altholz, "The Mind of Victorian Orthodoxy," *Church History* 51 (1982): 186-97; Walter H. Conser, Jr., *Church and Confession* (Macon GA: Mercer University Press, 1984); Ralph E. Luker, *A Southern Tradition in Theology and Social Criticism* (Lewiston NY: Edwin Mellen Press, 1984) chap.2; Daniel F. Rice, "An Attempt at Systematic Reconstruction in the Theology of Thomas Chalmers," *Church History* 48 (1979): 174-88. For the quotations see Wright, *Liberal Christians,* 20, and Perry Miller, ed., *American Thought* (San Francisco: Rinehart, 1954) ix. The note about Emerson's thesis is found in May, *Enlightenment,* 357. The final sentence of the paragraph is suggested by Holifield, *Gentlemen Theologians,* 71. For Carl F. H. Henry see his *God, Revelation and Authority* (Waco TX: Word, 1979) 3: chaps. 16-17, 27, and 4: chap. 1. Chapter 17 of volume 3 is significantly titled "Cognitive Aspects of Divine Disclosure." For Ronald H. Nash see *The Word of God and the Mind of Man* (Grand Rapids MI: Zondervan, 1982) 109, 111-12.

the late nineteenth and early twentieth centuries. Indeed, it is arguable that the rapid deepening of historical consciousness during those years was to some extent a direct product of economic and social turmoil. America had become a "distended society," a society split into a welter of contending factions and diverse cultures. In a setting of that sort it was difficult *not* to recognize the profoundly historical nature of the real world.[18]

The most striking social change was the relentless pressure of immigration. Although the percentage of foreign-born in the United States was scarcely larger in 1910 than it had been in 1860, the ethnic derivation of those who came around the turn of the century was markedly different. The new immigrants, who came primarily from Southern and Eastern Europe, injected unwelcomed diversity into American life, and by the end of the century initial distrust had swelled, in John Higham's words, "into a pressing sense of menace, into hatred, and into violence." For many reform thinkers the overriding problem of the age was the polarization of American society. As the apparent homogeneity of nineteenth-century life disintegrated, many who lived through the *fin de siècle* years felt the world of small towns, summer nights, and stable values slipping away. The smug certainties of Victorian culture simply did not fit social reality any longer.[19]

Another pressure that prompted thoughtful people to reassess older assumptions was the fragmentation of life in the cities. In many ways the nation's center of gravity shifted to the cities during the last twenty years of the century, and by 1920 a majority of Americans lived in what the Census Bureau defined as urban centers. The preeminent fact of life in the typical urban industrial setting was segregation according to occupational status, race, ethnicity, and religion. Added to this was the

---

[18]"The Distended Society" is the title of chapter 2 of Robert H. Wiebe's *The Search for Order* (New York: Hill and Wang, 1967).

[19]Maldwyn Allen Jones, *American Immigration* (Chicago: University of Chicago Press, 1960) 179, 208. John Higham, *Strangers in the Land* (New York: Atheneum, 1973 [1963]) 87, 38. For the erosion of Victorian values see May, *End,* part 2; Paul A. Carter, *The Spiritual Crisis of the Gilded Age* (Dekalb IL: Northern Illinois University Press, 1971) viii, 1-20; Daniel Walker Howe, "American Victorianism as a Culture," *American Quarterly* 27 (1975): 510; D. H. Meyer, "American Intellectuals and the Victorian Crisis of Faith," *American Quarterly* 27 (1975): 590, 594, 602.

emergence of distinct interest groups, as businessmen, farmers, laborers, white collar workers, and professionals acquired acute vocational self-consciousness. Although it is possible to overdramatize the social strain of the period, there is no question that reflective people were concerned about the apparent loss of community. Inevitably the "block universe" of orthodox rationalism became increasingly implausible.[20]

Shifting patterns of education in the latter years of the century also fostered recognition of the pluralistic character of the world. The spectacular growth of public education, which expanded the horizons of ordinary people, accompanied the emergence of the university system and the spread of the German pattern of graduate education. The latter especially facilitated advanced research in the social disciplines and spurred contact with the leading thought of Europe.[21]

These, then, were some of the social pressures that nurtured the conviction that cultural patterns are fluid and relative and pluralistic—which is to say, historically created. But the rapid growth of historical consciousness was also, and perhaps principally, a development internal to the history of ideas. It was the logical denouement of a cluster of closely related concepts that had been maturing since the Enlightenment.

Although the seeds of these concepts were scattered throughout the history of Western thought, the real roots of modern historical consciousness started to take form in the eighteenth century. More precisely, in the eighteenth century men and women in the West began to think in serious, systematic, and nontheological terms about the nature of historical process. Now it is quite true that the great speculators of

---

[20]For the shift to urban centers see Arthur M. Schlesinger, Sr., *The Rise of the City* (Chicago: Quadrangle Books, 1961 [1933]) esp. 79. For social strain see Wiebe, *Search,* 1-132; Alan Trachtenberg, *The Incorporation of America* (New York: Hill and Wang, 1982) 70-73, 79-81, 88-91, 98-100; Sam Bass Warner, Jr., *The Urban Wilderness* (New York: Harper and Row, 1972) 99, 110-11.

[21]For public education see Schlesinger, *Rise,* 162-201. Changes in American higher education are assessed in Richard Hofstadter, "The Revolution in Higher Education," in Arthur M. Schlesinger, Jr. and Morton White, eds., *Paths of American Thought* (Boston: Houghton Mifflin, 1970 [1963]) 273-83; and Laurence R. Veysey, *The Emergence of the American University* (Chicago: University of Chicago Press, 1965) 125-33, 264.

the Enlightenment, not to mention orthodox rationalists such as Butler and Reid, were more concerned with reason than history. Most considered history the arena in which reason is progressively exemplified; in Lord Bolingbroke's famous phrase, history is "philosophy teaching by example." Or consider Rousseau's memorable introduction to the *Discourse on the Origin of Inequality:* "Let us begin by laying the facts aside, as they do not affect the question"—which meant, of course, that history was to be measured by a standard external to itself. Nevertheless, eighteenth-century *philosophes* such as Montesquieu, Voltaire, and Hume (and Vico in the seventeenth century) did ponder the nature and meaning of history, and in time elaborated three notions important to the development of modern historical consciousness.[22]

The first of these notions was that cultural forms are peculiar to the particular settings in which they emerge. The Enlightenment formulation of this concept was still much more rationalistic than modern assumptions about the historical rootedness of culture. Even so, the *philosophes* helped to foster the recognition that all cultures are aboriginal, internally interdependent units. The conviction that there is such a thing as a discrete "climate of opinion," or a unique "spirit of a people," genetically tied to a particular time and place, is, in short, a direct legacy of the historical thought of the Enlightenment.[23] The second crucial notion, not introduced but importantly furthered by the *philosophes,* is that history involves developmental change. Precisely stated, history itself, distinct from reason—and distinct from "natural his-

---

[22]For the eighteenth-century sources of modern historical consciousness see R. G. Collingwood, *The Idea of History* (London: Oxford University Press, 1956 [1946]) 5, 82, 98-99, 103; Ernst Cassirer, *The Philosophy of the Enlightenment* (Princeton: Princeton University Press, 1951) 219-20; Peter Gay, *The Enlightenment* (New York: Random House, 1968 [1966]) 33, 451; *Dictionary of the History of Ideas,* s. v. "Historicism," by Georg G. Iggers, 458; Arthur O. Lovejoy, *Essays in the History of Ideas* (New York: G. P. Putnam's Sons, 1960 [1948]) 172-80; Maurice Mandelbaum, *History, Man, and Reason* (Baltimore: Johns Hopkins University Press, 1971) 52; Frank E. Manuel, *Shapes of Philosophical History* (Stanford CA: Stanford University Press, 1965) 95; Hans Meyerhoff, ed., *The Philosophy of History in Our Time* (Garden City: Doubleday, 1959) 4-5.

[23]Cassirer, *Enlightenment,* 213-16; Collingwood, *Idea,* 78; Gay, *Enlightenment,* 37-38; Mandelbaum, *History,* 54.

tory"—develops. Vico, for example, argued that history progresses in cycles but never repeats itself. The image is of a spiral: continuous, developmental change within a changeless, formal structure. Although they agreed that the laws governing social change are timeless, the *philosophes* also acknowledged that there really are new things under the sun. They impelled us to see, said Arthur O. Lovejoy, that the *plenum formarum* is not an inventory but a program to be fulfilled.[24] The third important contribution by the *philosophes* was the attribution of directionality—usually conceived as progress—to historical change. They argued that history not only develops, but develops toward something. The idea of direction in history was as old as the Book of Daniel, and it abounded in contemporary Christian works such as Bousset's *Discourse on Universal History*. But unlike Christian writers, the *philosophes* conceived the agency of historical change as radically immanent, and soon this came to mean inherently progressive as well.[25]

The intellectual revolution sparked in the Enlightenment became a veritable conflagration in the nineteenth century. Indeed, by 1913 Ernst Troeltsch was able to say that historical consciousness had come to be the fundamental feature of modern culture. The transformation Troeltsch had in mind was complex, but in very broad terms it consisted of an interplay between two more or less independent streams. One grew from the Anglo-French Enlightenment; philosophically it was linked with positivism. The other, beginning in the last third of the eighteenth century, centered in Germany and was associated with romantic idealism. Both traditions were profoundly influential in the

---

[24]Cassirer, *Enlightenment*, 214, 218-20, 226; Mandelbaum, *History*, 141; Manuel, *Shapes*, 79-91, 97-99; Meyerhoff, *Philosophy*, 5; Nisbet, *Social Change*, 114-22; Georg G. Iggers, *The German Conception of History* (Middletown CT: Wesleyan University Press, 1968) 30; Arthur O. Lovejoy, *The Great Chain of Being* (New York: Harper and Row, 1960 [1936]) 244; W. Warren Wagar, *Good Tidings* (Bloomington: Indiana University Press, 1972) 18-19.

[25]Cassirer, *Enlightenment*, 199, 207; Collingwood, *Idea*, 81; Mandelbaum, *History*, 53; Meyerhoff, *Philosophy*, 4-5; Nisbet, *Social Change*, 166-74; Georg G. Iggers, "The Idea of Progress," *American Historical Review* 71 (1965): 6. Ernest Lee Tuveson, *Millennium and Utopia* (New York: Harper and Row, 1964 [1949]).

United States, but at different times and among different groups of people.[26]

We shall glance at the idealist contribution first. The seminal minds in this tradition greatly enriched the Enlightened notions of the historicity of cultural forms and the developmental and directional thrust of historical process. Indeed, Johann Gottfried Herder might be considered the *paterfamilias* of modern historicism, for he contributed the image of history as a great tree, exfoliating in an endless profusion of unique and unrepeatable forms. More than anyone else, perhaps, Herder taught us to see that each culture is distinctive, and therefore comprehensible only in relation to its particular historical setting.[27] G. W. F. Hegel, in turn, radicalized the second notion—namely, that history is a process of ceaseless, unfolding development. He discovered, as Hans Meyerhoff put it, the realm of "pure historicity" from which there is no escape into a haven of eternal essences. In Hegel's work, reason, the core of reality, is immersed in the stream of historical change and can be apprehended only in motion. This developmental changefulness embraces humankind, whose awareness of history literally defines human nature.[28] Leopold von Ranke especially amplified the third notion, emphasizing the organic interconnectedness—the *inneren Zusammenhang*—of historical process. All generations, Ranke urged, are immediate to God. Thus the true task of the historian is not to fiddle with the bits and pieces but to grasp the historical situation as it *essentially* was; to

---

[26]For the cross-fertilization of these traditions see Mandelbaum, *History*, 5-20, 47-49, and H. Stuart Hughes, *Consciousness and Society* (New York: Random House, 1961 [1958]) 183-84. Some important figures, such as Ernst Mach and Edmund Burke, do not fit the pattern at all. Ernst Troeltsch, *Aufsätze* (1913) 628, is cited in Iggers, "Historicism," 457.

[27]For the measurable deepening of historical consciousness in the Idealist tradition see Collingwood, *Idea*, 87-88; Welch, *Protestant Thought*, 54; Franklin L. Baumer, *Modern European Thought* (New York: Macmillan, 1977) 294-301. For Herder and the concept of historical particularity see Cassirer, *Enlightenment*, 231; Iggers, *German Conception*, 30; Mandelbaum, *History* 58; Manuel, *Shapes*, 81-87; Meyerhoff, *Philosophy*, 10-11.

[28]Baumer, *European Thought*, 299; Collingwood, *Idea*, 117; Iggers, "Historicism," 460; Mandelbaum, *History*, 60; Meyerhoff, *Philosophy*, 6; Gerhard Masur, *Prophets of Yesterday* (New York: Macmillan, 1961) 58.

grasp, in short, the immanent unity that gives coherence and direction to the process.[29]

This developmental and progressive orientation made the German idealism attractive in the United States throughout the nineteenth century. The "ideal of a static society having been put away," said Vernon Louis Parrington a half century ago, "progress was assumed to be the first law of nature." Romantic historians such as Richard Prescott, Francis Parkman, and George Bancroft wrote the most popular books in America between 1830 and 1870. Bancroft, especially, American-ized the German feeling for the flowing, organic, interconnectedness of human experience. In his work and that of influential writers in other fields, such as Louis Agassiz, the "dynamic conception of nature" be-came a common currency of American thought, competing and in un-predictable ways interacting with religious and secular versions of orthodox rationalism. After the Civil War the idealist conception of progressive historical change fell into disfavor with most professional historians—who were, ironically, increasingly drawn to Scottish real-ism—but it became the dominant outlook among academic philoso-phers and a major strain in the ideas of leading social theorists. Indeed, progressive idealism in one form or another constituted an important part of the genteel tradition until well after the turn of the century.[30]

---

[29]For Ranke see Iggers, *German Conception,* 13-14, 65-68, 76-79; Wagar, *Good Tidings,* 178; Herbert Butterfield, *Man on His Past* (Cambridge: Cambridge Univer-sity Press, 1969) 103-108. For progressive idealism in general see Collingwood, *Idea,* 92; Lovejoy, *Essays,* 169-70; Manuel, *Shapes,* 118-19; *Dictionary of the History of Ideas,* s.v. "Romanticism," by Franklin L. Baumer, 204.

[30]For progressive idealism in popular and high culture see Miller, *American Thought,* ix-xiv; Schneider, *History,* 375-424, esp. 400; Wiebe, *Search,* 140-45; John Higham, *Writing American History* (Bloomington: Indiana University Press, 1970) 94. Amer-ican historians are discussed in R. W. B. Lewis, *The American Adam* (Chicago: Uni-versity of Chicago Press, 1955) 162-65; Harvey Wish, *The American Historian* (New York: Oxford University Press, 1960) 70; Henry Warner Bowden, *Church History in an Age of Science* (Chapel Hill: University of North Carolina Press, 1971) 16-25. "Dy-namic conception" is in Howard Mumford Jones, "The Influence of European Ideas in Nineteenth-Century America," *American Literature* 7 (1935-1936): 257. Vernon Louis Parrington, *Main Currents in American Thought* (1927), 2:iv-v, is quoted in Ga-briel, *Democratic Thought* (2d ed., 1956) 13.

The other major wellspring of modern historical consciousness was Anglo-French positivism. This tradition can be traced principally to Auguste Comte, Karl Marx, Herbert Spencer, and Charles Darwin. In their own ways these speculators vitally enriched the Western world's awareness of the concrete, developmental, and directional nature of historical process. The historicity of cultural forms loomed especially large in the work of Comte, whom Basil Willey significantly ranked as the central figure in the intellectual history of nineteenth-century Europe. Comte contended that the very structures of human cognition, as well as its applications, the sciences, are formed in the course of history. Marx, in turn, radicalized this conception by suggesting that the structures of thought are not only historically constituted, but historically interested. What appears to be truth is, for the most part, not truth but ideology.[31]

Like the idealists, the great thinkers in the positivist tradition also considered history a process of ceaseless development. They differed among themselves about what the historical entity is—for Comte, human knowledge; for Marx, economic production—but for all, history progresses by laws of necessary development. Spencer, especially, was responsible for fusing the doctrine of historical development with a cosmology of universal evolution. The sense that all things, great and small, are swept up in a single process of ascending cosmic change was his short-lived but important legacy to the deepening of historical consciousness. Spencer's ideas were published a decade before Darwin's, and Darwin himself was reluctant to expand on the philosophical implications of his own work. Yet Darwin's enduring achievement, John Dewey once noted, was to conquer "the phenomena of life for the principle of transition." Before Darwin, history had been conceived as a process of steady

---

[31]For Comte and the historicity of the forms of cognition see Mandelbaum, *History,* 64,67; Manuel, *Shapes,* 111; *Dictionary of the History of Ideas,* s.v. "Positivism in Europe to 1900," by Walter Simon; Basil Willey, *Nineteenth Century Studies* (New York: Columbia University Press, 1949) 188, 196-97. Note also Masur's judgment that Comte's philosophy of history constituted a "landmark in the development of historical consciousness in the West" (*Prophets,* 55-56). For Marx see Masur, *Prophets,* 64-65; Isaiah Berlin, *Karl Marx,* 3d ed.(New York: Oxford Press, 1963) 105-115; George Lichtheim, "The Concept of Ideology," in George H. Nadel, ed., *Studies in the Philosophy of History* (New York: Harper and Row, 1965) 160.

social development; after him it was more often conceived as only one dimension in the general process of natural, organic evolution.[32]

Finally, social thinkers in the positivist tradition, much like the idealists, found the mainspring of historical change embedded squarely in the process, which they too conceived to be essentially directional in nature. Unlike the idealists, however, most positivists considered the laws of historical change an extension of the laws of natural change (often based on a supposed continuity between biological and social evolution). This assumption was basic to positivist social thought on both sides of the Atlantic. The speculations of Herbert Spencer and Henry Adams, for example, illustrate a widespread tendency to envision history as directional development unfolding in strict accordance with natural law.[33]

The ideational roots of modern historical consciousness were, of course, more tangled than this schematization suggests. In the context of this study, however, the important task is not so much to unravel the various philosophical lineages as to note the common assumptions. By the end of the nineteenth century, most of the leading social thinkers in the United States and Europe were united by three convictions. The first was that patterns of belief and value are created in the matrix of history. For some this constituted a long stride toward total relativism. The second was that history is a process of continuous development. Few, if any, seriously believed in a "block universe" in which the

---

[32]For developmental laws see Berlin, *Marx,* 128-30; Mandelbaum, *History,* 64-67, 87-89, 93, 401 (but cf. 72-73); Wagar, *Good Tidings,* 27-34. For Spencer see Mandelbaum, *History,* 90-91; *Dictionary of the History of Ideas,* s.v. "Evolutionism," by Thomas A. Goudge; Richard Hofstadter, *Social Darwinism in American Thought,* rev. ed. (Boston: Beacon Press, 1955) 37. For Darwin see Goudge, "Evolutionism"; Hofstadter, *Social Darwinism,* 4; John C. Greene, *Darwin and the Modern World View* (Baton Rouge: Louisiana State University Press, 1961) esp. 95; Bert James Loewenberg, *Darwinism Comes to America* (Philadelphia: Fortress Press, 1969 [1941]) 30-33. John Dewey's classic essay, "The Influence of Darwinism on Philosophy," is reprinted in Miller, *American Thought;* see 218.

[33]For the intrinsic directionality of history see Nisbet, *Social Change,* 168-70 (but cf. 160-64 for pre-Darwinian theories of social evolution). For the link with natural change see Greene, *Darwin,* 100; Hughes, *Consciousness,* 37; Mandelbaum, *History,* 78; Stow Persons, *American Minds* (New York: Holt, Rinehart and Winston, 1958) 222-24.

last brick of history had been mortared into place. The third conviction, logically tied to the second, was what Ralph Henry Gabriel aptly called "cosmic constitutionalism." It assumed that the processes of history are propelled by directional laws that are essentially extrahistorical in nature. In time this last assumption—namely, that history has a preordained destiny—dropped from sight. By the 1920s most philosophers, historians, and social scientists had come to believe that the only logic history bears is what people commit to it, moment by moment. They realized that historical process is synchronic rather than diachronic; that the laws of history are functional rather than directional. And in turn a few—perhaps very few—gradually recognized that "development" too is a metaphor. Organic things develop, but history only changes.[34]

Historical awareness rarely arrived in a neatly-tied package. Different scholars stressed different components of the historicist world view. Henri Bergson and William James, for example, emphasized the third element, the radical openness of history, yet failed to press the first element, the historicity of culture, to the logical conclusion that persons are nothing but the sum of their historical experiences. Oswald Spengler and (the later) William Graham Sumner represent the opposite tendencies: stark ethical relativism coupled with more or less directional notions about historical process. Increasingly, however, a consistent and radical historicism, as evident in Max Weber and John Dewey, came to characterize the work of the leading social thinkers. Edward Purcell called it a sweeping turn to "non-Eucleadianism," by

---

[34]For the extrahistorical nature of the laws of history see Gabriel, *Democratic Thought, passim,* esp. 290; Loewenberg, *Darwinism,* 30-33; May, *End,* 153; Persons, *American Minds,* 323; Wagar, *Good Tidings,* 30-38. American social thinkers of the late nineteenth century who worked with this assumption include Richard T. Ely, Simon Patten, John Bates Clark, (the early) William Graham Sumner, John Bascom, Roscoe Pound, James Coolidge Carter, Josiah Royce, Charles Horton Cooley, Herbert Baxter Adams, John W. Burgess, Andrew Dixon White, Woodrow Wilson, and even the naturalist John Wesley Powell. The evaporation of the concept of development is described in Hughes, *Consciousness,* 428; Nisbet, *Social Change,* 224, 288; Noble, *Paradox,* 53-54. For the distinction in twentieth-century thought between synchronic and diachronic laws see Mandelbaum *History,* 114-15, and Nisbet, *Social Change,* 7, 168-70, 284-87, and chap. 8. For "law" in recent social scientific thought see Robert K. Merton, *Social Theory and Social Structure* (Glencoe IL: Free Press, 1957) 96-99.

which he meant that the possibility of a rational, objective ground for value judgments, the possibility of "a priori synthetic" knowledge of any sort, in any field (including mathematics and formal logic), was perfunctorily discarded by virtually all serious scholars.[35]

By about 1930, in short, historical consciousness had become, in Benedetto Croce's words, "pure and complete." The idea of the historical creation of culture had become an ideology of unflinching epistemic relativism. Even scientific knowledge had been chained to the perspective of the observer. It was, at best, a "convenient fiction" for cutting into the chaos of reality. The supposition that history is a process of developmental change had become the doctrine of the infinite plasticity of human nature. And the belief that history is directional had yielded to the view that history is not going anywhere, but is as random as the elements of nature. Eric Temple Bell, professor of mathematics at the California Institute of Technology and former president of the Mathematical Association of America, apparently spoke for the majority of professional scholars in 1930 when he concluded that "certainty has vanished, and there is no hope at present of its return in any form which we might recognize."[36]

This was the historicist legacy—what Joseph Wood Krutch rather melancholically called "the modern temper"—and thoughtful Chris-

---

[35]For Bergson see Masur, *Prophets,* 254, 260. For James see David W. Marcel, *Progress and Pragmatism* (Westport CT: Greenwood Press, 1974) 8-9, 25, 189, and Cushing Strout, "The Unfinished Arch: William James and the Idea of History," *American Quarterly* 13 (1961): 505-15. For Spengler see Wagar, *Good Tidings,* 163-64, 185. For Sumner see Hofstadter, *Social Darwinism,* 55, 60-65. For Weber see Hughes, *Consciousness,* 293, 331, 420. For Dewey see Marcel, *Progress,* 203-29, and Morton White, *Social Thought in America* (Boston: Beacon Press, 1957 [1947]) *passim.* Purcell's point is perhaps best made by pitting representatives of the older against the newer generation. Compare, for example, Richard T. Ely with Thorstein Veblen; Lewis Henry Morgan with Franz Boas; Albion Small with Robert E. Park; Roscoe Pound with Thurmond Arnold; Woodrow Wilson with Charles Beard (*The Crisis of Democratic Theory* [Lexington: University Press of Kentucky, 1973] 17-20, 47-106, esp. 53-54).

[36]Croce is quoted without attribution in Meyerhoff, *Philosophy,* 12. Eric Temple Bell, *Debunking Science* (1930) 39, is quoted in Purcell, *Crisis,* 59. More generally, see Russett, *Darwin,* chap. 8—significantly and aptly titled "The Demise of Certitude." On the literature of the development of historicism, see "Historicism: A Bibliographical Note," at the end of this book.

tians everywhere had to come to terms with it. By 1930, if not much earlier, it was clear that Protestant liberals had given their hearts to a thoroughly historical view of social reality. They made theistic modifications, to be sure, but by and large they were persuaded that knowledge of divine things, like knowledge of all things, must be found squarely in the flow of history if it is to be found anywhere at all.[37] Most Protestant conservatives and virtually all fundamentalists, on the other hand, rejected the whole business with scarcely a second thought. But there were a few conservatives, such as Augustus H. Strong, who took these questions with utmost seriousness because they knew that they had no choice. At the same time they clung to the conviction that the truths—or at least the essential truths—summarized in the great creeds of Christendom had somehow eluded the grip of historical process.

---

[37]Joseph Wood Krutch, *The Modern Temper* (New York: Harcourt, Brace and World, 1929). For the growth of historical consciousness in Protestant liberal thought see Welch, *Protestant Thought,* chap. 7; Sydney E. Ahlstrom, *A Religious History of the American People* (New Haven: Yale University Press, 1972) chap. 47, esp. 772-74; William R. Hutchison, *The Modernist Impulse in American Protestantism* (Cambridge MA: Harvard University Press, 1976) esp. chap. 2.

Chapter Two

Breaking the Shell
of Orthodox Rationalism:
The Education of the Old Strong

B Y THE MIDDLE of the nineteenth century romantic notions of epistemology and pedagogy were well established
in and around Boston, but few of their warming rays had
yet reached New Haven. Augustus Strong's education at Yale College
consisted of daily confrontations with classical languages, literature, and
the philosophical and theological implications of orthodox rationalism—all accomplished by rote recitation. "The system," he recalled
some fifty years later, "consisted simply of learning lessons from a textbook and reciting them to the tutor or professor. No discussion was
permitted at any time. . . . [No] question was asked by any student of
an instructor during the whole four years." Still more regrettable, said
Strong, was the failure of his teachers to convey any sense of the historical development or cultural impact of a topic or discipline. Stalwarts such as Timothy Dwight and Noah Porter "never . . . suggested
to us that a subject might have light thrown upon it by side reading.

. . . Never was the history of a science spoken of."[1]

After graduating from Yale in 1857, Strong took the year of travel in Europe customary for young men of his social class, then entered Rochester Theological Seminary. The dominant influence at Rochester at that time was Ezekial Gilman Robinson, president of the school, later president of Brown, and always a haunting presence in Strong's life. Robinson easily persuaded him that genuine education entails independent reflection and criticism; he also persuaded Strong that genuine knowledge properly begins with metaphysics. "It alone dealt with realities," Strong later remembered himself believing, and "one could have no firm footing in any other department of knowledge unless he had reached a good metaphysical foundation." For Robinson, however, the term metaphysics had a very precise meaning. Like many learned clerics of the day, Robinson had been deeply influenced by William Hamilton's synthesis of Scottish and Kantian epistemology. Thus he taught Strong to regard metaphysics not as the study of being, but as the study of the timeless and universal categories of thought through which being is known.[2]

Even so, during Strong's first pastorate at Haverhill, Massachusetts, he exhibited some awareness of the meaning of historical conditioning. Month after month the young pastor labored to teach the

---

[1]*AB,* 62-63,181. See also *PAR,* 443-60. For mid-nineteenth-century pedagogy at Yale (and elsewhere) see Mark A. Noll, "Christian Thinking and the Rise of the American University," *Christian Scholar's Review* 9 (1979): 4-8; J. David Hoeveler, Jr., *James McCosh and the Scottish Intellectual Tradition* (Princeton: Princeton University Press, 1981) 235.

[2]*AB,* 102. In regard to Robinson, Strong wrote: "Words and phrases which I must have heard from him in the classroom thirty-five years ago, and which have come to be a part of my mental furniture, I now recognize as not my own but his" (*MISC* 2:64; see also 58, 63). For Robinson's influence and thought, see Norman H. Maring, "Baptists and Changing Views of the Bible," *Foundations* 1 (July 1958): 56; Carl F. H. Henry, *Personal Idealism and Strong's Theology* (Wheaton IL: Van Kampen Press, 1951) 20-47. Strong believed that Robinson was, however, too much influenced by Hamilton's relativism. He especially disliked Robinson's view that humans have no knowledge of God's substance. Strong countered that knowledge of divine attributes necessarily entails a limited knowledge of divine substance (*MISC* 2:69-70; see also *ST,* 4).

congregation the difference between permanent and transitory norms in Scripture. He especially hoped to overturn the tradition against women speaking in the services. "I claimed that Paul's prohibition was only for the time and place for which he wrote," he recalled. "What was indecorous in apostolic times was now permissible and proper." Or so it seemed.

> At the next prayer meeting everybody was agog to see the denouement. I had no sooner taken my seat after the introductory exercises than a voluble young woman, who had . . . for months been aching for the chance, arose and poured forth an incoherent lot of sobs and protestations that made the judicious grieve and did the business for women's speaking for that evening and for many evenings after.[3]

After four years with the small congregation in Haverhill, Strong was called to the First Baptist Church of Cleveland, Ohio. Though he was only twenty-nine, the Cleveland church was one of the largest, wealthiest, and most prestigious in the denomination. He soon acquired a reputation for meaty, meticulously prepared sermons on the great themes of Christian faith. And he began to think broadly and deeply about the origin and nature of religious knowledge. There is no reason to believe that he was particularly sensitive to the problems raised by historicism, but he was beginning to spin a web of ideas about the way religious knowledge is acquired, and this web eventually ensnared some of the most troubling questions of the age.[4]

In his handwritten *Autobiography,* penned a half-century later for the interest of his children and grandchildren, Strong allowed that his scholarly efforts in Cleveland soon earned "some reputation" for erudition. Before long he was offered a professorship at Crozer Seminary, then the presidency of Brown. He declined these invitations, but when Ezekial Robinson became president of Brown in 1872, Strong was offered Robinson's vacated theology chair at Rochester. He liked the idea of returning to his old seminary, but dryly told the trustees that he could

---

[3]*AB,* 152-53.

[4]Ernest W. Parsons, "Dr. Strong as Preacher," *RTS Bulletin* [72] (supplement, May 1922): 16-18; Winthrop S. Hudson, *Baptists in Transition* (Valley Forge PA: Judson Press, 1979) 120.

not do theology very well unless, as he put it, "I had affairs in my own hands." So in 1872, at the age of thirty-six, Strong moved his rapidly growing family back to Rochester to begin his forty-year reign as president and professor of systematic theology.[5]

II

After the turn of the century some of Strong's friends suggested that he had crossed an intellectual watershed in the early 1890s. The extent to which he had truly scrapped the scholastic underpinnings of his 1888 collection of essays, *Philosophy and Religion,* and the first four editions of his *Systematic Theology* is perhaps debatable. Nonetheless, the hypothesis that Strong experienced a major change in the early 1890s is generally persuasive, and it allows us to analyze his early work—that is, the work forged in the quarter century between his graduation from seminary and the early 1890s—as a unit. The goal here is not to summarize Strong's early writing, which was a learned but quite conventional exposition of Reformed systematic theology. The aim, rather, is to see how modern notions of social and cultural process slowly, almost imperceptibly, undermined the elaborate framework of orthodox rationalism that he had inherited and used to uphold his philosophical and theological system.[6]

At first glance it is difficult to imagine a more ahistorical way to launch a system of theology than the one Strong chose. Like his great rival Charles Hodge, Strong declared on the first page of the first edition of his *Systematic Theology* that theology must be understood as a science, and any science worthy of the name "discovers facts and relations, but does not create them." The object of theological propositions, the reality to which they refer, he wrote, has an "existence entirely independent of the subjective mental processes of the theologian." Thus theological science is the description of objective ontological facts—facts

---

[5]*AB,* 181, 203.

[6]The depth and permanence of the change of the early 1890s is assessed in chapters 3 and 4. Outsiders' perceptions are discussed in chapter 5.

hung in timeless suspension above the limited and mutable eyesight of the observer.[7]

However, this prolegomenon was, in a sense, only window dressing. Like contemporary Protestant liberals—or New Theologians, as they were beginning to be called in the 1870s and 1880s—Strong clearly recognized that systematic theology must begin with serious inquiry into the anthropological sources of religious knowledge. But there was a difference. Liberals ordinarily claimed that theology must start with the affective or experiential sources of religious knowledge, while Strong believed that theology must start with the formal epistemic sources. Before we can know anything else, he averred, we have to figure out how the structures of the mind imprint themselves upon the process of knowing. What, in other words, is the nature of the mental grid that inevitably filters and shapes our knowledge of divine things?[8]

Examination of the principles or categories by which the mind knows reality is what Strong, following Robinson and other Hamiltonians, called metaphysics. For him metaphysics was the study of the "underlying facts of mind and matter," the analysis of the "great truths," "first truths," or "rational intuitions" inherent in thought itself. Thus Strong argued that notions such as law, causation, and order, which are cemented into human consciousness, form the presuppositional foundation for all knowledge, including religious knowledge.[9]

Strong bristled at the claim that "metaphysical and moral inquiry" is inferior as a source of knowledge to empirical natural research. He berated contemporary positivists, not because they were godless, but because they denied the usefulness of the metaphysical study of consciousness. Thus Comte's great failing, said Strong, was that he had failed to see that a "structural pre-equipment of mind is necessary in order to correlate and arrange phenomena. The very idea of unity by

---

[7]*ST*, 1-2. For comparison with Charles Hodge in particular, and the Princeton theology in general, see Mark A. Noll, ed., *The Princeton Theology* (Grand Rapids MI: Baker Book House, 1983) 25-45, 117-31.

[8]For the methodology of the New Theology see William R. Hutchison, *The Modernist Impulse in American Protestantism* (Cambridge MA: Harvard University Press, 1976) chap. 3.

[9]*PAR*, 2-3,15,20-22; *ST* (1907) 52.

which we classify facts must come to us from the unity of our own self-consciousness." Strong believed that Comte's rejection of notions such as consciousness, causality, and law had entangled him in a denial of logic itself: "Where there is no law, there can be no logic." Where there is no logic, even "mathematical truth is purely phenomenal."[10]

Now as it happens, said Strong, the metaphysical study of consciousness reveals that the premier "first truth" of consciousness is the presupposition that God exists. This presupposition logically and cognitively precedes all forms of religious knowledge. More precisely, it is the assumption that is necessary in order to make sense of any other cognitive act.

> The validity of the simplest mental acts, such as sense-perception, self-consciousness, and memory, depends upon the assumption that a God exists who has so constituted our minds that they give us knowledge of things as they are.

Even the logical operations of the mind, such as induction and deduction, can be taken seriously only by "presupposing a thinking Deity" who makes the universe to correspond to the "investigating faculties of man."[11]

These early reflections on the metaphysical study of consciousness were not, however, as antiseptically ahistorical as they seem. In at least two ways Strong compromised the timeless and universal nature of the principles of consciousness. One was deliberate, the other undoubtedly not deliberate.

---

[10]*PAR*, 8-11, 20.

[11]*ST*, 2, 29, 33. Some New Theologians, such as Newman Smyth, agreed that revelation presupposes an intuitive knowledge of God rather than the reverse. But Strong attacked Smyth's assertion that this primal intuition of God is noncognitive. Indeed, presuppositional knowledge of God, Strong boldly added, is knowledge of the divine substance itself (*ST*, 34-35, 4). For the large role of presuppositionalism in evangelical thought see George M. Marsden, "The Collapse of Evangelical Academia," in Alvin Plantinga and Nicholas Wolterstorff, eds., *Faith and Rationality* (Notre Dame IN: University of Notre Dame Press, 1983) 219-64. For Strong's contribution to that tradition see Kenneth S. Kantzer, "Unity and Diversity in Evangelical Faith," in David F. Wells and John D. Woodbridge, eds., *The Evangelicals* (Nashville: Abingdon Press, 1975) 47-52.

The first compromise was his affirmation that knowledge of God is presuppositional but not a priori. Experience awakens and deepens the "first truths" of consciousness, but experience does not create them. It is only in the ebb and flow of life that the God presupposition, like other "first truths," emerges—and certain kinds of experiences, such as confrontation with death, are more effective in this respect than others. "When we say that God is known [presuppositionally]," said Strong, "we do not hold that this knowledge will develope itself apart from observation and experience, but only that it will develope itself upon occasion of observation and experience." Strong thought that the same is true of morality. Everyone is born with a latent ability to make moral discriminations, but it is only in the flux of experience that this ability is awakened and nurtured.[12]

One could, of course, go too far. The moral philosophy of the positivists was, in Strong's estimation, downright pernicious. He thought that they made moral development radically historical, so that the "feeling of obligation is [nothing but] the result of ancestral experiences of utility." The great mistake of speculators such as Herbert Spencer (whom Strong especially loved to flog) was that they confused the formal intuition of right with advantage, and the formal intuition of wrong with disadvantage. Strong did not object to Spencer's historical interpretation of the material content of this or that particular moral prescription, but he resisted the idea that the formal ability to discriminate between right and wrong is itself a product of experience. "All the languages of mankind," he retorted, "distinguish between these two ideas and put an immeasurable gulf between them."[13]

Strong's second compromise with the modern view of history proved more portentous. By stipulating that religious knowledge, like all other forms of knowledge, is mined from the structure of consciousness, Strong made the study of consciousness—namely, metaphysics—logically and epistemically prior to theology. The unintended result was to establish the philosopher, and ultimately the secular scholar, rather than the theologian, as the final arbiter of truth and reality. By making the "first truths" of consciousness the gate to God and by making philosophers

---

[12]*PAR*, 86; see also *ST*, 30.

[13]*PAR*, 53-54.

the gatekeepers, Strong unwittingly placed unmediated religious knowledge—direct revelation, the whisper of the Spirit, or the decrees of the Church—in a derivative status. More seriously, he had effectively handcuffed knowledge of divine things to the historical development of consciousness itself. From there it was only a short step to the realization that human beings are, if not mere creatures of their own past, at least chained to the processes of their past.

III

When we turn from Strong's view of the relation between historical experience and the epistemic form of religious knowledge to his view of the relation between historical experience and the content—the actual "stuff"—of religious knowledge, we encounter, once again, a world without history. Or so it seems at first glance. But a second look reveals that modern notions of continuity and process were quietly, almost imperceptibly, at work.

Thoughtful Christians have always regarded human history as the locus of God's saving and revelatory activity. In the late nineteenth century, however, the question that most sharply divided liberal and conservative Protestant theologians was whether revelation emerges from within the historical process, as a new dimension of meaning and value, or whether it intrudes from outside the historical process, in the form of miracles and direct communications from God to his people. Until the early 1890s Strong, like most Reformed orthodox theologians, emphasized the latter—the interruptive, intrusive aspect of revelation. And while he never depreciated the revelatory value of miracles in the realm of nature, it is clear that in his view the miraculous process by which God's thoughts had been conveyed to the minds of the biblical authors was more significant.[14]

Unlike many of his orthodox contemporaries, Strong was not, however, especially interested in the method of biblical inspiration. He was quite content to define inspiration as "the divine influence which secures a correct transmission of the truth to the future"—and to let it go at that. But whether there had been a *correct* transmission of truth was

---

[14]For a general survey of these issues see H. D. McDonald, *Theories of Revelation* (London: G. Allen and Unwin, 1963) 119-36; chap. 6, esp. 196, 203-217.

not open for discussion. He was certain that the notion of inspiration was worthless if it did not mean that Scripture had been preserved from all error—which meant, of course, that the Bible originated wholly outside the normal modes of cultural change. "We do not admit the existence of scientific error in the Scripture," he flatly asserted, and he devoted a sizable part of the first edition of the *Systematic Theology* to a refutation of alleged flaws and inconsistencies.[15]

A curious turn of events in the late 1880s illumines the intensity of Strong's convictions about the plenary accuracy of the Bible. Hard feelings had developed between him and William Rainey Harper, who at this time was teaching Old Testament at Vassar, but soon was to become the first president of the Baptist-related University of Chicago. The background of that relationship is outside the scope of this study, but it suffices to say that Strong believed that Harper was unfit to call himself a Baptist precisely because he did not uphold the total trustworthiness of the Old and New Testaments. Strong demanded to know whether, in Harper's view, inspiration "guarantees the truth of the Scripture record, or whether it leaves room for error." Harper's lectures, he charged, "seem to intimate that . . . [inspiration] does not after all secure the absolute truthfulness of the Old Testament documents." If a mistake of any sort were admitted, even a minor mistake of attribution, said Strong, "I do not see what inspiration worth talking about is left after such an admission is made."[16]

Strong's conviction that the Bible had eluded the grip of historical construction showed up in numerous ways. Repeatedly he declared that the Bible is not a compilation of "merely human productions," but the "work of one divine mind." Not only is there perfect complementarity among the many authors, but the death of the last apostle—the last in-

---

[15]*PAR,* 150-53. See also *ST,* 95-104, and AHS, *Lectures on Theology* (Rochester NY: Press of E. R. Andrews, 1876) 51.

[16]Strong to William Rainey Harper, 8 January 1889 and 25 December 1888. For Strong's long and tortured relationship with Harper, see Lars Hoffman, "William Rainey Harper and the Chicago Fellowship" (Ph.D. dissertation, University of Iowa, 1978) 34-41, 109-116, and Conrad Henry Moehlman, "How the Baptist Super-University Planned for New York City Was Built in Chicago," *Colgate Rochester Divinity School Bulletin* 11 (1938-1939): 131.

spired writer—marked an absolute disjunction between the period of substantive revelation and the nonrevelatory ages that followed.[17]

For all practical purposes, then, in these early years Strong conceived of history not as an organic process, and certainly not as a web of meanings, but as a succession of discrete events—very much like a line of fence posts stretching off into the horizon. Here and there a post was missing. These were the places where God had broken into the line and revealed something of himself and his purposes. Most of these interventions had involved the disclosure of knowledge (otherwise unobtainable) to the writers of Scripture, but some also had involved the providential and miraculous rearrangement of social and natural sequences. Thus the material—the "stuff"—of religious knowledge had come from history but it was not of history. It was essentially different in origin and in kind.

Nonetheless, even in the 1870s and 1880s, when Strong's thinking was most monolithically ahistorical, deep in the interior the seeds of historical consciousness were beginning to sprout. For one thing, he was beginning to feel the cogency of an evolutionary interpretation of civilization. Strong was not, to be sure, a Reformed version of Henry Thomas Buckle. At this point he still thought, for example, that Adam and Eve were the literal parents of the race. He still believed that Providence, "in every century and through agencies *utterly insufficient of themselves,* summons new moral forces into being." And when he tried his hand at political economy he discovered, like most clerical economists of the day, that political economy is a universal science. "Since the laws of nature and the laws of mind are everywhere the same," he ponderously intoned, "there must be one Political Economy, as there is one Astronomy and one Moral Philosophy, for England and for India, for America and for Japan."[18] Even so, the "climate of the age" included a broadly evolutionary view of the progress of civilization, and Strong could hardly avoid its influence. "Evolution," he admitted (a bit too easily), "is only a mode of divine action, not in conflict with design, but a new illustration of it—a method of securing a result, and so the latest and best proof [of] a designing God." Moreover, organic, evo-

---

[17]*ST,* 104, 84-94.

[18]*ST,* 238; *PAR,* 29, 238, 444.

lutionary development applies to culture as well as biology. "No man can teach history who conceives of it as a record of isolated facts," for "where there is any degree of civilization, there are no sudden movements, no changes without cause, no revolutions without age-long preparation. History is no rope of sand, but an organic whole."[19]

The implications of the last passage are so startling one wonders if Strong fully realized what he was saying. One formula he often employed was to say that although divine truth never changes, human apprehension of it broadens and deepens through experience. Thus development in theological science means the same as development in the physical sciences. "What is originality in astronomy? Is it man's creation of new planets? No, it is man's discovery of planets that were never seen before, or the bringing to light of relations between them that were never before suspected."[20]

Still, we are left with a puzzle. Time and time again Strong insisted that neither Christian doctrine, nor the apprehension of Christian doctrine, is subject to development. In an 1875 address to fellow ministers, for example, he warned that one of the most insidious influences infecting the denomination was the growing assumption that "there is no fixed, complete and binding system of church organization revealed in the New Testament." Strong called his comrades to embrace the "warrior spirit that gives battle rather than yield one inch of truth." (And in a move calculated to do just that he treated pedobaptism in the *Systematic Theology* under the headings of "Heresy" and "Schism.")[21]

How then should we reconcile Strong's admission that the apprehension of divine truth is socially and developmentally conditioned with equally forceful claims, made on other occasions, that it is not? It may be unfair to expect consistency in addresses, sermons, essays, and books written for different audiences. Yet Strong was a sedulous scholar, who often memorized his sermons verbatim, and it seems unlikely that he would have played for a crowd. A more plausible explanation is that he was slowly coming to see that the human apprehension of divine truth,

---

[19]*PAR*, 28-29, 340.

[20]*CCEM*, 459; see also *ST*, 19. It is significant that this discussion of the progressive apprehension of fixed truth is not found in Strong's early *Lectures on Theology*.

[21]*PAR*, 246, 248; *ST*, 549-50.

however certain at the moment, however valid in context, ultimately is limited by one's perspective. Another way of putting it is to say that he never doubted that the barque is sturdy, indeed, flawless. But he also was beginning to suspect that it bobs and lurches and floats in the stream of history.

IV

As early as 1878 Strong became interested in questions of theological method. In a closely reasoned critique of Herbert Spencer's cosmology he argued that any inquiry into the nature of reality must be strictly inductive, always working backward "from effects to causes." Indeed, said Strong, this is precisely where Spencer went astray, for "the deductive element, rather than the inductive, is the determining characteristic of [his] scheme." Not surprisingly, Strong had great fun with Spencerian monsters such as the primal Unknowable, the persistence of force, and the law of progression from homogeneity to heterogeneity. Nonetheless, as Dwight Bozeman and others have shown, appreciation for inductive procedure was one thing; genuine commitment to historical-critical method was quite another.[22]

Strong did not publicly discuss biblical higher criticism, for example, until the mid-1890s, but privately he warned his protégé and onetime friend William Rainey Harper to be wary of it. Critics such as Ferdinand Christian Bauer and Crawford Toy were animated, said Strong, not by "literary considerations," nor by a true regard for the "conclusion of science," but by a "desire to get rid of the supernatural." In his view it was their assumptions, not their empirical findings, that led them to discover "myth and legend" and a "concoction of fables" in the Scriptural record. Strong occasionally jumped on the critical bandwagon when he thought that it would take him where he wanted to go. Yet he rightly sensed that sooner or later the methods of modern historical scholarship would create more problems for orthodoxy than they would solve. "Let us not 'bow to the passing Zeitgeist,'" he implored

---

[22]*PAR,* 40-41. Theodore Dwight Bozeman, *Protestants in an Age of Science* (Chapel Hill: University of North Carolina Press, 1977) 60-70, 138-59.

Harper. "[Let us stand] as simple Baptists always have . . . upon the consensus of all the ages."[23]

Because Strong did not say much about historical method before the 1890s, it is difficult to know what exactly he was thinking. Still, there are good reasons to believe that in his eyes the real danger of historical method was not the procedure itself—not the search for contextual connections and the like—but the cardinal assumption on which the procedure usually rested. And that assumption was, of course, that reason—critical, reflective, inquiring reason—is the principal instrument by which significant knowledge of the past, including significant religious knowledge revealed in the past, is attained. He freely acknowledged that reason "must examine the credentials of . . . revelation . . . and reduce its facts to order and system." In this sense reason is, admittedly, the "preliminary criterion" of truth. But Strong invariably added that reason's "highest wisdom" is to proclaim its own insufficiency. Those who fail to see this, those who make reason the "ultimate criterion" of truth, corrupt it, and thus turn it into a self-caricature that he derisively called "mere reasoning." Or, to put it a bit differently, Strong feared that those who used higher critical methods often failed to see that the fear of the Lord is not the end but the very beginning of wisdom.[24]

Nonetheless, deep within this fortress of conservatism, the lure of modern historical method persistently tugged. The nature of the lure is not easily defined, for it was more like an attitude than a precise idea. One might call it a habit of openness, a dislike for unwarranted certitude, a nose for the common sense of a situation. It was, in short, an instinctive aversion to formalism. At the very least, Strong's antiformalist attitude entailed a standing conviction that religious knowledge cannot be harvested in isolation from other fields of knowledge. "All history," Strong wrote, "all science, all master-pieces of human genius in painting and sculpture, in epic and tragic poetry, in eloquence and

---

[23]Strong to William Rainey Harper, 8 January 1889; see also Strong to Harper, 25 December 1888, and 4 January 1889.

[24]*PAR*, 573; see also *ST*, 16. The invidious distinction between reason and reasoning was a recurring feature of nineteenth-century orthodox rationalism; see Marsden, "Collapse," 239; E. Brooks Holifield, *The Gentlemen Theologians* (Durham NC: Duke University Press, 1978) 54.

state-craft and invention, can help the interpretation of the word of God." To accomplish this end Strong resolved early in his career to acquire a working knowledge of the natural and social sciences by working systematically through the standard handbooks on geology, mineralogy, meteorology, chemistry, astronomy, botany and political economy. With more than a bit of pride he later described the laboratory apparatus and the mineral, fossil, and biological specimens he had collected over the years, as "the prettiest and completest little collection I have seen."[25]

Still more important than breadth was Strong's habit of aggressive curiosity. In his estimation this was a token of the way persons disciplined their minds and their lives in general. He knew the difference between erudition and pedantry. A compulsive traveler and outdoorsman (and father of six children), he heartily disliked the scholar who smelt of the lamp. "The mere book-worm," he gibed, simply "cannot be a good interpreter" of the word of God. Rather one must be a "full man . . . in with the life of his times, knowing something by personal observation of its currents of opinion, mixing with cultivated people and . . . participating in the political and denominational movements of the day."[26]

Strong recognized that his eagerness to embrace all truth, wherever it might be found, had its pitfalls. Too often, he admitted, his sermons came close to "naturalism" and lacked spiritual fervor. This may have been true, but there can be little doubt that his real problem was a temptation of a very different sort. It was what William R. Hutchison has called the "modernist impulse"—a powerful inclination to find truth

---

[25]*PAR*, 326; *AB*, 180. An avocational but surprisingly extensive knowledge of the natural sciences was not unusual among learned conservatives like Strong; see Bozeman, *Protestants*, 7; William James Morison, "George Frederick Wright" (Ph.D. dissertation, Vanderbilt University, 1971) esp. 427; Ralph E. Luker, *A Southern Tradition in Theology and Social Criticism* (Lewiston NY: Edwin Mellen Press, 1984) chap. 2. On the other hand, it was precisely because conservatives such as Strong knew much about the content but very little about the methods of late nineteenth-century science that they soon found themselves in serious trouble; see James Ward Smith, "Religion and Science in American Philosophy," in Smith and A. Leland Jamison, eds., *The Shaping of American Religion* (Princeton: Princeton University Press, 1961) esp. 404.

[26]*PAR*, 326.

and value not only in the timeless revelation given in Scripture, but also in the environing web of history and culture, in the totality of the human setting.[27]

V

In retrospect it is clear that Strong's earliest work contained the seeds of at least three concessions to the modern view of historical process. The first, prompted by Hamilton's synthesis of Scottish and Kantian epistemology, was the claim that the basic building blocks of religious knowledge are embedded in the structure of consciousness. The second was a pronounced affinity for an evolutionary interpretation of civilization. And the third was the lure of the modernist impulse—a temptation to look to history and contemporary culture for amplification of the meaning of revelation.

Although each of these concessions was extremely limited, each was, in a sense, a crevice into which the "acids of modernity" had seeped. It would be an exaggeration to say that the whole structure of Strong's theology, which had been built on ahistorical assumptions, suddenly came tumbling down. But there can be little doubt that by 1890 the foundation had been very badly eroded.

---

[27]*AB*, 197; Hutchison, *Modernist Impulse.*

Chapter Three

Intimations of Christ in Creation: Beginnings of the New Strong

I
N THE LATE 1880s and early 1890s something remarkable happened to Augustus Strong. A sunburst seemed to irradiate his thought, casting the old doctrines in a new and more pleasing light. Publicly the turning point was a series of articles about cosmology published in the *Examiner* in 1894 and 1895 and reissued in 1899 under the title *Christ in Creation and Ethical Monism*. What is remarkable about these essays is that they revealed a powerful new impulse to conceive reality as one and to see the divine as immanent within the human historical process.[1]

---

[1]"Christ in Creation," *Examiner* (6 October 1894); "Ethical Monism," *Examiner* (1, 8, 15 November 1894); "Ethical Monism Once More," *Examiner* (17, 24 October, 3 November 1895); these essays were reprinted in *CCEM*, which I have used. They were also reprinted in *Ethical Monism, in Two Series of Three Each, and Christ in Creation, with a Review by Professor Elias H. Johnson* (New York: Examiner, 1896). Some of the ideas in the ethical monism articles were prefigured in Strong's 1893 presidential address to the American Baptist Missionary Union, "The Decree of God the Great Encouragement to Missions," reprinted in *CCEM*.

Although Strong left few explicit clues about his motivations, it is tempting to ask why this change took place so abruptly. One possibility is that he was influenced anew by his seminary mentor Ezekial Gilman Robinson. The latter died in June 1894, and about that time Strong first read Robinson's printed lecture notes on systematic theology, posthumously published in 1904 as *Christian Theology*. Although Robinson was not really a liberal, he was quite tolerant of the new currents of thought. Even in the 1850s, said Strong, Robinson had taught "a more modern system than was at that time taught in any other evangelical seminary of any denomination." Even so, it is unlikely that Robinson directly influenced Strong. The younger man disliked Robinson personally and for some reason considered him lax about doctrinal matters. Moreover, Strong almost certainly had sculpted his new cosmological ideas, which he called ethical monism, long before he was reintroduced to Robinson's notes.[2]

Another possible explanation for Strong's eager embrace of ethical monism is that by 1890 or so the external circumstances of his life had grown remarkably comfortable. His personal finances were more than ample, he was moving into the peak of his intellectual power, and his influence among Northern Baptists was unparalleled. In this situation an expansive and benign view of God's relation to the created order presumably would have seemed reasonable as well as congenial. Nonetheless, this explanation also falters. The late 1880s and early 1890s were years of severe turmoil in Strong's personal life and it is more likely that a monistic vision of reality afforded resources for healing and solace. The most acute disappointment of this period was the loss of faith by Strong's brilliant elder son, Charles. I shall probe the impact of that episode more deeply in a later chapter, but it suffices here to say that by Strong's own reckoning Charles's religious estrangement was the most painful ordeal of his life. Also about this time Strong's wife, Harriet, contracted a disease diagnosed as "cerebral meningitis." Though he remained deeply devoted to her until her death in 1914, he may have anticipated the long deterioration of her physical and mental health, which left her an

---

[2]*MISC* 2:63, 107; *AB*, 220; *ST* (1907) 205.

invalid and a virtual recluse for the last thirty years of her life.[3]

Another major disappointment of these years was Strong's inability to persuade John D. Rockefeller to establish a Baptist "super-university" in New York City. Strong rightly perceived that New York was rapidly becoming the leading commercial center of the Western world, and thus the logical site for a highly endowed coeducational institution offering only graduate education. It was to be, in short, the nation's preeminent university. Assuming that he would be president and William Rainey Harper vice-president, Strong was convinced that Baptists were in an auspicious position to seize the educational leadership of modern culture. "Because all truth is Christ's," he insisted, it is "our duty as Christians and as Baptists to provide the highest university training." The story of Strong's turbulent relationship with Rockefeller, and the "treacherous" decision by Harper to support an alternate plan to build the University of Chicago, is outside the scope of this study. It is enough to say that Strong's determination in this matter virtually consumed him. One of the principals in the negotiations described him as "daft," and another depicted him as "melancholy, a profoundly unhappy and disappointed man." Strong himself acknowledged that this one goal had preoccupied his thoughts for a decade. In time he was reconciled with Rockefeller and Harper, and grudgingly applauded the success of the University of Chicago, but he later admitted that he never quite got over the bitterness he had felt when he discovered that "after all I had done for fifteen years, my New York University was gobbled up and transferred to Chicago."[4]

---

[3]For the relationship with Harriet Strong, see *AB*, 157, 201, 330-31, 345, 349-50. At her death he wrote that he had been left "desolate," waiting "till the day dawn, and the shadows flee away." See also Leonard I. Sweet, review of *Autobiography of Augustus Hopkins Strong*, ed. Crerar Douglas, *Bulletin from the Hill* 54 (1982): 4.

[4]Strong's preoccupation with the Baptist superuniversity is evident in virtually all of his letters to William Rainey Harper, 1889-1890. For the AHS quotations see, respectively, "American Baptist Education Society," unpublished address, 29 May 1892, America Baptist Historical Society, and *AB*, 250. For the "daft" and "melancholy" remarks, see, respectively, Thomas W. Goodspeed to Harper, 22 January 1889, and Thomas T. Gates to Henry Morehouse, 3 January 1889, both quoted in Allan Nevins, *John D. Rockefeller* (New York: Charles Scribner's Sons, 1940) 2:223.

In the end, the reasons why Strong so abruptly adopted the philosophy of ethical monism are unknown. But there is no question that the change marked a striking transformation in his understanding of God and God's relation to the world. Even so, the depth and permanence of the transformation was, as we shall see, more elusive.

The term ethical monism was minted by Strong to describe and distinguish his viewpoint from personalistic idealism, which was associated with Borden Parker Bowne in the United States and Hermann Lotze in Germany. Probably the best definition of ethical monism is Strong's own. Each word carries considerable freight.

> *Ethical Monism:* Universe = Finite, partial, graded manifestation of the divine Life; Matter being God's self-limitation under the law of necessity, Humanity being God's self-limitation under the law of freedom, Incarnation and Atonement being God's self-limitation under the law of grace. Metaphysical monism, or the doctrine of one Substance, Principle, or Ground of Being, is consistent with Psychological Dualism, or the doctrine that the soul is personally distinct from matter on the one hand and from God on the other.

The first clause of the definition, which stipulates that the universe, matter, and humanity are a "graded manifestation of the divine Life" is denoted by the noun *monism.* The second clause, which asserts that (1) matter is a product or a manifestation of mind (although it is not reducible to mind), and that (2) minds are distinct from one another and distinct from God, is denoted by the adjective *ethical.* (Ethical is, in this case, a somewhat idiosyncratic term. Strong simply meant to emphasize the personal character of reality, without lapsing into the insubstantialism of Bowne's idealism.) Considered together, then, the two sentences affirm that the universe is made up of one thing (God), and

---

See also Conrad Henry Moehlman, "How the Baptist Super-University Planned for New York City Was Built In Chicago," *Colgate Rochester Divinity School Bulletin* 11 (1938-1939): 134; Lars Hoffman, "William Rainey Harper and the Chicago Fellowship" (Ph.D. dissertation, University of Iowa, 1978) 34-41. For the reconciliation with Harper, see Hoffman, 144, and AHS, "Appreciation [for William Rainey Harper]," *Biblical World* 27 (1906): 235-36.

that this one thing is manifested in distinct parts (divine and human personalities).[5]

All of this becomes clearer when we see that in Strong's view the cosmos is radically Christological. In the eternal dimension God the Father is pure potentiality, "latent, unexpressed, unrevealed," while Christ is God's objectification of himself to himself. In the temporal dimension Christ is God's objectification in the finite universe. "Since Christ is the principle of revelation in God," said Strong, "we may say that God never thought, said, or did anything except through Christ. . . . Creation, then, is the externalization of the divine ideas through the will of Christ." Creation is not, in other words, an emanation of divine energy but a distinct and separable product of divine self-limitation. Strong called this process the continuous "depotentiation of the Logos."[6]

The depotentiation of the Logos results in, among other things, multiple centers of consciousness. Strong called this psychological dualism, and this is what he meant to emphasize when he talked about the ethical side of ethical monism. The main point here, to use one of his favorite metaphors, is that individual souls relate to one another and to God just as islands in the sea relate to one another and to the undergirding firmament. Each is a distinct, autonomous entity, yet each is linked with the others because all share a common substance and because all are anchored in the same subterranean reality. The universe is, in short, qualitatively monist but quantitatively plural. Further, the world is quantitatively plural—or more exactly, dual—because matter is derived from the divine life. Strong did not mean to suggest that matter is either illusory or reducible to life. But he did believe that

[5]*ST* (1907) 90. For the influence of Lotze and Bowne on American Protestant thought, see William R. Hutchison, *The Modernist Impulse in American Protestantism* (Cambridge MA: Harvard University Press, 1976) 121-26, 130, 208-11. For a succinct summary of personalism, see Thomas A. Langford, *Practical Divinity* (Nashville: Abingdon Press, 1983) 119-24. For the surprising influence of this tradition on conservatives see Leo Sandon, Jr., "Boston University Personalism and Southern Baptist Theology," *Foundations* 20 (1977): 101-105.

[6]*CCEM*, 2-3, 29; see also *ST* (1907) 109.

matter ultimately comes from life, and is properly regarded as a manifestation or artifact of life.[7]

For Strong the fundamental import of ethical monism was, then, that Christ, the Logos, is the power that constitutes and sustains all things in the physical, cultural, and spiritual realms. Strong loved to stress this point, affirming again and again in sermons, essays, and lectures that Christ is the universal source of all creativity.

> He is the principle of gravitation, of mental interaction, of logical induction, of evolution, of moral unity. . . . No design? Rather there is nothing but design. The sunset clouds are painted by his hand. The laws of cohesion and of chemical union are laws of his mind and wisdom.

Upholding "all things by the word of his power," Christ's creative energy "pulses and throbs in all men everywhere. . . . The whole race lives, moves, and has its being in him; for he is the soul of its soul and the life of its life."[8]

In these years Strong was prone to describe Christ's being and activity in almost Bergsonian terms as the divine vitality that constitutes and pervades existence. Happily noting that theologians had "outgrown the old scholastic terminology of substance and qualities," he implored the church to go "back to the far simpler and more scriptural category of life and its powers," for the relation between Christ and the world is literally biological. "Christ and his people are one, in a deeper and more real sense than we have ever imagined," he wrote. "We are his brain, his tongue, his hands, for translating the decrees of God into history."[9]

---

[7]*CCEM*, 189-90; *ST* (1907) 106. In a letter to the Southern Baptist educator E. Y. Mullins, Strong wrote, "I hope you will not make the common mistake of supposing that my 'Monism' makes men 'parts of God.' Men are no more *parts* of God than my thoughts are *parts* of me. Men are *products* of God's mind and will, as my thoughts are *products* of my mind and will. . . . My 'Monism' is ethical—that is what my critics ignore. It recognizes that these products have a relative independence, so much so that men may resist God and resist him forever" (Strong to Mullins, 16 April 1912, Southern Baptist Theological Seminary Archives).

[8]AHS, "Address before the Ministers' Conference," unpublished address, 2 October 1893, American Baptist Historical Society; *CCEM*, 228.

[9]*CCEM*, 158, 28, 275-76; see also *OHCT*, 28.

More pertinent to our present concern is, however, the way that Strong's vision of a continuous, creative effusion—or, more precisely, "depotentiation"—of the divine vitality influenced his understanding of the relation between historical experience and the knowledge of divine things. He began by insisting that Christ is properly apprehended as the power of human consciousness. Human consciousness *is* Christ's self-limitation under the law of freedom. "If I can learn what [Christ] says in the constitution of the human mind, that will be authority for me." This assumption helped to solve some of the most nettlesome problems of philosophy, such as the validity of our knowledge of the external world and the validity of logical relations. Thus Strong argued that "we cannot explain the interaction between individual things unless they are all embraced within a unitary Being who constitutes their underlying reality." Likewise, "Christ is the principle of induction, which permits us to argue from one part of the system to another."[10]

The assumption that Christ is the connective tissue that makes epistemic transactions possible was, in Strong's hands, a claim with two sides. One side proclaimed human transcendence over history. "Though we have a finite and temporal existence," he explained, "we are not wholly creatures of time. To some extent we are above its laws. We have 'thoughts that wander through eternity,' a consciousness that we are too large for our dwelling-place." Indeed, we are conscious of phenomena such as intuition, memory, and judgment only because we stand above them, like a "rock apart from the stream."[11]

But there also was the other side of the claim—the side prefigured many years before in the affirmation that the knowledge of God is linked to the historical development of the mind. By the 1890s Strong had carried this idea to the startling conclusion that the Christ who constitutes the structure of consciousness is intrinsically historical, for Christ "is the animating spirit of [evolution], the inner force that moves all its wheels, the mind and heart and will that expresses itself in all its processes." Indeed, he wondered why Christians so often fought the idea of evolution, for it "reveals to us the method of Christ's working both in nature and in grace."

---

[10]*CCEM*, 123, 8-10, 12; see also *ST* (1907) 109.

[11]*MISC* 1:315-17, 170.

> We believe in a divine Christ who fills all things with his life and power, and who is conducting the movements of the planets and the march of human history. Nature reveals a present God, and evolution is the common method of his working.

Christ, in other words, manifests himself historically, and history is the manifestation of Christ.

> All reason and conscience, all science and philosophy, all civilization and education, all society and government, in short, all the wheels by which the world moves forward toward its goal have a living spirit within the wheels, and that living spirit is Christ.[12]

For the Victorian upper middle class, bathed in the warm sunlight of seemingly endless physical and spiritual progress, who could doubt that the world was moving forward, propelled by the living spirit of Christ? It was an exhilarating vision. But in some ways the momentum of the vision carried Strong farther and faster than he had bargained for.

II

The fundamental import of ethical monism was, then, that Christ, the Logos, is the spark of human consciousness. And consciousness, exfoliating in time, is historical process. But what did all this imply about history itself as the locus of revelation?

Given that Strong always considered himself an impeccably orthodox Reformed theologian, the natural place to seek the answer to this question is in his fully developed ideas about the origin of Scripture. Unfortunately this leg of the journey takes us into a jungle of revisions, ambiguities, and outright contradictions. Even giving him the benefit of the doubt, it is virtually impossible to emerge with a clear and consistent interpretation of his position. Yet it is precisely because of this turmoil that Strong's work is, even here, worth examining, for he powerfully influenced a generation of Protestant ministers who left few

---

[12]*CCEM,* 197, 74, 273-74; see also *ST* (1907) 107: "Ethical Monism holds that the universe . . . is but a finite, partial and progressive manifestation of the divine Life."

theological records but almost certainly passed along to their hearers similar perplexities about the place of tradition in the modern world.

It is helpful to observe how Strong defined inspiration in the 1876 *Lectures on Theology* and in all editions of the *Systematic Theology* through the 1899 sixth edition.

> By the inspiration of the Scriptures, we mean that special divine influence upon the minds of the Scripture writers in virtue of which their productions, apart from errors of transcription, and when rightly interpreted, together constitute an infallible and sufficient rule of faith and practice.

In the seventh edition, published in 1902, Strong repeated this definition. But he also did something quite curious. Beside the old formulation he now added what he called a "series of statements more definite and explicit than we have hitherto been justified in making." However, these "more definite" statements amounted to a new and quite different definition of the process by which God discloses truth.

> Inspiration is that influence of the Spirit of God upon the minds of the Scripture writers which made their writings the record of a progressive divine revelation, sufficient . . . to lead every honest inquirer to Christ and salvation. [13]

Note that this sentence differed from its venerable predecessor in three ways. First, it specified that the Bible is the record of revelation rather than revelation itself. Second, it added the term progressive. Third, and most significantly, it dropped the word infallible, stating only that inspiration renders Scripture sufficient unto salvation. In a codicil Strong now noted that we must admit that Scripture "is defective, yet it reflects [Christ] and leads to him."[14]

The cat was out of the bag! Careful readers of the greatly enlarged eighth edition of the *Systematic Theology,* which appeared five years later, found it strewn with telltale signs of serious turmoil in Strong's thinking. The original definition of inspiration had been jettisoned com-

---

[13]*ST,* 95; *ST,* (7th ed., 1902) 104a. I owe this point to Norman H. Maring, "Baptists and Changing Views of the Bible," *Foundations* 1 (October 1958): 39.

[14]*ST* (1902) 104b.

pletely, leaving the new formulation standing alone. An explanatory note, published in all previous editions of the *Systematic Theology*, had said that inspiration is the "divine influence which secures a correct transmission of the truth to the future," but "the truth" was now quietly revised to read "needed truth."[15]

These slight but crucial changes in the definition of inspiration triggered reverberations all down the line. One was a more historicized understanding of the method of inspiration. Strong now allowed, for example, that it was fruitless to speculate about such questions. "Perhaps," he wrote, "the best theory of inspiration is to have no theory"— although this healthy diffidence toward arcane matters did not dampen his willingness to publish fifty densely packed pages on the subject.[16] But the real import of Strong's growing historical consciousness was that it left him hopelessly undecided about the way that inspiration took place. Was it normally given in epiphany-like experiences directly superintended by the Holy Spirit? Or was it normally mediated through natural powers? At one end of the scale, he wrote, we have to recognize that on rare occasions God has shattered the continuity of history with a communication "uttered in an audible voice." At the other end of the scale we also have to recognize that "man has, indeed, a certain natural insight into truth." But *customarily* inspiration was closer to the latter, an internal illumination arising within experience. "As creation and regeneration are works of the immanent rather than of the transcendent God, so inspiration is in general a work within man's soul, rather than a communication to him from without." We must admit, he told the Rochester trustees in 1902, that "modern scholarship has modified our ideas with regard to the method of inspiration."[17] All of this was clear enough, but unfortunately Strong did not leave it there. On other occasions he argued that the *customary* method of inspiration had been, not

---

[15]*ST*, 95; cf. *ST* (1907) 196. Most objections against Scripture, Strong wrote in the first seven editions of *ST*, are urged on the basis of "certain errors in secular matters . . . . But we deny that such errors have as yet been proved to exist." In the same section in the eighth edition (1907), this denial quietly disappeared; see *ST* (1902) 105 and *ST* (1907) 222.

[16]*ST* (1907) 211; see also *CCEM*, 126.

[17]*ST* (1907) 209, 203, 211; *52d Annual Report* (1902) 33-34.

the awakening of natural powers, but the direct, unmediated instruction of the Scripture writers by God. Moreover he apparently saw no inconsistency in arguing that those who had established the canon in the second and third centuries also had been directly superintended by the Holy Spirit. Indeed he again attacked William Rainey Harper—this time publicly—for having the temerity to esteem "modern inspiration as better than that which is three thousand or more years old."[18]

Here it is important to see that Strong meant to draw a logical distinction between the method or manner of God's communication on one side, and the substantive information that was communicated on the other. Strong was certain that regardless of the method, inspiration resulted in (as a later generation would phrase it) propositional revelation. Inspiration conveyed not only values and feelings, but also empirical information expressible in verbal propositions. And this cognitively knowable information ultimately came from outside history and culture, for it was "truth beyond the power of man to discover or to understand."[19] But this immediately raises a thorny problem. Regardless of the method of divine disclosure, is revealed information protected from contamination? Is it, in short, inerrant?

Before the mid-1890s Strong gave little ground to biblical critics. He admitted insignificant "imperfections" in the text, and allowed that perfection is not logically demanded by the "dynamical" theory of inspiration anyway. But except for these fleeting concessions, he stoutly denied that the "autographs" of Scripture had been marred by substantive errors of any sort.

However, sermons and essays dating from the years around the turn of the century, as well as the seventh (1902) and eighth (1907) editions of the *Systematic Theology*, show that on the question of the accuracy of Scripture Strong's mind was very much on the move. The problem is to figure out which way. Sometimes he seemed to be retreating to the rigid defense lines of his early writing. "Do I say that there are errors in matters of historical detail, errors in . . . translations . . . errors in exegesis, errors in Logic? I say nothing of the kind." Moreover the eighth

---

[18]*ST* (1907) 200; *PL*, 11-12, 34; AHS, "Modifications of the Theological Curriculum," *American Journal of Theology* 3 (1899): 329; see also *ST* (1907) 196-97.

[19]*ST* (1907) 207; see also 206, 211.

edition of the *Systematic Theology,* like the first seven, was liberally salted with brave assertions that the Bible is without error.[20] Sometimes, however, Strong openly acknowledged that the Bible is not reliable in matters of history and science. Borrowing the words of his old friend George Park Fisher, he allowed that the infallibility of the Bible does not extend to "minutiae in matters of history and science," nor does it guarantee that "every doctrinal and ethical statement in all these books is incapable of amendment." Like an old soldier prudently abandoning indefensible outposts, Strong sometimes admitted that the Bible is marred by "imperfections of detail in matters not essential." This means, he invariably added, that it is "sufficiently correct and trustworthy to accomplish [its] religious purpose," but it does not mean that the perfection of Scripture necessarily goes beyond "moral and religious truth."[21]

Occasionally Strong tried to deal with scriptural inaccuracies by setting them in a more favorable literary context. What appears to be an error in the Bible, he very carefully explained, is in fact a failure to identify the literary form in which the so-called error occurs. "A myth," for example, "is not a falsehood; it is a product of mental activity, as instructive and rich as any later product, but its characteristic is that it is not yet distinguished into history and poetry and philosophy." Once on this path, however, Strong was drawn into more serious concessions. He was forced to admit the composite origin of the Pentateuch, the probability that Jonah was a parable and Job a "dramatic poem," the possibility that some or most of the books of the Bible had been written

---

[20]*CCEM,* 127-28. There are numerous examples. "Science has not yet shown any fairly interpreted passage of Scripture to be untrue" (*ST* [1907] 224). "The Inspiration of the Scripture writers . . . qualifies them to put the truth, without error, into permanent and written form" (*ST* [1907] 212-13). "With regard . . . to the great age of the Old Testament patriarchs, we are no more warranted in rejecting the Scripture accounts . . . than we are to reject the testimony of botanists as to [the height of] trees of the Sequoia family" (*ST* [1907] 229). See also the fiercely apologetic section in *ST* (1907), "The Supernatural Character of the Scripture Teaching," 175-90, and *PL,* 11.

[21]*ST* (1907) 202, 207, 198-99, 214; AHS, "Address before the Ministers' Conference." A front page editorial in the Southern Baptist *Western Recorder,* published in Louisville, Kentucky, blasted Strong for publicly admitting that the "Bible is not free from error" (*Western Recorder* [27 June 1901]: 1).

at different times and by different persons than tradition had ascribed, and even that the present canon is to some extent adventitious.[22]

With a lot of pushing and pulling we might be able to squeeze all these different opinions into a single uniform, but it probably would not be worth the effort. The truth is that Strong was twisting in the wind. He had come to intellectual maturity in the 1850s and 1860s when modern biblical scholarship in America was still in its infancy. By the turn of the century he was undoubtedly bewildered by the mountainous growth of critical studies and simply did not know how to forge a consistent response to the problems they posed. But more than that, the Bible was just too thickly encrusted with the presupposition that it had somehow originated outside the stream of history. Strong's growing historical consciousness therefore seems to have been deflected in another direction. He really did believe that Christ is the living spirit of the age, and before long that conviction powerfully influenced his view of the divinity immanent in the historical process itself.[23]

---

[22]*ST* (1907) 214, 223, 171-72, 145-46, 240-41, 238-39.

[23]The assumption that the Bible is wholly or virtually without error was nearly universal among orthodox rationalists such as Strong, and pervasive in Protestant popular culture as well. For orthodox rationalists see E. Brooks Holifield, *The Gentlemen Theologians* (Durham NC: Duke University Press, 1978) 98, and Mark A. Noll, ed., *The Princeton Theology* (Grand Rapids MI: Baker Book House, 1983) 19, 26. For Protestant popular culture see Ferenc Morton Szasz, *The Divided Mind of Protestant America* (University AL: University of Alabama Press, 1982) 17, and Martin Marty, "America's Iconic Book," in Gene M. Tucker and Douglas A. Knight, eds., *Humanizing America's Iconic Book* (Chico CA: Scholar's Press, 1982) 1-3, 19-22. Some historians, such as Ernest R. Sandeen and Timothy L. Smith, have argued, however, that the doctrine of biblical inerrancy was largely an invention of, or at least peculiar to, nineteenth-century Old School Reformed circles. For the historiography of this debate see George M. Marsden, "Everyone One's Own Interpreter?" in Nathan O. Hatch and Mark A. Noll, eds., *The Bible in America* (New York: Oxford University Press, 1982) 97-99. Although several antebellum biblical scholars, such as Theodore Parker, were aware of the new currents, for the most part higher criticism made little headway in the United States until the very end of the century; see Szasz, *Divided Mind,* 19-20, 31, 35-40, and Jerry Wayne Brown, *The Rise of Biblical Criticism in America* (Middletown CT: Wesleyan University Press, 1969) 180-82. For the advent of higher criticism among American Protestants in general and Baptists in particular see, respectively, Ira V. Brown, "The Higher Criticism Comes to America," *Journal of the Presbyterian Historical Society* 38 (1960): 193-212, and Norman H. Maring, "Baptists and Changing Views of the Bible," *Foundations* 1 (July 1958): 52-75 and 1 (October 1958): 30-61.

Chapter Four

The Vision of Divine Immanence: The Structure of Historical Process

THROUGHOUT THE 1890s Augustus Strong's mind seemed to soar free of the ahistorical constraints of Protestant orthodoxy when he reflected upon the seamlessness and revelatory richness of the historical process itself. The approaching dawn of a new century undoubtedly had something to do with it. Protestants of all theological persuasions appear to have felt some stirrings of the modernist impulse.[1]

It is not surprising, therefore, that Strong, like so many others, began to reconsider the ancient and venerable assumption that miracles were in some sense a violation of historical process. In the 1907 *Systematic Theology* he repeated his customary definition of miracle as an "event palpable to the senses, produced for a religious purpose by the immediate agency of God." Yet immediately he added an " Alternative and

---

[1]William R. Hutchison, *The Modernist Impulse in American Protestantism* (Cambridge MA: Harvard University Press, 1976) chaps. 2-4.

Preferable Definition" that characterized a miracle as an "event in nature, so extraordinary in itself . . . as fully to warrant the conviction . . . that God has wrought it." The key words here are "in nature" and "extraordinary." Strong's aim was to prune the concept of miracle as much as possible in order to strip away connotations of superstition and credulity, without sacrificing the conviction that discrete segments of history had been uniquely refulgent with the divine presence.[2]

Strong's response to this challenge was to depict a miracle as an intensification of God's normal and natural activity in the world. "What seems a sudden break and change," he suggested, "is only the putting forth in greater energy of the same divine will that constitutes the essence of nature." A miracle is, in short, "simply an extraordinary act of that same God who is already present in all natural operations." Once miracle is seen in this fashion, as a sudden focusing or intensification of God's universal presence, the "hard and fast line between the natural and the supernatural" drops away. "The supernatural," Strong wrote, "is in nature itself, at its very heart, at its very life; . . . not an outside power interfering with the course of nature, but an inside power vitalizing nature and operating through it."[3]

It should be stressed that Strong's effort to refine the orthodox view of miracles did not imply that miracles were fabrications. "Why should I doubt that God spoke to the fathers through the prophets?" "Why should I think it incredible that God should raise the dead?" Strong's point, rather, was that in essence this miracle was no different than the process in which Christ "in ten thousand fields is turning carbon into corn." The real problem with the concept of miracle, he thought, was

---

[2]*ST,* 61; *ST* (1907) 117-18. The desire to blunt the angularity of miracles is evident in the work of other conservatives of the period. See for example William James Morison, "George Frederick Wright" (Ph.D. dissertation, Vanderbilt University, 1971) 377-85; Steven Roy Pointer, "The Perils of History: The Meteoric Career of Joseph Cook" (Ph.D. dissertation, Duke University, 1981) 145-47. In this respect the difference between some conservative and some liberal Protestants becomes elusive. See, for example, Glenn Altschuler, "From Religion to Ethics: Andrew Dixon White and the Dilemma of Christian Rationalism," *Church History* 47 (1978): 315, 319.

[3]*CCEM,* 72; *ST* (1907) 118; *MISC* 1:230. See also *ST* (1907) 119; *CCEM,* 345; *OHCT,* 192, 244-45.

the common but unwarranted assumption that divine transcendence means "the entering in of power from without [space]." But what transcendence really means is that the "power latent is greater infinitely than the power exerted." And from this perspective, he confidently added, it is clear that "miracle is just as credible as [the] regular and uniform action" of nature.[4]

Thus it seems fair to say that by the 1890s Strong had grown keenly sensitive to the principle of the continuity of the historical process. Coupled with that new awareness was a greatly enriched appreciation for the revelatory values found in the stream of mundane events. Four currents are discernible.

The first was an inclination to blur the distinction between special and general revelation. Strong never admitted that the two forms of revelation could be fused, but sometimes, in practice, the boundary did appear to fade. The eighth edition of the *Systematic Theology* especially stressed the diffusion of God's self-revelation in sources other than Scripture. He now suggested, quoting Charles Briggs, that God reveals himself not only in Scripture and in Jesus Christ, but also in "universal nature, in the constitution of mankind, in the history of our race." This means, he added, that "not simply Scripture, but all knowable truth, is a revelation from God." Strong's sedulous reading of secular literature was rooted in the belief that all great writers had been, by definition, instruments of divine communication. He never doubted that "literature is theology"—or at least "all literary production that is worthy of the name." The classics may not be inspired in exactly the same way that Scripture is, but still there is a "Christological element" in the work of the best writers that "fits them to be teachers of the race." Because the "universe is moral and religious at its core," he wrote, all art-

---

[4]*ST* (1907) xii, 119; AHS, "Address before the Ministers' Conference," unpublished address, 2 October 1893, American Baptist Historical Society; see also *ST* (1907) 34. Strong made the same argument in reference to predictive prophecy in the Old Testament. "The instances of telepathy, presentiment, and the second sight which the Society for Psychical Research has demonstrated to be facts show that prediction, in the history of divine revelation, may be only an intensification, under the extraordinary impulse of the divine Spirit, of a power that is in some degree latent in all men" (*ST* [1907] 134). Even so, Strong was irresolvably ambivalent in this matter; compare *MISC* 1:230 with *CCEM,* 144, or *ST* (1907) 428-31 with *MISC* 1:40.

istry becomes the "imaginative reproduction of the universe in its ideal relations."[5]

Beside the tendency to blur special and general revelation, Strong also came to stress—and this is the second current in his thinking—the molten, developmental nature of the matrix in which revelation is conveyed. We encountered this theme in a different context in the previous chapter. There I noted the conviction that Christ is the substance or "Life" that constitutes the world, and that Christ ordinarily expresses himself developmentally. Thus the inner thrust of historical change is, strictly speaking, Christological. But there is more to it than this, for the Christological character of history means that history is inherently lawful. Simply put, "God makes the old the basis of the new, and the new an outgrowth from the old. In all ordinary cases God works from within and not from without." The key here is the evolutionary lawfulness of Christ's creative work.

> The passion for reality which inspires our generation is no longer content with legal fictions and arbitrary interventions. . . . It wants consistency and law. . . . All this it has when it recognizes the method of the immanent Christ to be the method of growth.

Strong was certain that the lawfulness of history renders it not static but dynamic, for history is continually charged by pulsations of creative energy from fountains deep within itself. The universe is not a plenum. Rather it is a "plastic organism to which new impulses can be imparted from [Christ] whose thought and will it is an expression. . . . Though these impulses come from within, they come not from the finite mechanism, but from the immanent God." When all of this is considered together, it means that historical change manifests continuity of plan, coupled with continuous increments of the divine energy. "Upon this plan all the rationality of evolution depends."[6]

---

[5]*ST* (1907) 25-26. *MISC* 1:255, 257.

[6]*CCEM,* 163, 193, 164. These remarks were made in 1898. Only five years earlier Strong had lamented that the theological world did not adequately recognize that the "God who is so near it, who constitutes its very life, and who is carrying forward its historic development, is none other than Christ" (*CCEM,* 292).

Before proceeding to the third current in Strong's view of the revelatory power of history, it is interesting to notice briefly how these ideas facilitated a more flexible understanding of human evolution. In the 1870s and 1880s he had persistently tried to separate animal and human evolution. But in the 1890s this resistance was rapidly eroded, and by the turn of the century Strong had come to believe that the human body had evolved in tandem with the "brute creation." The formation of man, he now thought, was a "*mediate* creation . . . presupposing existing material in the shape of animal forms." Yet Strong continued to insist that man's spiritual nature had been immediately imparted by God through a process "governed by different laws from the brute creation, yet growing out of the brute. . . . In other words, man came not *from* the brute, but *through* the brute." Thus in the matter of human evolution, as in so many areas, Strong was increasingly determined to walk a precarious tightrope between familiar orthodoxy and beckoning modernity.[7]

The third current in Strong's conception of the revelatory values in history was, however, spectacularly free of ambivalence. It was a roundhouse embrace of the spiritual progress evident in modern culture. Progress, he urged, is not linear advance, but the restoration of lost health. Everywhere Christ is striving to heal his own body, to heal a broken world. "Through all our modern literature and life Christ is working, gradually making all things new." He saw this restorative process in the growth of learning. The progress of science and philosophy, which Christians often fear, "may be only the form of Christ coming to us over the waves to rescue us." He saw the restorative pro-

---

[7] *ST* (1907) 466 (italics added), 469, 466-67. The clumsy integration of old and new views in *ST* (1907) is particularly evident in Strong's discussion of the development of the human body. After making a vigorous case for the evolution of the body, he concluded: "Apart from the direct agency of God, the view that man's physical system is descended by natural generation from some ancestral simian form can be regarded only as an irrational hypothesis" (*ST* [1907] 470). Apparently Strong meant that the body *appears* to follow a natural trajectory, but, like the creation of the soul, is guided by God's immediate intervention. However that may be, Strong also argued, much like Thomas Huxley and Lester Frank Ward, that the evolutionary process eventually reached a point of critical momentum at which it transcended itself in freedom and rationality in mankind. See AHS, Introduction to *Control in Evolution*, by George Wilkins (New York: A. C. Armstrong, 1903).

cess in the expansion of the church, and even more importantly, in the "great efforts outside the church to improve government, to right social wrongs, to diffuse the spirit of kindness between employers and employed." Christ, Strong wrote,

> is moralizing the nations, giving a new sense of community, increasing sympathy with the wronged and oppressed, bringing the classes and masses together, educating the race, and preparing the way for freedom and true religion.

We normally associate the modernist impulse with liberals and humanists like Lyman Abbott and Octavius Frothingham, but none of these outdid the conservative Strong. "Of all days since man trod this planet," he exploded, "this is the greatest day"![8]

Just as history is Christ, so progress is Christ. "Not the victim of a past process," Christ "adds to the process, and the successive additions from his living energy are the secret of evolution . . . guiding it to a preordained and rational end." Strong judged that the interpenetration of the Logos in history, which continuously fuels the engines of progress, was one of the great insights that contemporary religious thought had "rescued from neglect"—except that the Christocentrism of the New Theologians was not nearly radical enough. "I would go back to Christ as to that which is original in thought, archetypal in creation, immanent in history; to the Logos of God, who is . . . the heart of the universe."[9]

It is precisely because Christ is at the "heart of the universe" that the church must come to grips with the normative authority of contemporary culture. No liberal made the point more cogently.

> Christianity must take possession of all the culture of the world, or she must utterly give up claim to be divine. She must appropriate and disseminate all knowledge, or she must confess that she is the child of ignorance and fanaticism. She must conquer all good learning, or she must herself be conquered.

---

[8]*CCEM,* 108-109; *MISC* 1:310; *CCEM,* 479.

[9]*MISC* 1:227; *CCEM,* 193, 141. Strong believed that progress is inconceivable without creative infusions from the immanent Logos because history is naturally devolutionary; See *MISC* 2:118.

In Strong's mind modernism was not an option but an obligation. "The impulse to this revision is *itself* divine; an impulse from Christ himself." To resist the modernist yearning is, in other words, to resist Christ. To fail to see Christ "in the whole continuous process of history . . . [is] to substitute a sort of half-atheism for real theism."[10]

This leads finally to the fourth current in Strong's conception of the revelatory power of historical process. The first three currents—his tendency to blur special and general revelation, his insistence upon the molten nature of history, and his espousal of the modernist impulse— were clear streams letting in the light of contemporary social thought. But the fourth stream was an abiding conviction that the onward, upward rush of history carries within itself an old-fashioned gospel whose truth never changes.

Sometimes he talked about the tension between fluid history and fixed doctrine as if it were merely a matter of separating the two: *adiaphora* change according to the times, but the essentials somehow escape social construction. This formula was useful enough for graduation addresses, but in more thoughtful moments he knew that the account was not settled so easily.[11]

Strong clearly saw that the task was to establish a ground for permanence. He growled about "professedly Christian teachers who so emphasize the element of change in the history of doctrine that all permanence is virtually denied." For these teachers there "is no such thing as objective truth." "Ethical and religious doctrine are in constant flux. Even Christ and Christianity are held to be merely temporary phases of evolution, and both may be outgrown."[12]

Now it is quite true, said Strong, that science has proved that the phenomena of the physical world are "all instances of a flux of particles." And it is true that "so-called permanence is an illusion created by our short-sighted imaginations." But the nature of the external world is beside the point. A valid metaphysic must begin with consciousness,

---

[10]*CCEM*, 141, 106; *MISC* 1:116 (italics added); *OHCT*, 152-53.

[11]See, for example, his last address to a graduating class at RTS, in *MISC* 2:492-93.

[12]*MISC* 1:290-91.

because consciousness "knows and dominates physical nature." More exactly, it is precisely because consciousness is to some extent outside nature and history that observation of nature and history becomes possible. "Can any becoming be observed unless there is an abiding intelligence in the observer[?] Only when I stand on the rock apart from the stream can I see the rush of the water flowing by." In human consciousness, in short, "we find something abiding . . . a personal identity, which subsists through change and in spite of change." More than this, he went on, the concept of development is meaningless unless there is "something to develop." He summed up his objections with the judgment that the "very conception of change, if the change is not capricious and useless, implies a law behind the phenomena."[13]

Although Strong did not bring in the heavy artillery of ethical monism to combat radical historicism, ethical monism did inform his thinking. Of the two words, ethical and monism, Strong confessed, the "more practical, the more valuable . . . is the former," for it denotes the duality of spirit and matter and the plurality of God and individual minds in a qualitatively monistic universe. Nonetheless, the multiple forms of reality presuppose a single underlying substance. "Matter and mind, man and God, have underground connections . . . because all things . . . have their being in God." Perhaps this is why consistent historicism never had a fighting chance in Strong's world. He could write and preach with memorable eloquence about the evolutionary Christ who suffuses contemporary culture with his presence. Yet underneath it all is the timeless and unconditioned unity that defines but is not defined by historical process. Here and there Strong could well afford to meet the New Theologians more than half way because he never really believed that history is the ultimate category of understanding. Under it all, "Christ and his truth still remain." Or, as he told the American Baptist Missionary Union in his final presidential address, "history, with all her vicissitudes, including the rise and fall of empires and civilizations, is the working out of his plan."[14]

In summary, then, ambivalence or doubleness of this sort ultimately bifurcated Strong's mature sense of history as a source of reli-

---

[13]Ibid., 291-93.

[14]CCEM, 53-54; OHCT, 260; CCEM, 303.

gious knowledge. Miracles were unabashedly downplayed. The distinction between special and general revelation was blurred, the fluidity of the social context was stressed, and the normativeness of contemporary culture was affirmed. Yet all these claims were pitted against a more fundamental claim. In the final reckoning, he seemed to say, history is a shallow stream rippling across the bedrock of God's changeless truth.

II

By the early 1890s Strong had become acutely aware of the insufficiency of ahistorical methods in biblical and theological scholarship. The whole aim of his theological efforts, he wrote in 1897, was to "rescue theology from the realm of mere abstractions and to show its connections with literature and life." This is not to suggest that he ever countenanced a wholesale break with the Baconian methods that saturated nineteenth-century orthodox scholarship. Indeed, until 1912 or so he was only dimly aware of the way that critical methods actually functioned in advanced scholarly circles. But overall he was more pragmatic, and probably did more to discredit narrowly inductive ways of doing theology than he himself ever imagined. [15]

Strong's greatly mellowed attitude toward biblical higher criticism is a case in point. Determining the extent of the "human element" in the Bible is a purely empirical task, he wrote in 1893. "It is simply a question of fact . . . not to be decided *a priori*." At the end of the decade he was prepared to admit that "modern theology has immensely gained in candor and insight by acknowledging that the same method of human growth that was adopted by the incarnate Word was also adopted in the production of the written word." And in the final edition of the *Systematic Theology* he slipped in an unprecedented (and remarkably objective) section on the nature and purpose of higher criticism. Calling it "structure-critique," he insisted that it portended no "terrors to one who regards [it as part] of Christ's creating and educating process." Taking his own words to heart, the following year he bravely wrote that

---

[15]*AB*, 220.

he was "prepared now to acknowledge all that the higher criticism can prove as to the composition of the sacred documents."[16]

Strong almost certainly knew that some of his own faculty members were on the cutting edge of critical biblical scholarship in America. While it is true that some of them were, or became, more radical than he wanted or expected, it is also true that he consistently encouraged unfettered biblical study at Rochester. "What Scripture is, and how the Scripture was composed and put together," Strong told the trustees in 1898, "is a matter of history, and to investigate these matters fully is a duty to truth and to God."[17]

Although Strong's own exegesis and exposition of Scripture was never well-informed by critical considerations, with the passage of years he became more and more convinced that the serious theologian must exhibit a disciplined receptiveness to all aspects of human achievement and learning. One manifestation of this conviction was his growing appreciation for catholic churchmanship and deepening concern that Christians conserve the great insights of the past rather than dissipate their energies attacking error. Those who go through life wearing the blinders of zealous orthodoxy usually forget, said Strong, that "Christ is larger than all our conceptions of him."[18]

---

[16]AHS, "Ministers' Conference"; *CCEM,* 206; *ST* (1907) 169, vii; *AB,* 346.

[17]*48th Annual Report* (1898) 38-39. For the growth of religious liberalism at RTS and, particularly, the critical methods championed by Rauschenbusch, Moehlman, and Walter Betteridge, see LeRoy Moore, Jr., "The Rise of American Religious Liberalism at the Rochester Theological Seminary" (Ph.D. dissertation, Claremont Graduate School, 1966) chap. 3. Strong's manner of expression in these years—the tone and nuance of his phrases—is significant. "I am pleased with your declaration that Scripture is the expression of man's past experiences of truth," he told E. Y. Mullins. "God has not left each individual to work out all knowledge for himself . . . Christ is 'the lamp' of the heavenly city—light concentrated and made visible" (Strong to Mullins, 21 April 1913, Southern Baptist Theological Seminary Archives).

[18]*CCEM,* 477-78. Strong often illustrated his own position by contrasting it with authors with whom he disagreed, but almost always the intent was constructive— more like a joust than an attack. Thus it is not surprising that he came to have deep reservations about Howard Osgood, the most conservative member of the RTS faculty, because Osgood was "exceedingly quick to perceive untruth [in others]" (*OHCT,* 88). Ezekial Gilman Robinson fell into Strong's disfavor for the same reason; see *AB,* 220-21.

Beside the growing desire for catholic churchmanship, Strong began to reassess the role of reason itself. From the beginning he had maintained that reason is the initial arbiter of theological truth. Indeed, "theology claims to be a science because it is the recognition, classification, and interpretation, by reason, of objective facts concerning God." But now he was more inclined to say that there are several ways to skin the theological cat—and ratiocination is, at best, only one of them.

> States of the sensibility are needed to know music; a feeling for beauty is requisite to any understanding of plastic art; and the morally right is not rightly discerned except by those who love the morally right. In a similar way there are states of the affections which are necessary to know God.

Theological discernment requires the "mind's whole power of knowing." The intellect must be enlightened by the "eyes of the heart" if it is to yield "knowledge of religious truth."[19]

To some extent all of this was standard fare, for Protestant theologians had always insisted that doctrinal knowledge must be supplemented by the inward witness of the Spirit. Yet this is not exactly what Strong was talking about. Rather he was pointing to a strictly human quality, an affective power or sensibility that grows with experience and is necessary for the discernment of religious truth. Still faithfully reflecting the threefold faculty psychology of British-Scottish moral philosophy, he explained that "faith is an act of the affections and will, as truly as it is an act of the intellect." Thus Romanists, Campbellites, and Princeton Calvinists erred by making faith "merely intellectual belief in the truth, on the presentation of evidence." Strong suggested that in reality William James was closer to the truth when James asserted that "often enough our faith beforehand in an uncertified result is the only thing that makes the result come true . . . . If your heart does not *want* a world of moral reality, your head will assuredly never make you believe in one."[20]

19*CCEM*, 138-39.

20*ST* (1907) 840-45. Although he could quote persons like James when it suited his purposes, it should be said that Strong's psychological theory remained closer to that of contemporaries like Francis Wayland and Noah Porter; see D. H. Meyer, *The Instructed Conscience* (Philadelphia: University of Pennsylvania Press, 1972) 45, 48.

Strong's estimation of specific persons may be a clearer reflection of his thinking than any number of formal statements in the *Systematic Theology*. He was sure that liberals such as Lyman Abbott and R. J. Campbell suffered from "much misunderstanding of Christian doctrine," but he also was sure that they had their priorities right, for they understood that "Christianity is more than talking or thinking or doing. It is a life." Liberal colleagues such as William Arnold Stevens, Cornelius Woelfkin, and Walter Rauschenbusch easily won his heart, not because they were liberals, but because in their private lives they consistently manifested, as he put it, "spiritual gifts" and a "loving spirit."[21]

Strong revealed a great deal about himself and his convictions about the proper way to do theology when he talked about his sons Charles and John—each of whom seems to have embodied exactly half of his personality. His relationship with Charles will be discussed more fully in a later chapter. Strong attributed Charles's loss of faith partly to Charles's lack of appreciation for imagination, intuition, and affection. "He depreciates insight," Strong complained. "He is critical rather than constructive. He does not see that imagination is only creative reason, that it penetrates into the meaning of the world as mathematics cannot." In contrast, Strong thought that his younger son John, who remained devoutly evangelical, possessed "imagination as well as logic, sympathy as well as acumen." Strong admitted that John's intellectual prowess might not be equal to Charles's, but that hardly mattered, for John had other gifts. "Imagination and affection are with him great aids to the attainment of truth." Strong never changed his mind about this matter. On the eve of his eighty-first birthday he still would write, "John is a son after my own heart, in that his affections give him access to theological truth."[22]

It cannot be said that historical method—at least in the conventional meaning of the phrase—ever became a conspicuous part of Strong's mental furniture. But it can be said that as he grew older, he came to understand, with increasing clarity, that religious knowledge

---

[21]For "it is a life" see *OHCT*, 84. For Stevens see *AB*, 228. For Woelfkin see *55th Annual Report* (1905) 39; 1918 diary. For Rauschenbusch see *53d Annual Report* (1903) 32; *RTS Bulletin* [68] (November 1918): 76; 1918 diary.

[22]*AB*, 257-58, 204-205, 268, 351.

cannot be mechanically deduced from Scripture or induced from nature. The method must be at least as rich as the reality one seeks to know. Of course he had always insisted that reason alone is inadequate. He had vigorously disagreed with biblical critics such as Crawford Toy and William Rainey Harper, for whom, he thought, there were no mysteries, only unsolved problems. But in these later years the thrust was different. By the turn of the century Strong clearly was more worried about the pretentiousness of rationalistic orthodoxy. In his mind modern scholastics had sadly forgotten that divine things are known only by bringing to bear the totality of the human experience—imagination, affection, sensibility, as well as reason. Long ago, he wrote in his *Autobiography* in 1897, "I set out to be a man of faith, to be a great believer, to hold the truth in love." There was in that statement more, perhaps, than met the eye.[23]

---

[23]*AB*, 221. Recently several historians have argued that the leading orthodox rationalist writers were more attuned to the full range of human emotions and sensibilities, both personally and in their theological work, than is commonly assumed. See Andrew W. Hoffecker, *Piety and the Princeton Theologians* (Grand Rapids MI: Baker Book House, 1981); Mark A. Noll, ed., *The Princeton Theology* (Grand Rapids MI: Baker Book House, 1983) 33, 44.

Chapter Five

The (Changing) Spirit of the Age:
The Response to Strong
in American Protestantism

I N HIS *RECOLLECTIONS* Washington Gladden described the
first stirrings of historical consciousness in the churches in the
late 1870s as "a going in the tops of the trees." It may be too
much to say, as some historians have, that by the 1920s the winds of
change were smashing American Protestantism with hurricane force.
But there can be no doubt that between the 1870s and 1920s the ve-
locity of the transformation did increase at an astonishing rate.[1]

When the first edition of Augustus Strong's *Systematic Theology*
reached the review pages of the journals in the late 1880s, most, but
not all, of the critics were unconcerned about the problems raised by
historical consciousness. When the eighth edition of the *Systematic The-*

---

[1]Washington Gladden, *Recollections* (1909) 262-66, as quoted in William R.
Hutchison, *The Modernist Impulse in American Protestantism* (Cambridge MA: Harvard
University Press, 1966) 77. For a poignant firsthand account of the religious turmoil
of these years see Gaius Glenn Atkins, *Religion in Our Times* (New York: Round Table
Press, 1932) esp. 35, 86, 283.

ology was reviewed a quarter century later, most, but not all, of the critics had become acutely sensitive to them. It would appeal to our aesthetic sense if the trajectory of heightening awareness were a neatly ascending arc, but it was not. The reviews of Strong's publications in the late 1890s are curiously difficult to categorize; perhaps the inchoateness of the response at that stage is itself an indication of the inchoateness of cultural change. Nonetheless, on balance, the review literature did become increasingly perceptive about, and astringent toward, Strong's work. The shifting concerns of the critics are, in short, an index of the speed and power of the forces sweeping across American Protestant thought.

The publication of the *Systematic Theology* in 1886 propelled Strong into the major league of the theological profession, or so one would judge by the flurry of reviews. Fellow Baptists found little to criticize, and they certainly had no objection to the extremely cautious way he handled problems raised by historicism. The *Watchman,* for example, commended the book as "emphatically conservative"—indeed, just the sort of material a student "ought to commit to memory." Strong's counterpart at Newton Theological Institution, Alvah Hovey, was impressed by his ability to wed the "Christian thought of centuries" to the needs of the present. Elias H. Johnson, systematic theologian at Crozer, would later dissociate himself from Strong, but at this point he was quite willing to applaud the *Systematic Theology* as "far and away the best book on theology for a pastor to have." Even so, Johnson seems to have sensed that something was amiss with the premises of Strong's thought. "A prudent radical," he warned, "had better take care how he throws stones at the windows of [such] a bold conservative."[2]

---

[2]G. D. B. Pepper, "Strong's Systematic Theology," *Watchman* (18 November 1886): 1; Alvah Hovey, review of *ST, Baptist Quarterly Review* 8 (1886): 567-69. Elias H. Johnson, "Dr. Strong's Theology," *Baptist Quarterly Review* 12 (1890): 396-98, is a review of the nearly identical second edition of the *ST* (1889) and *PAR*. Some copies of *PAR* contain an appendix of several dozen excerpts from personal letters to Strong and excerpts from published reviews of *ST*. All are laudatory and some are from notable figures, such as William G. T. Shedd, Henry Martyn Dexter, Moses Coit Tyler, and Charles H. Spurgeon. A comparison of some of these excerpted reviews against the original sources reveals that the scissored versions reprinted in *PAR* often misrepresent the intent of the reviewer. Nevertheless the appendix indicates the breadth of Strong's audience.

Francis L. Patton, soon to become president of Princeton College, bestowed the blessing of orthodox Presbyterians. Patton naturally dissociated himself from some of Strong's substantive theological views—when Strong calls pedobaptists "heretics and schismatics," he groaned, "we feel within us the promptings to an unusual form of speech"—but in general he found the book valuable. Patton was satisfied that Strong had generally steered clear of the "new theories" about the origin of man; that his "defense of Inspiration . . . is the best that we have seen"; and that his argument for the presuppositional knowledge of God was "discriminating." Benjamin B. Warfield, the new professor of Didactic and Polemic Theology at Princeton Seminary, lavished praise on Strong's *Philosophy and Religion,* published two years after the *Systematic Theology.* Judging it full of "common sense and sound thinking," Warfield was particularly impressed with Strong's view of inspiration, which he found "singularly clear and satisfactory." The conservative *Lutheran Quarterly* was similarly unconcerned about Strong's working assumptions. The Gettysburg theologians were astonished by his "startling" insensitivity to the significance of the sacraments, but otherwise approved the *Systematic Theology* as a kind of publication "very much needed just now amid the general haze in the theological world."[3]

Although no one considered Strong too daring on historical questions, some found him not daring enough, and others found him hopelessly old-fashioned or even confused. George Frederick Wright, the very prominent Congregationalist editor of *Bibliotheca Sacra,* and in many ways a behemoth like Strong, regarded Strong's work as "one of the most important contributions made in recent years." But Wright drew the line at theistic presuppositionalism. The ultimate presupposition, Wright countered, is knowledge of ourselves, and from this we infer knowledge of God. In Wright's view Strong did not understand that our knowledge of God must grow from experience rather than some structural "pre-equipment" of human consciousness. The *Methodist Review* was more blunt about Strong's shortcomings, especially his superficial treatment of the issues raised by modern biblical criticism.

---

[3]Francis L. Patton, review of *ST, Presbyterian Review* 8 (1887): 365-67; Benjamin B. Warfield, review of *PAR, Presbyterian Review* 9 (1888): 679; unsigned review of *ST, Lutheran Quarterly* 17 (1887): 132-34.

Although the reviewer tried to soften his criticisms by saying that they were "as a few 'dead flies' in a large mass of very precious ointment," his characterization of Strong as a "Pharisee of the most straitest sect" clearly stood as the final verdict.[4]

By far the most substantive response to the *Systematic Theology* came from Yale's George B. Stevens, who focused on Strong's expositions of original sin and the sacraments, but used these issues to address a more fundamental problem. In regard to original sin, Stevens singled out Strong's claim that mankind had sinned in Adam "not individually, but seminally." Stevens realized that Strong's aim was to implicate humanity in Adam's fall without implicating individuals, and especially individual infants, in Adam's guilt. But he was not impressed. "These are words," Stevens retorted. "Tell us, were we there or were we not?" Unfortunately, Strong wanted it both ways: he wanted the scholasticism of Augustine—a view Stevens considered "an absurdity" in the modern world—and he also wanted a "real *historical connection*" with Adam in the same way that we have a real historical connection with our grandfathers and inherit their actual traits. Stevens concluded that Strong perpetually oscillated between "two irreconcilable standpoints," clinging to the "relics of scholasticism" while trying to embrace the "realism of modern science and philosophy."[5]

Stevens was even more querulous toward Strong's restrictive view of the Lord's Supper. Again, his critique was aimed not so much at the doctrinal position itself as the ahistorical assumptions that undergirded it. In the first place, Stevens charged, Strong has "treated the Bible as a body of proof-texts" by "garbling a few words here and a few there and twisting them out of all relation to the matter which the Scriptures have in hand." Still more regrettable, said Stevens, was Strong's imprisonment in the " 'Zeitgeist' of a former age." He fails to see that there is "too much Christian life and thought and feeling in the world to make any [a priori] theory effective, whatever a supposed 'logic' may say."[6]

---

[4][George Frederick Wright], review of *ST*, *Bibliotheca Sacra* 44 (1887): 306-309, 323; unsigned review of *ST*, *Methodist Review* fifth series 68 (1886): 2:940-41.

[5]George B. Stevens, "Strong's Systematic Theology," *New Englander and Yale Review* new series 10 (1887): 38-39.

[6]Ibid., 46-47; see also Stevens, "Strong's Philosophy and Religion," *New Englander and Yale Review* new series 12 (1888): 421-31.

Andover Seminary's Willis A. Anderson was equally perceptive. He found Strong's doctrine of Scripture "disappointing," and judged his treatment of the relation of revelation to history (as well as ethics and science) especially inadequate. Strong simply dogmatizes about inerrancy, Anderson complained. He fails to see that the "question is not whether the Bible is inspired, but what inspiration is." Yet Anderson also discerned that a butterfly was struggling to emerge from the cocoon of orthodox scholasticism. Throughout the *Systematic Theology*, Anderson lamented, "so much of truth is interwoven that at first glance one does not perceive how much it has been lost by being forced into the limitations of Augustinianism. The flowers are crushed, but their fragrance exhales from every page. . . . The requirements of his system are too much for him."[7]

In 1899 Strong published *Christ in Creation and Ethical Monism*. One of the minor curiosities of American religious history is that this volume, which was immeasurably more imaginative than any edition of the *Systematic Theology*, produced scarcely a ripple among the critics. Progressive theological journals barely noticed its existence. Conservative journals instantly eyed it with suspicion: any book with monism in the title could not be harmless. Both camps focused almost exclusively upon the speculative metaphysical assertions of the volume and neither seemed to notice that it was filled with halting but important concessions to the epistemic assumptions of modern thought.

The few liberals who reviewed the volume predictably chided Strong for identifying substance with God in a pre-Kantian fashion, or for giving theological answers to philosophical questions. Conservative reviewers were equally unhappy, but for a different reason: they suspected incipient pantheism. The sour reaction of the usually liberal *Methodist Review* was typical. The writer, A. J. F. Behrends, who had been one of Strong's students, said that he had read the articles with "incredulous amazement." Labeling the book "injurious" and "subversive," Behrends declared that "to fight [Strong's] doctrine is to fight for God." Princeton's Benjamin B. Warfield, whose erudition rivaled Strong's, worried about the defection of an old ally to the camp of the enemy. "The accession of so winning a writer to the ranks of the ethical monists

---

[7]Willis A. Anderson, review of *ST, Andover Review* 8 (1887): 96-97.

is a circumstance of first-rate importance," he growled. "Dr. Strong's 'ethical monism' is pantheizing idealism saved from its worst extremes by the force of old habits of thought; and, of course, it must eat deeper into the system or again recede from it."[8]

Strong's fellow Baptists were no longer so sure that they wanted to claim him either. Baylor's church historian, Albert Henry Newman, spoke for the denomination's Southern wing in the *Review and Expositor.* Newman had once been Strong's student and, later, faculty colleague at Rochester. By any reasonable measure of such things he was temperamentally and doctrinally more conservative than his teacher. Yet Newman regarded Strong's work as relatively uninformed by history— both in the straightforward sense that it did not exhibit sufficient acquaintance with the events of the past, and in the deeper sense that he was insensitive to the genetic unfolding of ideas. Here Newman was inching pretty close to the real issue at stake, but there is no reason to believe that he discerned its import more clearly than Strong did.[9]

Northern Baptists generally implied that Strong had become a dangerous influence in their midst. Jesse B. Thomas, writing for the *Watchman,* avoided outright disavowal of *Christ in Creation* only by acrobatically supposing that Strong really did not mean what he was saying. "He is still a dualist and an Augustinian," Thomas averred. "He has, apparently, added monism as a hypothetical periphery, within which his theology may dwell peaceably with current physical and metaphysical dogma." Strong's old friend Alvah Hovey was less inclined to finesse the matter. Hovey acknowledged that Strong had "set the truths of Christianity in a clearer rational light," and in itself, this

---

[8]A. J. F. Behrends, "Ethical Monism," *Methodist Review* 77 (1895): 357, 369, 361; see also M. Valentine, review of *CCEM, Lutheran Quarterly* 30 (1900): 279-84. The first Warfield quotation is from an unsigned review of *CCEM* (undoubtedly by Warfield) in *Presbyterian and Reformed Review* 12 (1901): 325-26. The second is from a review of *ST* (5th ed., 1896), *Presbyterian and Reformed Review* 8 (1897): 356-58.

[9]Albert Henry Newman, "Strong's Systematic Theology," *Review and Expositor* 2 (1905): 44-45, 50, 58-59, 61, 64, 66. One measure, perhaps, of Strong's stature is that E. Y. Mullins, president of Southern Baptist Theological Seminary and editor of the *Review and Expositor,* immediately wrote to Strong and offered him an opportunity to reply, at whatever length he desired; see the letter of Mullins to Strong, 7 February 1905, SBTS Archives.

was good. But Hovey countered that the kind of "metaphysical speculation" Strong had flirted with usually did "very little . . . for the cause of true religion."[10]

The most thoughtful response came from Crozer's Elias H. Johnson, a keenly intelligent but unreconstructed orthodox rationalist. A half-dozen years earlier Johnson had expressed reservations about the boldness of Strong's speculations. Now the reservations turned into dismay. Again and again Johnson wrestled Strong to the ground, charging him with internal contradictions, nonsensical definitions, outrageous exegeses of biblical texts, and, in general, a lot of fuzzy thinking obscured by a winsome prose style.

> Such ambiguity leaves his whole philosophy in the air, floating . . . like some spider-web, but just as intangible, and just as unserviceable for those who have no knack at levitation, and who do care a little whither the freshening monistic breeze would carry them.

Johnson found the speculativeness of ethical monism especially distasteful. Theological construction, he complained, should not require us "to climb up Matterhorns of speculation, panting in the rarified air, with our hearts in our throats, and under the guidance of occult or ambiguous phrases." Here, he charged, Strong had fallen into the same trap that had ensnared many liberals.

> All the New Theology we have occasion to dread consists of inferences from the infinite. . . . If Dr. Strong had kept clear of inference concerning matters no one has any means of knowing about, he would not have startled so many of us. . . . And if the rest of us could be content with a proper Christian agnosticism . . . our doctrinal refinements would not prove so often an argument for the infidel, and a bewilderment to the unbeliever.[11]

---

[10]Jesse B. Thomas, review of *CCEM, Watchman* (9 August 1900): 11-12; Alvah Hovey, "Dr. Strong's Ethical Monism," *Watchman* (13 December 1894): 10; (20 December 1894): 10. A third installment of Hovey's review, which I have not quoted, appeared in the issue of 27 December 1894, 11-12. An unsigned editorial in 1907, probably by Edmund F. Merriam, proclaimed that everyone "must acknowledge the beauty and adequateness of a system of thought which brings God into unity with the world and man" (*Watchman* [19 September 1907] 7).

[11]Elias H. Johnson, *Ethical Monism* (New York: Examiner, 1896) 44, 51, 57.

What is most startling about the reviews of *Christ in Creation and Ethical Monism* is how wide of the mark they really were. Except for occasional quibbling about traducianism or some other doctrinal heirloom, most of the critics were preoccupied with the possibility that ethical monism would escalate into pantheism. The historicist seeds strewn throughout the book passed virtually unnoticed. By identifying God not only with the substance of the world, but also with the temporality of the world, Strong had implicated the divine in the machinery of historical process. Yet no one raised this point. No one noticed that Strong had made serious concessions to the modern conviction that society is the workshop in which culture is forged, or that these concessions had put an intolerable strain upon the entire system. No one saw, in short, that it was history, not pantheism, that was wedging itself between Strong and his old comrades.

Conservative reviews of the massive eighth edition of the *Systematic Theology* (published in 1907) were largely insensitive to the problems raised by historicism. The Cincinnati *Journal and Messenger,* a fountainhead of Southern fundamentalism in the 1920s, gave Strong a thumping round of applause for holding "firmly to the fundamental doctrines." Baylor's Calvin Goodspeed, Oberlin's George Frederick Wright, and the *Watchman's* Edmund F. Merriam responded a bit more thoughtfully to Strong's exposition of human evolution, but all three smugly concluded that he had so domesticated the animal that orthodoxy had nothing to fear. Merriam said nothing about Strong's view of the origin of Scripture; Wright judged it one of the strongest parts of the *Systematic Theology,* while Goodspeed (more perceptively) concluded that the great man had fallen into hopeless inconsistency. Yet all of these reviewers were more concerned with doctrinal than epistemic issues. Caspar Wistar Hodge, speaking for Princeton, was interested in neither, but continued to insist that the central problem was metaphysical. The question, Hodge asserted, "is whether, when God created the world, He created a something which was not part of Himself and which has some principle of relative persistence." Indeed, nothing better illustrates the unworldliness of the Princeton posture in 1910 than Hodge's deep concern over what he saw as Strong's objectionable tendency to confuse "Infralapsarianism" with "Hypothetical Universalism."[12]

---

[12]"Dr. Strong's Theology," *Journal and Messenger* (Cincinnati OH), 31 January

Not surprisingly liberal reviewers had a much tighter grip on the real issues at stake. Most were acutely conscious that Strong had smuggled a farrago of historical and ahistorical premises into a single theological system. Auburn's Herbert Youtz, for example, admitted that Strong possessed "great philosophical powers" and a "feeling for reality that is sadly wanting in some modern essays in theological interpretation that are tuned to the present *Zeitgeist.*" But the tragedy, as Youtz saw it, was that the *Systematic Theology* "aids us very little in . . . the age that has dawned," for Strong "pours his old wine into the old bottles, and even retains the old labels and corks." Clarence Beckwith at Chicago Theological Seminary was pleased that ethical monism and universal evolution had become, he thought, the guiding principles of Strong's mature thought. But he argued that Strong had only patched new ideas onto the old quilt. "One wonders . . . how deep and far-reaching the changes would be," Beckwith asked, "if Dr. Strong were now to rewrite his entire system in the light of his newer principles." The awkwardness of the *Systematic Theology* also troubled George W. Taft, editor of the Baptist *Standard* in Chicago. "Everything is grist that comes to his mill," Taft observed. "He is an evolutionist, but evolution sits lightly on his theological system. . . . The bridge is still incomplete and unusable."[13]

Strong's dilemma was diagnosed with surgical accuracy by William Adams Brown at Union Seminary in New York. The final edition of

---

1907, 6; Calvin Goodspeed, review of vols. 1 and 2 of *ST* (1907), *Review and Expositor* 5 (1908): 246-47; [George Frederick Wright], review of vol. 1 of *ST* (1907), *Bibliotheca Sacra* 64 (1907): 774. See also Wright's review of vol. 2, *Bibliotheca Sacra* 65 (1908): 591. See also Edmund F. Merriam, "President Strong's Theology," *Watchman,* (29 August 1907): 7; Caspar Wistar Hodge, review of vols. 1 and 2 of *ST* (1907), *Princeton Theological Review* 6 (1908): 338. See also Hodge's review of vol. 3 (1909) in *Princeton Theological Review* 8 (1910): 334. On the other side of the theological fence, George William Knox at Union Seminary in New York snidely remarked that in Strong the "human and the divine are in a rare combination, defying all hostile science, a combination which is invincible" ("Some Recent Works on Systematic Theology," *Harvard Theological Review* 1 [1908]: 193).

[13]Herbert Alden Youtz, review of *ST* 3 (1909), *American Journal of Theology* 13 (1909): 469-70; Clarence Beckwith, review of *ST* 2 (1907), *American Journal of Theology* 12 (1908): 502-504. George W. Taft, "Two Remarkable Men and Their Books,

the *Systematic Theology*, he noted, is an "interesting example of the way in which the new view-point affects a scheme of doctrine originally wrought out under very different presuppositions." Brown pointed to the tensions in Strong's treatment of miracle and inspiration as glaring examples of the stress between old and new assumptions. Since miracle was now defined not as an act of God upon nature but as a heightened manifestation of God's presence in nature, and since inspiration was now defined not in terms of scientific accuracy but in terms of religious efficacy, Brown wondered why Strong did not toss out the old definitions entirely. "These changes . . . are far-reaching in importance, involving the entire shifting of the basis of authority from an external and dogmatic basis to one which is spiritual and inherent." Ultimately, Brown thought, the system failed to deal adequately with religious experience—a failure epitomized by Strong's jump from proofs for the existence of God to proofs for the validity of Scripture, with no supportive chapters on religious experience. Strong's clumsy attempt to paste together the Logos and the historic Jesus, he added, similarly resulted from insensitivity to the historicity of Christianity itself.[14]

An unnamed reviewer for the *Standard* picked out the malfunction in the mechanism as would a jeweler with a pair of tweezers.

> Dr. Strong began his theological thinking under the influence of a method which was then universal, but which has now been largely abandoned. According to this ideal, theology consisted in the expo-

---

Augustus Hopkins Strong and William Newton Clarke," *Standard* (25 January 1913): 607-608, is the second in a two-part series; the first appeared 18 January 1913. Scotland's James Hastings was bewildered by the contrast between Strong's "impersonal, absolute, rigidly theological" attitude and his "marvelous knowledge of theological literature and . . . faculty of discrimination." Even so, he wryly noted, here "we have all the material, and we do not need to go hunting among our books for it; we do not need to have other books. . . . There is nothing in the English language like this book" (review of *ST* 1 [1907], *Expository Times* 19 [1907-1908]: 30, and review of *ST* 2 [1907], *Expository Times* 19 [1907-1908]: 317-18). See also Hastings's review of *ST* 3 (1909), *Expository Times* 20 (1908-1909): 466.

[14]William Adams Brown, "Recent Treatises on Systematic Theology," *American Journal of Theology* 12 (1908): 154-55.

sition of the material which is found in the Bible as an authoritative compendium of supernatural information. The human and historical elements . . . were scarcely considered at all.

In the meantime, said the reviewer, "biblical scholarship has passed from the conception of the Bible as a collection of timeless and eternal divine oracles to an appreciation of the vital, historical religious experience recorded in the Bible." Although Strong had felt the influence of these movements, his "recognition of the methods of modern scholarship is a 'concession' rather than a positive possession. . . . He has simply modified the older theory of inspiration, but has not felt the power of the historical method."[15]

The reviewer went on to argue that Strong's diffidence about historical method had robbed ethical monism of its real power. His "present interest," the critic noted, is to comprehend the "Eternal Christ" as the "immanent Power in nature and history." But the " 'proof-text' method . . . has made his work unreadable for the biblical scholars. . . . To cite half a dozen brief biblical passages out of context and with no hint of the historical situation . . . will seem to most biblical students today a totally inadequate method of expounding scripture." Thus, in Strong's hands, doctrine has become "an inscrutable mystery, laid upon the believer as a burden, rather than offered as a positive help to the religious understanding of God."[16]

Strong was stung. He told the Rochester alumni that the "conservatives at Waco and Princeton think me too radical, and the radicals of Union and of Chicago think me too conservative." In the *Autobiography* he was more blunt. There he groused that the ethical monism articles had provoked "many ignorant denunciations" in which he had been smeared as a "pantheist and a Buddhist." The ugliness of the critical response to the eighth edition of the *Systematic Theology* also took a heavy toll. Shortly after its publication he admitted, " I am disposed to leave theology and philosophy behind and to go back to the solid ground of nature." Even so, there is no reason to believe that the reviews had any measurable impact upon Strong's thinking. The uproar over ethical

---

[15]Unsigned review, *Standard* (25 April 1908): 980.

[16]Ibid.

monism did induce him to downplay it as "only tentative," but he never retracted nor modified a single line. The same was true of the *Systematic Theology*. "I am more and more convinced that I have taught the essential truth," he reflected with typical self-confidence in 1908. "I am willing to make my *Systematic Theology* my monument."[17]

The third volume of Strong's "monument" and the first volume of *The Fundamentals* both appeared in 1910. Because the stated aim of the latter was to show off the heavy artillery of Protestant orthodox apologetics, and because the editor, A. C. Dixon, was a friend and fellow Northern Baptist, it is puzzling that Strong did not contribute. In 1910 the modernist-fundamentalist controversy was only a muffled rumble on the horizon. Strong undoubtedly heard it in the distance, but his absence from the roster of worthies in *The Fundamentals* suggests that at that point he still did not intend to be drawn into the storm.[18]

Yet events often overwhelm the best of intentions. Strong was too much a part of American Protestantism to be left out. The story of how he became entangled in the conflict is not only the final chapter in the story of his career, but also an important chapter in the story of the conservative confrontation with history. Even so, long before the religious press started to register the acrimonious exchanges of the controversy, Strong knew from personal experience that this war, like all wars, would prove more costly than most combatants imagined.

---

[17]AHS, "Dr. Strong at the [Alumni] Dinner," *RTS Record* 3 (June 1908): 14; *AB*, 255, 345. See also *45th Annual Report* (1895): 31-32, for discussion of the reaction the ethical monism articles provoked. In an autobiographical essay written in 1913, Strong made no retractions; see *OHCT*, 30.

[18]I do not know if Strong was invited and declined, or was never invited to contribute to the *Fundamentals*. Although he was friendly with the editor, A. C. Dixon, as well as with many others who soon became leaders of the fundamentalist movement, at that time Strong was not part of the informal network that was rapidly hardening into a fundamentalist coalition. For the intense maneuvering circa 1910 see Ferenc Morton Szasz, *The Divided Mind of Protestant America* (University AL: University of Alabama Press, 1982) 81-83.

Chapter Six

The Price of Knowing: Private Crisis and Public Confrontation

NEAR THE TURN OF THE CENTURY Augustus Strong became acutely aware that historical consciousness always comes with a price tag. Whether he chose to accept or reject the historicist's verdict on the origin of religious knowledge, he learned that simply to become cognizant of the problem is invariably a costly business. He also learned that the first and final payments would have to be made at home.

Strong's first child, Charles Augustus Strong, proved to be a person of exceptional gifts. In 1885 he graduated *summa cum laude* from Harvard College. Like his friend and classmate George Santayana, Charles had concentrated in philosophy at a time when Harvard was, thanks to teachers like Josiah Royce and William James, undoubtedly the most exciting place in the United States to study the subject. After graduate work in France and Germany, Charles taught psychology and philosophy at the University of Chicago and at Cornell and Columbia Universities. William James once described him as one of the most formidable thinkers of his generation. "He goes by points," James noted, "pinning each one definitely, and has, I think, the very clearest mind I ever knew." Although Charles eventually authored a charming book of philosophical fables (in addition to numerous technical studies), he appears to have had a rigorous analytical intelligence. James counted Charles among his "dearest friends," but found his "unremitting, untiring, monotonous addiction" to truth exhausting. More than once Augustus Strong lamented that his son's aptitude for intuitive and imaginative insight was persistently overwhelmed by his passion for "precision and clearness."[1]

This yearning for antiseptic clarity of thought seems to have been the decisive factor in Charles's rejection of Christian belief. After graduating from Harvard (and before his sojourn in Europe), Charles had returned to Rochester Seminary to study for the Baptist ministry. For one year he attended all mid-week prayer meetings and taught two church school classes every Sunday. But nagging doubts about the possibility of supernatural revelation finally drove him to admit to himself and to his father that his fundamental convictions were no longer orthodox. Charles believed that withdrawal from seminary and an open profession of agnosticism was the only honorable option. George Santayana, who modeled the protagonist of *The Last Puritan* after Charles, later remarked that "modernist compromises and ambiguities were abhorrent to his strict honesty and love of precision. [For Charles] you mustn't preach what you don't believe." But the decision to renounce Christianity was not easy. Charles's biographer judged that the emotional strain of the ordeal, and especially the strain of telling his father, permanently impaired his health.[2]

For Augustus Strong the hurt was equally deep. Although he had six children, Charles clearly was—and, for that matter, always would

---

[1]William James, *The Letters of Williams James,* ed. Henry James (Boston: Atlantic Monthly Press, 1920) 2:229-30, 282, 310; see also 198, 225, 295, 301, 309, 315, 337. For Strong's remark see *AB,* 257-58. For biographical information on Charles Strong see *Dictionary of American Biography,* s.v. "Strong, Charles Augustus." See also Bruce Kuklick, *The Rise of American Philosophy* (New Haven CT: Yale University Press, 1977) 360, 362, 649.

[2]George Santayana, *Persons and Places: The Background of My Life* (New York: Charles Scribner's Sons, 1944) 249-53. I owe the point about *The Last Puritan* to Crerar Douglas, editor of *Autobiography of Augustus Hopkins Strong* (Valley Forge PA: Judson Press, 1981) 380. Data on Charles Strong is taken from *AB,* 261-62 and *DAB.*

be—the apple of his eye. Indeed, Strong rarely missed a chance to boast about Charles's intellectual prowess and scholarly achievements. Nonetheless, shortly after Charles's decision to leave the seminary, Strong asked the First Baptist Church of Rochester to withdraw the "hand of fellowship" from Charles because he had "ceased to believe in the . . . fundamentals of doctrine." Strong later wrote that the episode had been "the greatest disappointment and sorrow" of his life. In time the birth of a granddaughter stirred hope in Strong's heart that Charles would find that "the new outlet to his affections" would be

> of great service to his religious life. Shut up to intellectual work, the emotional side of his nature has never had sufficient development . . . . A little child upon his knee, pleading with him, asserting her will against his, putting the utmost faith in him . . . will teach him more of religion than all his researches.

Strong never ceased to believe that Charles would change. In his eightieth year he admitted that he still lived in the "hope that before I die Charles will see 'the light of the knowledge of the glory of God in the face of Jesus Christ.' "[3]

It never happened. To the end of their lives father and son inhabited, as Edmund Gosse said of himself and his Plymouth Brethren father, "opposite hemispheres of the soul." Strong did not live to see the publication of Charles's last work, *A Creed for Sceptics* (1936), nor to read Charles's autobiographical statement that he had been driven to reject Christian faith by the "unnaturalness of the suppositions" in his father's *Systematic Theology*. Yet one suspects that Strong would not have been dismayed. Charles's "filial loyalty and persistent search for truth," he wrote in his old age, "are signs of Christ's working in him, though he is . . . unconscious of their Author."[4]

---

[3]Letter from AHS to Prudential Committee, First Baptist Church, Rochester NY, 9 July 1916. However, the church's minutes of 4 November 1891 indicate that the decision to withdraw fellowship from Charles was at Charles's own request. Other quotations are from *AB*, 262, 351, 264.

[4]Charles Augustus Strong, "Nature and Mind," in George P. Adams and William Pepperell Montague, eds., *Contemporary American Philosophy* (London: George Allen and Unwin, 1930), 2:313; AHS's remark is in *AB*, 351. Edmund Gosse's remark is in *Father and Son* (New York: Oxford University Press, 1974 [1907]) 165.

The most interesting aspect of this story is Strong's guilt about his own role in Charles's spiritual odyssey. By 1900 Strong had come to believe that his own crustiness about doctrinal rectitude had been one of the forces that had alienated Charles from the church. "At that time," he wrote in reference to Charles's years at Harvard, "I was myself less open to modern ideas than I have been since. . . . I became alarmed at Charles' tendencies. . . . It was all a mistake on my part, and I now greatly regret that I did not leave him to . . . the Spirit of truth." By 1916 growing remorse finally prompted Strong to ask the First Baptist Church of Rochester to rescind the excommunication of Charles, which had taken place exactly twenty-five years earlier. Most pertinent to our present concern is the reason he gave for the retraction.

> Times have changed during these last twenty years. Churches think less of mere formulas of doctrine, and more of the spirit of a man's life. I believe that my son shows in his life the work of Christ's spirit; and that a reversal of the Church's action, and his restoration to church-fellowship, may themselves be a help to the settlement in his mind of some of the speculative problems that have vexed him.
>
> I now wish to confess my own wrong in the matter. . . . I would now be more lenient and forebearing and hopeful in cases where there is no moral delinquency, and where the defect is only intellectual misunderstanding. I am nearing my fourscore years, and I would like to celebrate my eightieth birthday with this burden off my mind.[5]

"Where the defect is only intellectual misunderstanding"! It is ironic that a man whose main claim to fame was the construction of the monumental *Systematic Theology* would, in the end, characterize a rejection of the whole edifice of Christian doctrine as "only intellectual misunderstanding." Yet those who knew Strong well probably were not surprised. "I have never understood that my calling was to make simple theologians," he wrote in his *Autobiography*. The goal had always been simpler and deeper. "I have aimed to give my students something to preach, but also to convince them that without love truth cannot be rightly seen and without God truth is an abstraction and not a power."[6]

---

[5]AHS to Prudential Committee, 9 July 1916; see also *Minutes*, First Baptist Church, Rochester NY, 23 July 1916.

[6]*AB*, 221.

II

The most portentous public crisis of Strong's mature years was the rapid change in the theological complexion of Rochester Theological Seminary after his retirement in 1912. Strong had hoped that the school would continue to exhibit a healthy mix of theological positions within a framework of basic orthodoxy. "I do not expect that my teaching in all its details will be perpetuated in the Seminary," he announced at his retirement banquet, "but I have faith in God that this Seminary will be preserved from essential error, and that an ever increasing number of men will go out from its walls to proclaim the gospel of the grace of God." Yet, even then, Strong's optimism was shadowed by a premonition of troubled times ahead. "These forty years have been a time of unrest in the theological world," he reflected, and in his mind the root of the unrest was not difficult to find. "The modern world," he wrote, "takes less interest in questions of doctrine than of old,—a sort of pragmatic estimation of truth by its present cash values has taken the place of the former belief that no word of God is devoid of power."[7]

As the months passed Strong's worst suspicions were confirmed. The trustee's decision not to make his younger son John president of the seminary was, in his mind, an unmistakable omen that the old-fashioned gospel would not be preserved. John had earned a Ph.D. in New Testament at Yale, and had taught at Rochester since 1904. His piety and pastoral gifts were highly regarded but his scholarship and administrative skills apparently were not. Strong said nothing in public, but privately his resentment boiled over. "There has been a reaction from my theology," he wrote to John in 1913, "and you have felt its ill effects. It may be best to let the new influences have their way—I doubt whether there is any use fighting against them."[8]

---

[7]AHS, *RTS Record* 7 (May 1912) : 21-22.

[8]AHS to John Henry Strong, 13 December 1913. For biographical data on John Strong see *Thirty Year Record of the Class of 1890* (New Haven: Yale College, 1922), and Frank Otis Erb, "Rochester Alumni and Education," *RTS Bulletin* [75] (May 1925): 139. For John's piety and Strong's effort to make him president of RTS see LeRoy Moore, Jr., "The Rise of American Religious Liberalism at the Rochester

Perhaps not, but everyone knew that Strong's ghost still stalked the halls. When the trustees finally settled on Clarence Barbour in 1915, Barbour went out of his way to secure Strong's blessing. The older man assured Barbour that he would "support and stand by any man whom the Board of Trustees may select, and if they select you, you may count on my loyal backing." But Strong admitted that he was troubled about Barbour's theological views.

> You are too much under the influence of the Chicago School of Theology. It is said that the recent appointments to professorships are all of men who are unwilling to say that they believe in the preexistence, deity, virgin birth, miracles, physical resurrection, objective atonement, omnipresence, of Jesus Christ. The Chicago men, it is said, are practical Unitarians, and that the Seminary has already gone over to the unevangelical wing of Christendom. Since you have not stemmed the tide, but have helped it on, you are under suspicion as thinking more of the temporary popularity of the institution than of its conformity to the Scriptural model. You could easily set yourself right in this respect by standing up in your inaugural address . . . for the old fashioned evangelical faith.

Barbour replied with a warm—and adroitly evasive—profession of evangelical faith, but Strong was not taken in. After Barbour took over Strong became more and more convinced that the seminary was hurtling toward "practical Unitarianism." In public he continued to hold his tongue, but privately he was increasingly apprehensive about the theological drift at Rochester.[9]

One indication of Strong's unease was the rift that developed between him and Walter Rauschenbusch, who had been his student and whom he had appointed to the Rochester faculty in 1897. Strong had always been fond and supportive of the younger man. In 1912 he had

---

Theological Seminary" (Ph.D. dissertation, Claremont Graduate School, 1966) 161-67. Strong himself wrote to John, "People think perhaps that you are better fitted for the pastorate than for teaching. The choice of electives by the students might indicate this. All concede that the Seminary would sustain a great loss, if you leave it, for your character and personal influence is most highly esteemed" (AHS to John Henry Strong, 13 December 1913).

[9]Clarence Barbour to AHS, 9 January 1915; AHS to Barbour, 13 January 1915; Barbour to AHS, 18 January 1915; American Baptist Historical Society.

assured Rauschenbusch that his *Christianizing the Social Order* "is a great book, and I am proud of you." Rauschenbusch, in turn, had told others that he hoped that the new president would be "as wise and tolerant as Dr. Strong." In 1917 Rauschenbusch dedicated his *Theology for the Social Gospel* to Strong "with reverence and gratitude." But this time the admiration was not returned. Strong acknowledged that he was honored by the dedication, but icily added, "I have a book of my own in press which will show you better my attitude toward the theological problems of the day." Rauschenbusch was understandably hurt. Strong's diary suggests that the relationship was patched up at the time of Rauschenbusch's final hospitalization, and it shows that Strong deeply grieved when Rauschenbusch died in the summer of 1918. Even so, one must wonder what Strong meant when at Rauschenbusch's funeral he prayed, "Whatever of shortcoming or of defect may have been his, Thou canst rectify and remedy."[10]

A long, bitter passage Strong added to his *Autobiography* in 1917 shows how much he resented the turn of events at Rochester. Undoubtedly his feelings were complicated by the realization that to a great extent there was no one to blame except himself. The financial independence of the seminary, which dissolved the school's answerability to the churches, was an achievement of his administration. He believed that he had not pressed vigorously enough for the election of his son John, or of a progressive conservative such as E. Y. Mullins to

---

[10]AHS to Walter Rauschenbusch, 30 December 1912, is quoted in Moore, "Religious Liberalism," 244. Rauschenbusch to George Cross, 5 June 1912, is quoted in LeRoy Moore, Jr., "Academic Freedom," *Foundations* 10 (1967): 64-79. AHS to Rauschenbusch, 25 December 1917, is quoted in Moore, "Religious Liberalism," 245. AHS, "Prayer," *RTS Bulletin* [68] (November 1918): 11. See also AHS, 1918 diary, *passim.* Rauschenbusch's dedication read, "THIS BOOK IS INSCRIBED WITH REVERENCE AND GRATITUDE TO AUGUSTUS HOPKINS STRONG: FOR FORTY YEARS PRESIDENT OF ROCHESTER THEOLOGICAL SEMINARY, MY TEACHER, COLLEAGUE, FRIEND, HUMANIST AND LOVER OF POETRY, A THEOLOGIAN WHOSE BEST BELOVED DOCTRINE HAS BEEN THE MYSTIC UNION WITH CHRIST" (Rauschenbusch, *A Theology for the Social Gospel* (New York: Macmillan, 1917) v. Although there was strain between Strong and Rauschenbusch, Strong never considered him as dangerously liberal as George Cross. Conrad Moehlman once told Winthrop S. Hudson that Strong's attitude toward Rauschenbusch was always tempered by Rauschenbusch's willingness to pray to Jesus (interview with Hudson, 23 June 1978).

the presidency. That failure, he groused, was "one of the great mistakes of my life. . . . I mourned over the result." Beyond these recriminations, he knew that many of the faculty members who espoused liberal or radical positions following his retirement were men whom he had hired. Nor could he fathom why President Barbour failed to repudiate their views. Under Barbour's administration, he wrote, many "soon gave evidence in their utterances that a veritable revolution had taken place in the attitude of the Seminary toward fundamentals of the Christian faith."[11]

In Strong's estimation the appointment of George Cross to replace him in systematic theology was the most egregious mistake in the seminary's history. "I regard that election as the greatest calamity that has come to the seminary since its foundation. It was the entrance of an agnostic, skeptical, and anti-Christian element into its teaching, the results of which will be only evil." It is significant that Cross's central shortcoming, in Strong's eyes, was his distorted understanding of the origin and nature of revelation itself. Cross's "view of Scripture as only the record of man's gropings after God instead of being primarily God's revelation to man," Strong wrote, "makes any systematic theology impossible and any professorship of systematic theology to be only a history of doctrines."[12]

This attack on Cross is particularly important, for it shows that by 1917 Strong clearly understood the difference between liberal and orthodox conceptions of the origin and nature of religious knowledge. But did he understand the meaning of the difference? Did he perceive that liberals reached different conclusions in doctrinal matters because they had different assumptions about the way religious knowledge is acquired in the first place? Did he discern, in short, that the fracture between liberalism and orthodoxy was essentially epistemic rather than doctrinal? Although he never phrased it exactly that way, there is little

---

[11]*AB,* 356-57. Teachers Strong hired who became liberal or very liberal included, in addition to Rauschenbusch and Moehlman, Walter Betteridge, Joseph W. A. Stewart, and Cornelius Woelfkin; see Moore, "Religious Liberalism," chap. 3. For Strong's effort to make the seminary financially independent of the churches see Moore, "Religious Liberalism," 146-53, and *MISC* 1:150-59.

[12]*AB,* 357.

doubt that he was finally coming to see the true nature of the problem, and to see it with painful clarity.

III

If Augustus Strong had died in the 1890s he might have been conveniently tagged by historians as an essentially conservative thinker whose erudition and largeness of spirit had led him now and then to dally in the meadows of the New Theology. But events after 1910 denied Strong the luxury of "evangelical liberalism" or "progressive orthodoxy" or some such compromise. In ways that he had never bargained for, he was forced to choose sides on a score of doctrinal and ecclesiological issues. More crucially, he also was forced to find for himself, if not a solution, at least a working accommodation to the dilemma of historical consciousness.

Strong had never had much taste for theological controversy, but during the World War he came to the conclusion that extreme theological liberalism—or modernism, as it was frequently called—was mushrooming out of control. The catalyst that provoked this judgment was a worldwide tour of Baptist missions that Strong and his second wife made in 1916 to celebrate their marriage and his eightieth birthday. The tour left him gravely alarmed. In his view liberalism on the foreign mission field was wrecking the labor of decades. Unable to bite his tongue any longer, Strong finally vented his anger in 1918 in *A Tour of the Missions.*[13]

Actually, this polemic—which one reviewer lustily cheered as a "fearful arraignment" of the depradations of liberalism—had been simmering for more than a decade. In the preface to the eighth edition of the *Systematic Theology,* written in the summer of 1906, Strong had warned that the church was heading for a "second Unitarian defection,"

---

[13]For the growth of liberalism on the mission field see William R. Hutchison, "Modernism and Missions," in John K. Fairbank, ed., *The Missionary Enterprise in China and America* (Cambridge MA: Harvard University Press, 1974) 110-31, and Hutchison, "The Moral Equivalent for Imperialism," in Torben Christensen and Hutchison, eds., *Missionary Ideologies in the Imperialist Era* (Aarhus, Denmark: Aros Publishers, 1982) 167-77. For liberalism among Baptist missionaries see Roland Tenus Nelson, "Fundamentalism and the Northern Baptist Convention" (Ph.D. dissertation, University of Chicago, 1964) 268-69.

and he hoped that his *Systematic Theology* might "do something to stem this fast advancing tide." By 1918 he knew, however, that neither he nor anyone else had done much to stem the tide. He also understood that the doctrinal deviations of liberalism were the symptom rather than the essence of what had gone wrong.[14]

In *A Tour of the Missions* Strong contended that modern scholars had effectively been paralyzed by their exclusive use of historical method in the interpretation of Scripture. He readily admitted that historical method had proved its worth, and as a result, "any honest Christian . . . has the right to interpret Jonah and Daniel as allegories" or to believe that "there may be more than one Isaiah." Indeed, there is "room for the most thorough investigation of the times and ways of revelation, for recognizing the imperfection of beginnings and the variety of the product." But modern biblical critics had gone astray, he charged, not because they followed historical method, but because they followed nothing else. "Proceed[ing] wholly by induction," they had confined themselves to "what can be seen immediately around [the data]." They therefore failed to allow for the possibility that "certain truths . . . cannot be reached by induction" and must be discerned "by intuition, long before induction begins." Strong still believed that the most fundamental of these truths is God's existence. Honest acceptance of this primal truth, known by "universal intuition," would lead eventually to repentance, and the conviction that the "Bible is Christ's revelation of God, and not merely a series of gropings after truth on the part of men."[15]

This was the heart of the matter. If history is the exfoliation of Christ's life in time, Strong wondered how critical historical method could be "really historical" if it *presupposes* that "physical forces are in the end the supreme determinants of history"? The biblical scholar, he countered, "must begin his investigations with one of two assumptions: Is the Bible only man's word? or, Is it also Christ's word? Is it a mere product of human intelligence? or, Is it also the product of divine

---

[14]*ST*(1907) viii-ix. "Fearful arraignment" is from [Victor I. Masters], "Dr. A. H. Strong's Terrible Arraignment of Destructive Criticism," *Western Recorder*, (21 October 1926): 11.

[15]*Tour*, 186, 175, 167-70.

intelligence?" The problem with historical method as it is usually employed, said Strong, is that it simply presupposes the former. "It sees in Scripture only a promiscuous collection of disjointed documents, with no living tie to bind them together, and no significance beyond that of the time in which they were written." But Christ's "presence in human history . . . has given *unity* to his continuous revelation." Thus Scripture cannot be "interpreted as a promiscuous congeries of separate bits; for a divine intelligence and life throb through the whole collection."[16]

Clearly the specter that haunted the octogenarian Strong was not the critical methodology of biblical and historical scholarship per se but the naturalistic assumptions that often accompanied it. This "perverted historical method," as he called it, was the very foundation of modernistic liberalism, and unlike the more benign liberalism of the 1880s and 1890s, it threatened his life's work. "What sort of systematic theology is left us?" he demanded. "There is but one answer: No such thing as systematic theology is possible." The liberal teacher in the liberal seminary, steeped in historicist assumptions, is a "blind leader of the blind."

> Having no system of truth to teach, he becomes a mere lecturer on the history of doctrine. . . . Ask him if he believes in the preexistence, deity, virgin birth, miracles, atoning death, physical resurrection, omnipresence, and omnipotence of Christ, and he denies your right to require of him any statement of his own beliefs. He does not conceive it to be his duty to furnish his students with any fixed conclusions as to doctrine but only to aid them in coming to conclusions for themselves.

Indeed, teachers of this sort, who dissect Scripture as if it were a "cadaver," destroy what they touch.

> The result of such teaching in our seminaries is that the student . . . has no longer any positive message to deliver . . . and at his graduation leaves the seminary, not to become preacher or pastor as he had once hoped, but to sow his doubts broadcast, as teacher in some college, as editor of some religious journal, as secretary of some Young Men's

---

[16]*Tour,* 170-77. "Physical forces" from AHS, " 'The Battle of the Huns,' " *New York Times,* 13 October 1918, sec. 3, 2.

Christian Association, or as agent of some mutual life insurance company.[17]

Strong's sarcasm undoubtedly cut close to the quick for many people, including Clarence Barbour, who had been a YMCA secretary before coming to Rochester. But Strong was playing for keeps. "This method of interpretation," he went on, "is like a blinding mist which is slowly settling down upon our churches, and is gradually abolishing . . . all definite views of Christian doctrine." On the mission field education and social service are displacing evangelism. Missionaries, "having nothing positive to preach, choose rather to teach." When they teach they "cannot help revealing their mental poverty, and disturbing the simple faith of their pupils." A thousand pages of liberal-conservative disputation were distilled in one final, bitter observation: "This method of Scripture interpretation makes evangelism an enterprise of fanatics."[18]

Even as Strong wrote these words, the clouds of the fundamentalist controversy were billowing high on the horizon. Except perhaps for the Northern Presbyterians, no denomination was more severely disrupted than the Northern Baptists. Many of the players on both sides had once been Strong's students, and now they were fighting for the disparate implications of the theology he had taught them. Not surprisingly, many of his public utterances were used freely, even loosely, by both factions as they sought to fortify their positions in the public mind. We need therefore to examine the roots of the controversy that marred the Convention's annual meetings at Buffalo and Des Moines in 1920 and 1921 in order to understand some of the things that Strong did and said and apparently thought in these final years. In retrospect it is clear that the story of Strong's growing consciousness of history was part of a larger story of cultural change and conflict in American Protestantism.

---

[17]*Tour*, 187-90.

[18]*Ibid.*, 191-95. Strong privately wondered "whether Dr. Barbour, with his compromising spirit, will have power to keep our students true to Christ" (*AB*, 357); see also Moore, "Religious Liberalism," 232.

Chapter Seven

Tradition against History:
Strong and the
Fundamentalist Controversy

THE LONG TRAIN RIDE HOME to New York City gave the editor of the *Watchman-Examiner* a chance to reflect on the tumultuous events he had just witnessed at the 1920 annual convention of Northern Baptists in Buffalo. Eventually Curtis Lee Laws would have second thoughts about the company he was keeping, but for now he was pleased to call himself and his colleagues "fundamentalists" in the fight against modernity. For good or ill, the label stuck.[1]

---

[1] Laws is usually given credit for inventing the term "fundamentalism" but it should be stressed that originally it did not have the connotations of militancy and narrowness that it now has. Indeed, Laws said that he chose the word precisely because it did not have the reactionary implications associated with words such as conservative, premillennialist, or Landmarker. Laws, "Convention Sidelights," *WE*, (1 July 1920): 834. The train setting is described in Joseph Stowell, *Background and History of the Association of Regular Baptist Churches* (1949) 18, as cited in Donald Tinder, "Fundamentalist Baptists in the Northern and Western United States" (Ph.D. dissertation, Yale University, 1969) 5. Laws's eventual alienation from the hard-liners is discussed in Norman Maring, "Conservative But Progressive," in Gilbert L. Guffin, ed., *What God Hath Wrought* (Chicago: Judson Press, 1960) 17.

The emergence of a fundamentalist faction in American Protestantism in general, and among Northern Baptists in particular, has been traced by a number of able historians—and, not surprisingly, different historians have discerned different forces behind the controversy. Social cleavages, cultural strain, doctrinal disagreement, even personal animosities have been emphasized by one scholar or another. Although each of these interpretations has merit, I would argue, along with Winthrop S. Hudson and George M. Marsden, that the most persistent cause of conflict was a growing divergence over the nature of biblical authority. More often than not, the central question was whether the Bible is a direct—and therefore inerrant—communication from God, or whether it is the principal record of humanity's faltering quest for God. Probably very few conservative Baptists in the early 1920s had ever heard of writers like Max Weber or Karl Mannheim, but their Baptist instincts were sound. They knew that contemporary culture was increasingly inhospitable to their deepest convictions. Another way of putting it is to say that the forces that prompted the formation of the Baptist Fundamentalist Fellowship in 1920, and repeatedly threatened to fracture the Northern Baptist Convention throughout the decade, ultimately grew from divergent perceptions of the historicity of religious knowledge.[2]

---

[2]Winthrop S. Hudson, *Religion in America* 3d ed., rev. (New York: Charles Scribner's, 1981) 279; George M. Marsden, *Fundamentalism and American Culture* (New York: Oxford University Press, 1980) 103-108. All of the major book-length studies of fundamentalism devote substantial attention to its growth among Northern Baptists; see Marsden, *Fundamentalism,* esp. chaps. 12 and 18; Stewart G. Cole, *The History of Fundamentalism* (Westport CT: Greenwood Press, 1971 [1931]) chap. 5; Norman Furniss, *The Fundamentalist Controversy* (Hamden CT: Archon Books, 1963 [1954]) chap. 6; George W. Dollar, *A History of Fundamentalism in America* (Greenville SC: Bob Jones University Press, 1973) chaps. 8-9; Ernest R. Sandeen, *The Roots of Fundamentalism* (Chicago: University of Chicago Press, 1970) 260-64; see also Robert G. Torbet, *A History of the Baptists* (Valley Forge PA: Judson Press, 1963 [1950] 427-39. Several Ph.D. dissertations trace the story in detail, each from a different angle; the most important include Tinder, "Fundamentalist Baptists"; Walter E. W. Ellis, "Social and Religious Factors in the Fundamentalist-Modernist Schisms among Baptists in North America" (University of Pittsburgh, 1974); Roland Tenus Nelson, "Fundamentalism and the Northern Baptist Convention" (University of Chicago, 1964). Recent article-length studies include Maring, "Conservative But Progres-

For Baptists, the turmoil created by growing historical consciousness was most acutely manifested in a forty-year struggle for control of
the seminaries. The opening shot was fired in 1882 when Ezra P. Gould
was asked to leave Newton Theological Institute. Fourteen years later
Hamilton Theological Institute forced out Nathaniel Schmidt. Both
men were biblical scholars who had adopted higher-critical views. The
next major round came in 1905 when William Rainey Harper, president of the University of Chicago, transferred George Burman Foster—
who was about as radical as a theologian could be and still claim to be
a Baptist—from the Divinity School to the Department of Comparative
Religion. Harper hoped to make Foster less visible and the university
less vulnerable, but things did not work out that way. The following
year Foster published *The Finality of the Christian Religion*, a strenuously
historicist interpretation of the origin and evolution of Christianity. The
volume provoked a storm of criticism among Northern Baptists and led
to his permanent expulsion from the Chicago Baptist Minister's Meeting in 1909.[3]

These early victories notwithstanding, conservatives correctly read
the writing on the wall. Fearing that they would soon lose control of
the seminaries, they founded Boston Missionary Training Institute (now
Gordon-Conwell Theological Seminary) in 1889, Kansas City Baptist
Theological Seminary in 1902, and Northern Baptist Theological Seminary in Chicago in 1913. Each of these efforts was designed to bring
Baptist theological education into alignment with Baptist orthodoxy as
represented in the New Hampshire Confession of 1833. Beyond that,
and more precisely, each reflected a commitment to teach the uncon-

---

sive," and Ernest R. Sandeen, "The Baptists and Millenarianism," *Foundations* 13
(1970): 18-25. Contemporary assessments include Robert A. Ashworth, "The Fundamentalist Movement among the Baptists," *Journal of Religion* 4 (1924): 611-31; Ernest DeWitt Burton, "Recent Trends in Northern Baptist Churches," *American Journal
of Theology* 24 (1920): 321-38; Edward B. Pollard, "Baptists and Fundamentalism,"
Homiletic Review 87 (1924): 265-67; Charles Hillman Fountain, *The Denominational
Situation* (Plainfield NJ: n.p., 1920).

[3]These events are described in several sources. See, for example, Norman H. Maring, "Baptists and Changing Views of the Bible," *Foundations* 1 (July 1958): 63-64;
Cole, *History*, 89-90; Nelson, "Fundamentalism," 106-119; Larry E. Axel, "Conflict
and Censure," in Peter Iver Kaufman and Spencer Lavan, eds., *Alone Together* (Boston:
Beacon Press, 1979) 94-95.

ditioned timelessness of the revelation found in Scripture. Members of the faculty of the new Chicago seminary, for example, pledged themselves to be "loyal to the Word of God," by which they meant the "positive, changeless and glorious doctrines of grace as opposed to the negations of the new rationalism."[4]

After the World War, declining enrollment in the older, better known Baptist seminaries fueled grass roots suspicion that the schools were weakening the faith of their students. Renewed determination to reverse this trend prompted the organization of the Baptist Fundamentalist Fellowship in the winter of 1920. Led by Jasper C. Massee, pastor of Baptist Temple in Brooklyn, the Fellowship met in Buffalo in June 1920, immediately preceding the denomination's annual convention. The purpose of the Pre-Convention Conference, as it came to be called, was to "restate, reaffirm and re-emphasize the fundamentals of our New Testament faith" in light of the "havoc which rationalism is working in our churches." Three hundred participants were expected, but ten times that number showed up, and the Pre-Convention Conference nearly overshadowed the convention itself as the most exciting show in town.[5]

The speakers at the Conference made their points in different ways, and branded their enemy with different epithets—rationalism, natu-

---

[4]The Northern Baptist Theological Seminary pledge is in the school's *First Annual* (1914-1915), as quoted in Cole, *History,* 90. In the late nineteenth and early twentieth centuries a network of denominational and nondenominational Bible schools grew up in an effort to offset the drift of the older seminaries. See S. A. Witmer, *The Bible College Story* (Manhasset NY: Channel Press, 1962) esp. 89-90, 158-64; Virginia Lieson Brereton, "Protestant Fundamentalist Bible Schools" (Ph.D. diss., Columbia University, 1981). Developments in the Northern Baptist Convention are summarized in Tinder, "Fundamentalist Baptists," chap. 10.

[5]The "Call to the Buffalo Conference" was issued 21 April 1920. It was printed in *WE* (20 May 1920): 652, and in the *Baptist* (12 June 1920): 2. For the signers see *Baptist Fundamentals* (Philadelphia: Judson Press, 1920), preface. For the circumstances surrounding the Call, see Ashworth, "Fundamentalist Movement," 614-15, and C. Allyn Russell, *Voices of American Fundamentalism* (Philadelphia: Westminster Press, 1976) 119, 248n. For the perceived threat to the seminaries see Tinder, "Fundamentalist Baptists," 274-77, and Clark H. Pinnock, "The Modernist Impulse at McMaster University," in Jarold K. Zeman, ed., *Baptists in Canada* (Burlington, Ontario: G. R. Welch, 1980) 203.

ralism, modernism, and the like—but in the end there was virtual una-
nimity that the acid that was eating out the heart of Baptist faith was
the willingness to historicize God's revelation to humankind. Thus in
the opening address Massee pinpointed the "presence in our schools of
the radical, scientific attitude of mind toward the Bible" as the most
pernicious trend of the day. John W. Porter, editor of the Louisville
Western Recorder, similarly admonished his Northern brethren to remember that truth "is a finality. . . . It cannot in the very nature of the
case be 'progressive,' but is a fixed and unchanging quantity." A. C.
Dixon, by then a teacher at the Bible Institute of Los Angeles, unequivocally attributed the historicist attitude to Satan. Whenever man
listens to God's word, said Dixon, Satan comes along and "calls in
question the fact of revelation." Satan asks, "Are you sure that God has
spoken at all? Does God speak directly to his creatures? Is there such a
thing as a revelation from God?"[6]

There where numerous speakers that day, but the Conference spot-
light was saved for the legendary William Bell Riley, who targeted "The
Menace of Modernism in Baptist Schools." Riley predictably assailed
the modernist effort to discredit beloved truths such as the deity of Jesus, but he aimed his most lethal barbs against those who undermined
the Bible's inerrancy. Modernists, he charged, evade the issue when they
ask: "Where shall we find our infallible interpreters of this inspired volume?" Rather the fundamental question "is an altogether different one—
have we an inspired and an infallible volume to interpret?"[7]

Riley was by now an old hand at this kind of fire-eating, Bible-
thumping oratory. Before the next speaker could get to the podium the
Conference had broken into a tumultuous demand that the denomination must investigate its schools. When a resolution to this effect was
presented to the full convention the following day, the convention minutes judiciously indicate that it was "discussed." However, one observer described the scene as "pandemonium," another lamented that
the crowd of 4,000 "was transformed into a shouting, hissing, ap-
plauding bedlam . . . [whose] behavior was shameful," and another

---

[6]*Baptist Fundamentals,* 5, 114, 122.

[7]William Bell Riley's address was published with the less inflammatory title,
"Modernism in Baptist Schools," in *Baptist Fundamentals,* 167, 171.

wrote that "no gathering of Baptists since Civil War days has developed tenser moments or more bitter antagonisms." In the end a bipartisan committee was appointed to investigate "the loyalty of our Baptist schools to Jesus Christ and his gospel."[8]

The peace patched together in Buffalo did not last long. Before the summer of 1920 was over harsh words again were flying in the denominational press. The intensity of fundamentalist concern is poignantly illustrated in an "Open Letter" Massee sent to Baptist colleagues several weeks after the Buffalo convention. It dealt with his son, who had attended an unnamed "Christian college" and, Massee related,

> did come home to me with question marks written over the entire question of the inspiration, authenticity, veracity and reliability of the Bible. . . . He did return to me profoundly convinced that the dominating attitude of the school which he attended toward the Bible was a scientific one rather than a spiritual one.

Eventually the boy regained his faith, but Massee had no difficulty diagnosing the illness besetting Christian schools: "When the false scientific attitude of mind toward the Bible obtains, students are not instructed to approach the Word of God with reverence, with love and with [un]questioning faith in its divine origin." Indeed, the denomination's "chief passion," he bitterly charged, apparently is "to supplant the Bible in our schools by the more or less modified Darwinian theory of evolution."[9]

In theory Massee was the official chairman of the Fundamentalist Fellowship, but William Bell Riley and John Roach Straton (the latter the pastor of Calvary Baptist in New York City) were the real field mar-

---

[8]For the full text of the resolution see *Annual of the Northern Baptist Convention, 1920,* 60-61. See also 48 for the fundamentalists' counterresolution. The setting is described in Curtis Lee Laws, "The Conference on Fundamentals," *WE* (1 July 1920): 838-40; Laws, "Convention Sidelights," *WE* (1 July 1920): 834; Laws, "The Northern Baptist Convention," *WE* (1 July 1920): 843; Homer DeWilton Brookins, "Northern Baptists at Buffalo," *WE* (1 July 1920): 837; cf. Fountain, *Denominational Situation,* 38.

[9]J. C. Massee, "Convention Rumors," *Baptist* (24 July 1920): 909; Massee, "The Churches and the Schools," *WE* (17 March 1921): 336; Massee, "An Answer to the Board of Education," *WE* (16 June 1921): 752-53.

shals. Straton was not a learned man, but he argued the fundamentalist case with considerable acuity. In every field of thought, he acknowledged, "human consciousness continues to play a great part," yet in medicine, law, and the sciences "there are, nevertheless, final and axiomatic principles and truths which can never be transcended and which stand, therefore, as ultimate authority." Unfortunately modern theology fails to see that "if the consciousness of the individual is the seat of authority and the court of final appeal, then we have anarchy in the religious world." Riley similarly diagnosed the cleavage in the denomination as a fracture between "German rationalism" and the "old evangelical faith," a fracture between the "philosophy of Descartes and the so-called science of Darwinism." Yet for Riley the basic issue was even simpler than that. "In the last analysis," he judged, "it comes wholly to one question. . . . Is the *book* we call the Bible divinely and infallibly inspired, a God-given revelation, or is it a purely human product, revealing the mental development of man in the process of evolution?"[10]

Fighting over the same issue erupted again at the second Pre-Convention Conference that gathered in Des Moines in June 1921, just before the annual meeting of the Northern Baptist Convention. The heat was oppressive and there were occasional outbursts of abusive language, but the proceedings generally proved less volatile than they had been the previous summer in Buffalo. This time the great flamethrowers— Dixon, Straton, and Riley—were absent from the roster of speakers. Yet the same anxiety about Scripture was manifest. Again Massee gave the keynote address, and again he singled out the "teachings permitted in our denominational schools"—namely, "that the Bible is as other literature, that it is not of divine origin"—as the root of the trouble.[11]

The muggy weather soon took its toll. The regular convention, which began the following day, was marked by shouting, jostling, and

---

[10]John Roach Straton, "Is It Right and Wise to Investigate Our Theological Seminaries?" *Baptist* (28 August 1920): 1072; William Bell Riley, "What Are the Real Questions Before the Northern Baptist Convention?" *Baptist* (18 June 1921): 627.

[11]*Baptist Doctrines* (n.p.: n.p., 1921) 14, 16. For the setting see Curtis Lee Laws, "Convention Sidelights," *WE* (7 July 1921): 834-35; Laws, "Fundamentals Conference at Des Moines," *Baptist* (2 July 1921): 684; Homer DeWilton Brookins, "The Northern Baptist Convention," *Baptist* (2 July 1921): 837-41.

acrimonious exchanges. The main event was, of course, the report of the school investigation committee. Their nearly unanimous conclusion proved to be surprisingly irenic. "Here and there," said the report, "doubtless is a teacher who has departed from the Baptist faith or has lost the Savior's spirit." But the report also scored the rancorous attitude of some fundamentalist teachers, noting that "no one is as yet so evidently the sole repository of divine revelation as to warrant his denouncing as infidels those who disagree with him." In the end the committee gave the schools what appeared to be a generally clean bill of health: "For the most part our schools of all grades are doing a work of which the denomination may well be proud."[12]

The committee's inclination to see a little fault on both sides and a lot of good everywhere had the unexpected effect of roiling the waters even more. Although Curtis Lee Laws's *Watchman-Examiner* was pleased with the "poise and sanity" of the report, many fundamentalists instantly dismissed it as a whitewash. Soon the moderate fundamentalist leader Frank Goodchild, who had chaired the investigating committee and written its final report, started to backpedal. What the committee tried to say, Goodchild very carefully explained, is that it is the duty of individual Baptist communities—not the Convention—to purge the schools of heretics. And before the year was out even Helen Barratt Montgomery, centrist president of the Convention, openly sided with the fundamentalists. "I believe that the time for the various boards of trustees to clean house has arrived," she declared. "The cleaning cannot be too thorough to suit the denomination."[13]

This long and increasingly heated controversy over theological regularity in Baptist seminaries, including the dispute about what the school report did or did not mean to say, was complicated by growing demand for theological regularity among Baptist missionaries and renewed pressure for an official creed. And the situation was further com-

---

[12]*Annual of the Northern Baptist Convention, 1921,* 92-93.

[13]Curtis Lee Laws, "Convention Sidelights," *WE* (7 July 1921): 835; Frank M. Goodchild, "A Correction," *WE* (15 December 1921): 1587; Helen Barratt Montgomery, [To the Editors], *WE* (29 December 1921): 1650.

plicated when the aged but redoubtable Augustus H. Strong finally decided to step into the ring.[14]

II

One month after the second Pre-Convention Conference, Strong published a broadside in the *Watchman-Examiner* significantly titled, "Confessions of Our Faith." In it he revealed that the previous summer he had declined an invitation from J. C. Massee to write the preface for *Baptist Fundamentals,* the collected speeches of the first Pre-Convention Conference. "I had read the newspaper accounts of that Conference and was displeased with the narrow views with regard to evolution and higher criticism which some of the brethren had there expressed," Strong explained. "Higher criticism has its rights, and instead of denouncing it we must concede that it has thrown valuable light upon the methods employed in the composition of Scripture." He went on to say, however, that neither evolution nor higher criticism could alter the cardinal doctrines of Christianity: the deity, incarnation, virgin birth, miracles, vicarious death, physical resurrection, second coming, and omnipresence of Jesus Christ. Strong then dropped what must have been the major bombshell of the summer in the Northern Baptist Convention.

> It must be evident to all who read this article that I agree far more fully with Dr. Massee concerning the fundamentals than I do with the opposite party. . . . I wish now therefore to set myself, with the qualifications I have just mentioned, squarely on the side of those who demand that our Baptist institutions should be true to the faith . . . and that none who is unable or unwilling to confess that faith should have place in the government or in the instruction of those institutions. This seems to me only the conclusion of common honesty. . . . I see therefore in the present uprising of our denomination, in spite of its incidental narrowness and shortsightedness, a movement of the Spirit of Christ. . . . Let us purge our institutions of men who are unwilling to confess their faith. Let us send out to our missions only those who have a definite gospel to proclaim. And let us inaugurate this change by the adoption of a "Confession of Faith."[15]

---

[14]These later events are recounted in Tinder, "Fundamentalist Baptists," 327-31, and Robert G. Torbet, *Venture of Faith* (Philadelphia: Judson Press, 1955) 406-11.

[15]AHS, "Confessions of Our Faith," *WE* (21 July 1921): 910.

So there it was. Augustus Strong seems at last to have taken sides, and rather decisively at that. In the words of one recent historian, it was "a sour note to finish on."[16]

But appearances can be deceiving. In the first place it should be noted that Strong refused to write the preface for *Baptist Fundamentals,* and refused to be associated publicly with the Fundamentalist Fellowship, until he was satisfied that he could do so without scandalizing his commitment to the evolutionary nature of history and the legitimacy of historical method. Moreover, he did not link himself with the Fellowship until *after* the moderates in the group—principally Curtis Lee Laws and Frank Goodchild—had gained control (albeit temporarily). It is true, of course, that Goodchild and other moderates had second thoughts, and that hard-liners such as Riley, Dixon, and Straton eventually grabbed the leadership of the Fellowship, but all this transpired after Strong had died. The plain truth is that in the late summer of 1921, when Strong cast his lot with the fundamentalists, they undoubtedly seemed to be running the most respectable game in town. Strong had every reason to believe that he could champion their cause without compromising his intellectual integrity.[17]

There is, however, another and more compelling reason why Strong should not be written off as a sour partisan of rigid fundamentalism in the last years of his life. The passing of the old order at Rochester, and the weakening of traditional Protestantism in general, weighed heavily on his mind, but it did not preoccupy him. He was still the same Augustus Strong who had seen the divine energy in the processes of his-

---

[16]LeRoy Moore, Jr., "Another Look at Fundamentalism," *Church History* 37 (1968): 200.

[17]Strong also said that the articles published in *Baptist Fundamentals* turned out to be less "narrow and inconsiderate" than he had expected, and this is why he agreed to speak in favor of the Fellowship. This statement hardly can be taken at face value. The speeches by Riley, Dixon, and Myers were, by any reasonable measure of such things, vengeful attacks on everyone slightly left of themselves. What Strong undoubtedly had in mind were the devotional addresses by Frederick L. Anderson, Thomas Jefferson Villers, Emory W. Hunt, Seldon W. Cummings, and J. Whitcomb Brougher on prayer, evangelism, and so on; see "Confessions of Our Faith," 910.

tory. And like a great nova, the vision flared most brilliantly in the final years of his life.

For many liberals, faith in the upward spiral of history crashed against the hard reality of the World War. For many fundamentalists, especially premillennialists, the war heightened anticipation of the imminent end of history. But for Strong, the conflict enhanced a long-standing conviction that humanity is organically fused with Christ, and that Christ's creative and redemptive power is progressively unfolding in the course of human affairs. "The great war," he told Baptists in France in 1920, has "deepened our sense of the unity of humanity and our own responsibility for the condition of the world." And the ground of that unity is Christ, the "Creator and Life of humanity . . . whose Spirit is moving in all the races of mankind." In Strong's mind the truly fundamental question of the age was not whether progress would come, but whether individual men and women would resist the flow of history. "Shall we be lacking in this great united effort of Christendom? Shall we willingly be left stranded on the shore as this great movement of the world toward God goes on?"[18]

Strong's thinking in the years of his retirement thus seems to have swung like a pendulum between two great concerns. The first was the doctrinal deviations of contemporary theology, fostered, in his judgment, by the growth of "perverted historical method." The second was a conviction, reinforced by the experience of the war, that Christ is the immanent energizing force in history. In his mind these issues were inseparable. The modern inability to see the Christological essence at the center of history was precisely why historical method had become, more often than not, "perverted" and destructive.

As things turned out, however, neither the highly publicized "Confessions of Our Faith" article, nor the sermons preached in France during his last visit to Europe, was Strong's final word on either subject. The final word was a series of homilies jointly published, significantly enough, in the conservative *Watchman-Examiner* and the liberal *Baptist* in the winter of 1921. In these homilies Strong's valedictory judgment was that fundamentalists and liberals had failed to appreci-

---

[18]Undated handwritten manuscript of a sermon preached in France, probably in June 1920. See also *WSIB* 27, 116-17.

ate, respectively, the historical and doctrinal dimensions of the Incarnation. The former, he thought, really should be called "literalists" because they had lost sight of "the omnipresent and eternal Christ, who has supervised in past ages the evolution of Scripture, so that it represents himself in all the forms of human composition." The latter had lost their doctrinal bearings, ironically, for precisely the same reason: they had lost sight of "that same eternal and omnipresent Christ who in Scripture represents himself as the only life and light of men." Both groups, he concluded, were "sincere but imperfectly informed."[19]

Written only weeks before his death, the tone of these articles was typically irenic; the argument was typically strung between the poles of doctrinal regularity and historical awareness. Strong's evenhandedness almost certainly was rooted in a desire to be impartial. There were friends and former students on both sides for whom he felt affection. Yet there is no reason to doubt that in this final statement he truly spoke his mind. He was too honest to dissimulate and too eminent to need to. What we cannot be certain of is the exact form of the underlying impulse.

Did Strong's evenhandedness reflect a conviction that the tension between ancient doctrine and modern assumptions really was resolved by the interpenetration of Christ, history, and the created order? Or did it reflect persisting ambivalence about the fundamental issues involved? Without question Strong himself would have said that the former was the case. A diary he kept for the year 1918, when he was eighty-two years old, shows him following the writings of the noted holiness missionary Mary Slessor, attending church three times each week, and entertaining fundamentalist leaders such as J. Whitcomb Brougher and W. A. Matthews. But the diary also shows him systematically rereading the Shakespeare corpus, buffing up his French, pondering a new book by Harry Emerson Fosdick, and entertaining noted liberals such as Cornelius Woelfkin and Rufus Jones. Someone has said that one

---

[19]*WSIB*, 62-63. Published posthumously in 1922, *WSIB* consists of ten short essays written by Strong in the fall of 1921 on the main themes of Christian faith. They were serialized in *WE* (3 November 1921 to 5 January 1922) and in the *Baptist* (5 November 1921 to 14 January 1922).

measure of a man's concern is what he is willing to fit into an already overburdened schedule. One suspects that Strong's concerns were more tautly stretched than he was ever quite willing to admit.[20]

---

[20]AHS, 1918 diary.

Chapter Eight

Shadows of Faith:
The Legacy of Augustus Strong

I N THE THICKENING HAZE of the liberal-conservative confrontation in the Northern Baptist Convention, Strong's effort to wed tradition and modernity was not what most persons were looking for. This is not to say that all others were blindly partisan. Many honorable men and women desperately hoped to find a way through the crisis. Rather the point is that no one seems to have believed that Strong offered the solution. No one—or at least no one of stature—sought theoretical guidance in his work in the way that liberals looked to Horace Bushnell or conservatives to Charles Hodge. If the reviews of Strong's *Systematic Theology* and *Christ in Creation* ten and twenty years before are a reliable indication, conservatives were virtually blind to whatever value there may have been in his integrative effort, and liberals considered it naive if not preposterous.

Even so, Strong did, ironically, have a significant following. Partisans on both sides frequently paraded his name when it suited their purposes. Liberals used him to establish their legitimacy, while conservatives used him to certify their credibility.

The maneuvering of Henry Clay Vedder is a good example of the way that liberals exploited Strong's reputation. A prominent church historian at Crozer Theological Seminary, Vedder was not exceptionally liberal, but he was, nonetheless, a favorite target of fundamentalist criticism. In the fall of 1920, while the school committee was investigating Crozer, Vedder decided to set the record straight. "It has come to my knowledge that a number of persons are busily circulating secret reports that I do not believe in the inspiration and authority of the Bible," he testily announced in the *Baptist*. Vedder then made it clear that he was prepared to go to the mat with his accusers—if Strong would be, in a sense, the referee.

> For a modern attempt at a scientific definition of inspiration, I accept without amendment the words of my theological teacher, Dr. Augustus H. Strong, whose orthodoxy nobody will impugn: "That influence of the Spirit of God upon the minds of the Scripture writers which made their writings the record of a progressive divine revelation." . . . So far as I know, I accept these words in exactly the same sense that Dr. Strong uses them. If he is orthodox in his teaching about the inspiration and authority of the Bible, I cannot see how I can be heretical.

Vedder then explained what he—and ostensibly Strong—meant by the phrase "progressive divine revelation": "Since the revelation of God was progressive, we find imperfections in its earlier forms." This led Vedder to conclude that the "old method of citing 'proof-texts' hit-or-miss from Genesis to Revelation is impossible to one who really understands the Bible. That is the significance of Dr. Strong's phrase, 'taken together.' "[1]

Vedder did not bother to mention that Strong himself frequently used prooftexts, nor that as recently as 1916, in the preface to his work on American poets, Strong had endorsed the use of prooftexts. Nor did he mention the sizable doctrinal differences between himself and Strong, evident in Vedder's 1922 textbook *The Fundamentals of Christianity*—which, like Rauschenbusch's *Theology for the Social Gospel,* was lovingly

---

[1] Henry Clay Vedder, "What I Teach about the Bible," *Baptist* (30 October 1920): 1357. For fundamentalist criticism of Vedder see J. C. Massee, "An Answer to the Board of Education," *WE* (10 June 1921): 753, and William Bell Riley, "Modernism in Baptist Schools," in *Baptist Fundamentals* (Philadelphia: Judson Press, 1920) 183.

dedicated to Strong. But all that is another story. In the heat of battle, Strong's presence obviously made good company.[2]

J. F. Vichert was another liberal who used Strong's reputation as a shield against fundamentalist criticism. Vichert had been one of the principal protagonists on the liberal side in the seminary controversy in 1918. He was dean of Colgate, where for many years William Newton Clarke's gentle reconstruction of systematic theology had been nurtured. Shortly after Strong's death Vichert too sought to legitimize his view of Scripture by associating it with Strong.

> Careful, critical study of the Scriptures . . . [coupled with] sane, reverent, constructive scholarship has done much to help us into a better understanding . . . of the Bible. This is reflected in the admirable article on that subject in these columns a few weeks ago by the late Dr. Strong.

This much was eminently fair. But Vichert could not resist adding that "absolute liberty of conscience under Christ is, according to Dr. Strong, the right of every Baptist." It is quite true that in earlier years Strong had made comments of this sort, usually for the benefit of Presbyterian readers. But in the context of the fundamentalist controversy he also insisted—and Vichert hardly could have missed it—that liberals had wildly abused the Baptist notion of "soul liberty."[3]

Fundamentalists did their share of name dropping as well. A week before the first Pre-Convention Conference in Buffalo, J. C. Massee defended the gathering on the ground that they, like "Dr. Augustus Strong," knew something had to be done to stop the "drift toward rationalism." Massee failed to mention, however, that Strong had done nothing to support the organization of a fundamentalist faction in the Northern Baptist Convention. Yet this did not prevent the incantation of his name in the speeches given at the Buffalo Pre-Convention Conference. William Bell Riley freely quoted from Strong's *A Tour of the*

---

[2]Vedder's dedication read: "TO MY TEACHER IN THEOLOGY, AUGUSTUS HOPKINS STRONG, D.D., L.L.D., READER, IF YOU FIND HERE AUGHT GOOD AND TRUE, THANK HIM. IF YOU FIND UNTRUTH AND HERESY, BLAME ME!" Vedder, *The Fundamentals of Christianity: A Study of the Teaching of Jesus and Paul* (New York: Macmillan, 1922) v.

[3]J. F. Vichert, "Fears and Hopes of a Fundamentalist," *WE* (2 March 1922): 226.

Missions in order to prove that Rochester, among other schools, had fallen into evil ways. Seldon W. Cummings, urging Baptists to cultivate the habit of prayer, noted that both Dr. Augustus H. Strong and Jesus had stressed the value of prayer. At the Des Moines Pre-Convention Conference the following year, Jacob Heinrich defended the authenticity of the New Testament canon. While acknowledging that 2 Peter, Jude, 2 and 3 John, and Revelation were "frequently held to be spurious," Heinrich disposed of these objections by pointing out, without further ado, that these books had been accepted as genuine by Dr. Strong.[4]

If Strong's name was useful to the fundamentalists while he was alive, it proved even more useful after he died. Ernest Gordon's assault on liberalism, published in 1926 as *The Leaven of the Sadducees,* contrasted the current sorry state of Rochester Theological Seminary with its strength and theological integrity when Strong had been at the helm. Victor I. Masters, the combative editor of the Louisville *Western Recorder,* also upheld Strong's memory. A 1926 speech by a faculty member of McMaster University, which purportedly linked Strong to the " 'New Scholarship' of German rationalism," prompted Masters to rush to Strong's defense. Since it is the method of "Modernists" to belittle the intelligence of conservatives, Masters began, "we want every reader to know that Dr. Augustus H. Strong . . . is considered by many the greatest Baptist theologian America has produced." Yet everyone knows, continued Masters, that Strong never condoned the "dastardly work of the destructive critics in their use of the so-called historical method to explain away the Scriptures." Across town, at Southern Baptist Theological Seminary, the voices were more moderate, but there too nothing but praise for Strong's work was heard. Speaking for the *Review and Expositor,* John W. Johnson wrote that Strong had kept a "clear . . . perspective [on] his own time and the crucial philosophical

---

[4]J. C. Massee, "Should Baptists Confer?" *Baptist* (12 June 1920): 696; William Bell Riley and Seldon W. Cummings in *Baptist Fundamentals,* 181-82 and 103, respectively; Jacob Heinrich in *Baptist Doctrines* (n.p.: n.p., 1921) 62. Significantly, Riley attacked E. Y. Mullins for compromising with Darwinism, but he never mustered the courage to attack Strong—who was, if anything, more deeply committed to evolutionary ways of thinking than Mullins. Roland Tenus Nelson, "Fundamentalism and the Northern Baptist Convention" (Ph.D. dissertation, University of Chicago, 1964) 331.

and theological issues involved in it." Although Princeton's Caspar Wistar Hodge still could not bring himself to admit that Strong had ever known much about philosophy, Hodge warmly acknowledged, nonetheless, that now "his work is done, and it was a great work."[5]

It was a remarkable feat. One scarcely can imagine persons more culturally and theologically diverse than Henry Vedder, Victor Masters, and Caspar Hodge. Yet all claimed Strong as one of their own. The puzzle is to figure out why. As the Northern Baptist Convention tumbled through the stormiest years of its history, how—or why—did Augustus Strong become the man for all seasons?

One might surmise that his eminence was, to some extent, related to personal attributes such as his reputation for piety, his imposing appearance—a mane of snow-white hair and athletic physique at the age of eighty-five—and, undoubtedly, lingering memories of his prowess in the pulpit and in the caucus rooms of countless Baptist conventions. Hundreds had been his students at Rochester, and probably many of them continued to venerate him for that reason alone. Above all was his erudition. No Protestant conservative in America, with the possible exception of Warfield, had manifested greater familiarity with contemporary theological and imaginative literature. In the final analysis, however, Strong's appeal to persons on both sides of the fence was essentially a matter of theological identity. Both groups had ample reason to believe that in his heart of hearts he was one of them.

---

[5]Ernest Gordon, *The Leaven of the Sadducees* (Chicago: Bible Institute Colportage Association, 1926) 189; [Victor I. Masters], "Dr. Strong's Terrible Arraignment of Destructive Criticism," *Western Recorder* (21 October 1926): 11; John W. Johnson, "Prerequisites to an Understanding of the System of Theology of Augustus Hopkins Strong," *Review and Expositor* 19 (1922): 336-40; Caspar Wistar Hodge, review of *WSIB, Princeton Theological Review* 20 (1922): 681-82. For the controversy at McMaster see Clark H. Pinnock, "The Modernist Impulse at McMaster University," in Jarold K. Zeman, ed., *Baptists in Canada* (Burlington, Ontario: G. R. Welch, 1980) 199. Again it is interesting that Masters, like Riley, attacked E. Y. Mullins for compromising with evolutionary notions, but he overlooked the same tendencies in Strong's work; see William E. Ellis, "Edgar Young Mullins and the Crisis of Moderate Southern Baptist Leadership," *Foundations* 19 (1976): 176-77. For an example of Strong's considerable influence among conservative Protestants as late as the 1940s see Henry Clarence Thiessen, *Introductory Lectures in Systematic Theology* (Grand Rapids MI: Eerdmans, 1949) *passim,* esp. preface.

II

In this book I have tried to tell the story of one man's growing awareness that "history is ourselves." Simply summarized, Augustus Strong had received an impeccable classical education, solidly grounded in the ahistorical principles of orthodox rationalism. But with the passage of years his epistemic assumptions inexorably shifted. By the 1890s he had made major concessions to the modern view of historical process as the matrix in which religious knowledge, like all other modes of knowledge, is formed. Even so, a crisis developed as Strong gradually realized that his new epistemic principles would not support the old system of doctrine. He was forced to choose between incompatible worlds as he came to see that the great scholastic superstructure of the *Systematic Theology* was built on a foundation unable to bear that kind of weight.

Logically, he should have either discarded the new epistemology or substantially modified the old doctrinal system. But he did neither. It would be inaccurate to say that he left the antipathies wholly unresolved, locked in opposition. At several points in this study we have seen that, in the end, Strong did draw back from modern assumptions by insisting that Christ, the Logos, ultimately fills and informs the flow of history. But the important question is this: why was he so attracted to the modern view of history in the first place? If he was not willing to take modernity with unconditioned seriousness, why did he flirt with it at all?

To begin with, Strong always disliked the rigid and loveless attitude that so often seemed to go along with doctrinal regularity. He invariably found it easier to put up with "loose liberals" than with "cramped conservatives." Although he did not formally espouse the doctrine of future probation, much less universal salvation, as a practical matter he seems to have been confident that men and women who, like his son Charles, lacked Christian faith but manifested a Christlike spirit in their lives would nonetheless be found in the "New Jerusalem."[6]

---

[6]See for example *AB*, 315.

Beyond this elusive dispositional factor, Strong was temperamentally predisposed to believe that modern culture is suffused with progressive divine revelation. He read omnivorously, preached constantly, traveled incessantly, accumulated a modest personal fortune, and could not bear to be anywhere except in the driver's seat of every organization he joined. One of the chief benefits he had derived from travel in Europe, he wrote in his *Autobiography,* was "ease in conversation" and the ability "to mingle with men." A "proper knowledge of the world," Strong added with more than a trace of smugness, "is essential to confidence in one's own powers." And that was a view that persisted to the end. Writing to his daughter in his eighty-third year, he urged her to remember that confidence is, after all, "the secret of command over others." A memorial Strong wrote for William Rainey Harper in 1906 undoubtedly summed up many of the qualities he saw in himself. Harper's "love of learning," Strong asserted, "was not the love of a recluse. . . . He had great power of subduing to his own purpose and largeness of view the ablest of [men]. . . . Industry never went farther, nor economy of time. He believed in well stoking the engine and then running at full speed."[7]

Strong's zeal for life in the modern world extended to many of the social and cultural values of contemporary America. His children were educated at Exeter, Andover, Rochester, Harvard, Yale and Vassar. He supported full equality for women, denounced postwar anti-Semitism, and repeatedly advocated ratification of the Treaty of Versailles. "We belong to universal humanity," he wrote in the summer of 1920, and "we must take our share of responsibility for the government of the world." On another occasion he insisted, typically, that "we can save our own national life only by standing for the national life of others." Strong cannot be considered an active proponent of the Social Gospel, but he unfailingly endorsed the economic and political implications of the Social Gospel. In the realm of "manners," as it might be called, he manifested a taste for fine wine and good opera that is inconceivable among fundamentalists like William Bell Riley and A. C. Dixon. All together, it would appear that Strong was drawn to the modern view of

---

[7]*AB,* 141; AHS to Laura Strong, 10 April 1918; AHS, "Appreciation [for William Rainey Harper]," *Biblical World* 27 (1906): 235-36.

history at least partly because he was very much at home in the modern world. For those who were well-born and well-placed, the Gilded Age was an exhilarating time to be alive—and there is every reason to believe that he relished every minute of it.[8]

There is, then, considerable evidence that Strong was temperamentally, socially, and culturally predisposed to feel the stirrings of the modernist impulse. Yet it would be a mistake to leave it there, for along with these ingredients was another, less definable, but probably more important factor. Succinctly stated, the mature Strong found many of the hallmarks of modern thought, and especially the Protestant liberal rendering of those hallmarks, intellectually compelling. On the highly charged question of human evolution, for example, he never yielded an inch to the fundamentalists. From the 1880s onward he averred that human beings, like all organisms, undergo progressive development because evolution is an ingredient in the immanent Logos. He consistently defended critical methods of biblical and theological scholarship, and readily acknowledged corruptions and inaccuracies in the biblical text. He continued to emphasize, as he always had, the role of "religious sympathy" in the discernment of theological truth. In the last two or three years of his life he even began to talk about the authoritative function of the collective Christian consciousness—or, as he put it, the "general consent of believers as to the meaning of Scripture." Although in most creedal matters Strong remained unequivocally traditional, on the important question of Last Things he stuck with old-fashioned postmillennialism. And while he technically affirmed the doctrine of the vicarious atonement, his actual explication of this notion was so Bushnellian that one wonders if the conservatives and fundamentalists

---

[8]For Strong's progressive views of women's suffrage and higher education see *AB*, 305; "The Baptist Social Union," unpublished address, November 1892, American Baptist Historical Society; letter to Laura Strong, 10 January 1918; letter to William Rainey Harper, 18 November 1888. The first AHS quotation is from "My Views of the Universe in General," *Baptist* (29 May 1920): 625-26. The second is from "Motoring in Europe," typed manuscript [1919], American Baptist Historical Society. For his attitude toward the Social Gospel see, for example, the *57th Annual Report* (1907) 33. That Strong's personal mores were nonparochial is evident throughout the *AB* and in letters to Laura Strong, 6 August 1920, and Mary Strong, 13 June 1920.

who later lionized Strong truly understood—or for that matter, even cared about—his views of the issue.[9]

All of this is to say that only the most determined reductionist could doubt that Strong was powerfully influenced by what he read—and read he did. A lifetime of disciplined engagement with a wide range of theological and imaginative literature marks every page of the Strong corpus. The final edition of the *Systematic Theology*—lumbering and tortured as it is—exhibits an astonishing breadth of familiarity with American and European liberals such as Abbott, Bowne, Caird, Dorner, Martineau, Robertson, Schleiermacher, and Smyth. Indeed, except for the orthodox war-horse William G. T. Shedd, no one is more frequently quoted and discussed in the *Systematic Theology* than the British Unitarian James Martineau and the "mediating" German theologian Isaac A. Dorner. Even letters and diary entries from the last months of Strong's life are peppered with sprightly observations on contemporary politics, Einstein's relativity theory, and the probable author of certain Shakespearean plays.[10]

But simply to say that Strong read modern social thinkers and found their ideas compelling is a bit misleading. It suggests that the relation between Strong and Protestant liberalism was essentially adversarial—that Strong was only marauding in enemy territory. There is, however, a more fruitful way to look at it. Recently several historians have shown that in the late nineteenth and early twentieth centuries many liberals and conservatives discerned the inner spiritual nature and defined the most pressing spiritual needs of the age in remarkably similar ways. From this perspective it appears that Strong's affinity for some of the most cherished notions of Protestant liberalism is better understood as a symptom of an underlying perceptual unity. This is to say, in other words, that when we make tuning adjustments for differences of idiom,

---

[9]Strong reaffirmed his acceptance of evolution and higher criticism in "My Views of the Universe in General" and in *WSIB*, 8, 49-51. The role of religious sympathy and the Christian consciousness were prominent themes in the Wilkinson Lectures, given three weeks before his death—although he clearly saw the "general consent of believers" as a two-edged sword that also cut against the conclusions of the critics. See esp. Wilkinson Lectures, 1:17, 2:14-15. For his final eschatological views see "My Views of the Universe in General," and *WSIB*, 104.

[10]See virtually any of the extant letters to his children; see also 1918 diary.

Strong, like many contemporary liberals, was swept up in a powerful longing to hear the rhythms of the divine in the cadence of modern life. At the same time and in much the same way both groups became fascinated with the work of God's Spirit in present culture. This fascination led, in turn, to a fresh understanding of the meaning of religious experience and to a renewed insistence that history unfolds within a dialectic of divine judgment and promise.[11]

A complex blend of personal, social, and cultural factors seems, then, to have stirred and deepened Strong's consciousness of history. But why did he not go all the way? Why was he unable to make a clear commitment to a liberal understanding of history as the matrix of religious knowledge? Two major reasons are, I think, discernible. The first might be described as a need to preserve the coherence of the system of meanings inherited from his family and early mentors, and the second as a need to protect the integrity of his deepest and most ineffable religious experiences.

For most human beings, to abandon one system of meanings for another is not simply to choose a different way of looking at the world, but to choose another identity, another life. And the reason is not difficult to find. Individuals are implicated in symbol networks they inherit rather than select. "The enactments of our personality and character are involuntary, often compulsive," culture critic Eugene Goodheart has written. "We are not free to choose what we are or even what we will do. We cannot simply wish away traditions that we have grown to dislike." Indeed, our traditions "still possess us, [even] if we do not possess them." Or as Karl Mannheim put it a half century ago, persons find at their disposal "only certain words and their meanings . . . [which] determine to a large extent the avenues of approach to the surrounding world." If this analysis is valid for Augustus Strong, like everyone else,

---

[11]Others who have made this point include William R. Hutchison, "The Moral Equivalent for Imperialism," in Torben Christensen and Hutchison, eds., *Missionary Ideologies in the Imperialist Era* (Aarhus, Denmark: Aros Publishers, 1982) 167-77; Ernest R. Sandeen, "The 'Little Tradition' and the Form of Modern Millenarianism," *The Annual Review of the Social Sciences of Religion* 4 (1980): 165-81; Daniel Day Williams, "Tradition and Experience in American Theology," in James Ward Smith and A. Leland Jamison, eds., *The Shaping of American Religion* (Princeton: Princeton University Press, 1961) 449-59.

the inventory of words and meanings that defined his "avenues of approach to the surrounding world" were established for the most part in his youth and adolescence.[12]

The probable nature of those avenues has been illumined by William R. Hutchison's analysis of the early lives of two hundred-fifty prominent liberals and conservatives of the late nineteenth century. Hutchison discovered that nontheological variables such as formal and informal education, religious experience, family style, and personality type were strongly associated with one theological preference or the other in later life. In regard to education, for example, Hutchison found that liberals, more often than conservatives, came from professional families, were influenced by a free-thinking relative or college teacher, and pursued graduate study beyond seminary, often in Europe. When we look at Strong's situation we find, not surprisingly, that his father was a prosperous but not professionally educated newspaper owner in Rochester. Moreover, there is no evidence that Strong was influenced by a free-thinking relative or college teacher. He did travel in Europe after seminary, but by his own admission he did little except talk with friends and generally have a good time. The second major variable was the intensity of the conversion experience. Liberals tended to have no conversion experience or a less definable experience than conservatives. Strong, in contrast, described three distinct experiences, each deeper and more ineffable than the former. The third major variable was the nature of the childhood home. Liberals ordinarily came from child-centered, "Bushnellian" homes guided by a genial, not-too-strict father, while conservatives ordinarily came from strict, closely knit families dominated by a pious mother. Although it is risky to speculate about the emotional texture of Strong's childhood home, it is surely significant that in Strong's *Autobiography* his father is rarely mentioned but many memorable passages describe his mother, her impact upon his life, and the terrible loss he felt at her death. The fourth major variable was personality type. Liberals tended to be described by biographers (in or-

---

[12]Eugene Goodheart, *Culture and the Radical Conscience* (1973) 9-10, as quoted in Martin Marty, "America's Iconic Book," in Gene M. Tucker and Douglas A. Knight, eds., *Humanizing America's Iconic Book* (Chico CA: Scholars Press, 1982) 12; Karl Mannheim, *Ideology and Utopia,* trans. Louis Wirth and Edward Shils (New York: Harcourt, Brace and World, 1936) 3.

der of frequency) as "genial," "energetic," "dignified," and "humorous." Conservatives tended to be described (in order of frequency) as "rigid," "controversial," "gracious," and "dignified." Here Strong seems to fit the liberal personality profile somewhat better, but the latter set of traits were not wholly absent.[13]

All in all, it is clear that Strong was nurtured within a universe of conservative—or more precisely, conservatizing—cultural values. This is not to say that he was fated in some mechanical way to follow an orthodox rather than a liberal or otherwise unorthodox trajectory. The point rather is that Strong's formative experiences made one set of options consistently more plausible than another. We need not assume that all knowledge is socially constructed in order to recognize, as Hutchison put it, that persons often divide themselves into broad groups for whose members a given symbolic issue involves the preservation of an "entire system of cultural values."[14]

Finally, though, I suspect that there was another, more important reason why Strong shrank from consistent and radical historical consciousness. His personal religious experience held him fast to the conviction that knowledge of God ultimately transcends time and place. With the passage of years Strong became more aware of the meaning of historical process, but he also became more aware of the immediate, intimate, "biological" nature of the union with Christ. Reflecting, perhaps, the influence of the burgeoning holiness movement, in 1913 he described humanity as a "dead and shattered vine, plucked up from its roots in God." "But in Christ," he added, "God has planted a new vine,

---

[13]William R. Hutchison, "Cultural Strain and Protestant Liberalism," *American Historical Review* 76 (1971): 399-403, 406-411. See also Thomas A. Symington, *Religious Liberals and Conservatives* (New York: Teacher's College, Columbia University, 1935) esp. 40-49. For Strong's early years see *AB*, chaps. 1-3. For his conversion experiences see *AB*, 86, 163-65, 176, and the 1913 autobiographical essay in *OHCT*, 6-24. For the relation to his mother see *AB*, *passim*, esp. 295. For the social standing of the Strong family see Paul E. Johnson, *Shopkeeper's Millennium* (New York: Hill and Wang, 1978) 125-29. Strong's brother, Henry, was president of Eastman Kodak. For the relatively high social position of Northern Baptists in general in the late nineteenth century see Winthrop S. Hudson, *Baptists in Transition* (Valley Forge PA: Judson Press, 1979) 120.

[14]Hutchison, "Cultural Strain," 389.

a vine full of his own divine life, a vine into which it is his purpose one by one to graft these dead and withered branches, so that they may once more have the life of God flowing through them."[15]

In the *Autobiography* Strong wrote that his initial conversion in a Finney revival had been a dry, self-willed, "New School conversion." Authentic Christian life did not begin until he learned, in an epiphany-like experience years later, that "Christ interpenetrates and energizes [us]," becoming " 'closer than breathing, nearer than hands or feet.' " This *"union of life,"* Strong concluded, is the "central truth of all theology and of all religion. From it radiate all the other doctrines of Christianity." And though it contradicted one of the central premises of his systematic theology, at the age of seventy-one Strong would admit, "my philosophy has grown out of my religion. . . . I find recorded [in Scripture] what I have felt in my own heart. Deep answers unto deep."[16]

From this perspective it is easier to see why Strong was, finally, unwilling to embrace fully the modern world. However much religion is woven into the pattern of ordinary affairs, it begins in the realm of the unconditioned. He would have agreed with Durkheim's perception that there is "something eternal in religion which is destined to survive all the particular symbols in which religious thought has successively enveloped itself." It is undeniably true that from the 1890s onward Strong perceived, in a way that most conservatives never would, that "history is ourselves." But he also perceived, in a way that most modern-thinking men and women never would, that history itself is an artifact of a nonhistorical reality. "We mark the passage of time," he mused, "and we write our histories. But we can do this only because in our highest being we do not belong to space and time, but have in us a bit of eternity." Strong sailed uncharted seas but steered by familiar stars.[17]

---

[15]AHS, *Union with Christ* (Philadelphia: American Baptist Publication Society, 1913) 7-8.

[16]*AB,* 83-86, 163-64, 346-47.

[17]*MISC* 1:170; Emile Durkheim, *The Elementary Forms of Religious Life* (1912) 427, as quoted in Robert A. Nisbet, *The Sociological Tradition* (New York: Basic Books, 1966) 226.

Chapter Nine

Alternate Altars:
The Forms
of Historical Consciousness

AUGUSTUS STRONG'S CONFRONTATION with history was part of a larger confrontation between conceptual worlds. To put his story in perspective, and to appreciate the dimensions of this larger confrontation, we need to look at the ways other thoughtful Protestants responded to the same pressures. At the risk of considerable oversimplification, I suggest that four distinct and persistent patterns are discernible. I shall call them consistent ahistoricism, accommodating ahistoricism, accommodating historicism, and consistent historicism.

The central, defining feature of consistent ahistoricism was uncompromising resistance to the deepening historical consciousness of the age. But there were different ways to resist. At one extreme was a handful of learned and articulate intellectuals who not only rejected the notion of historicism, but mounted a vigorous counterattack. J. Gresham Machen, the Princeton biblical scholar mentioned at the beginning of this book, probably was the only one of these intellectuals who was widely known in the general culture. Machen's views were, however, common currency in Old School Presbyterian and Christian Reformed circles. The fundamental philosophical foundation of his position was orthodox rationalism, but the more proximate theological foundation was the "Didactic and Polemical Theology" fashioned by a group of exceptionally gifted scholars who taught at Princeton Theological Seminary in the middle and later years of the nineteenth century. One of the last of these was Strong's old rival, Caspar Wistar Hodge, Jr.[1]

In a 1912 essay aptly called "The Finality of the Christian Religion," Hodge summarized the Princeton apologetic. One of the central questions of the age, he began, is "whether Christianity is historically conditioned . . . or whether it is, as it claims to be, the one final religion." Lest anyone misconstrue the terms of the discussion, Hodge promptly explained that "one final religion" means that Christianity is "unsurpassable" and "exclusive," the product of a "special supernatural revelation . . . independent of and underivable from other religions." The question can be rightly answered, he averred, only if we acknowledge that the historical or ahistorical origin and nature of Christianity is a *purely historical problem,* provable or disprovable with purely historical methods of investigation. For one thing, said Hodge, Christians themselves have never (until recently) regarded Christianity merely as a relative improvement over other religions. Rather they have always insisted that the nerve of their religion is the historically demonstrable fact that God was supernaturally incarnated in Christ, that Christ is the only means to God, and that man is eternally lost without Christ's mediation. Thus the "essence of the Christian religion" is and always has been the conviction that Jesus Christ was the exclusive, unique, and final revelation of the "extramundane and infinite" God. Hodge challenged liberal critics of orthodoxy to apply to the primary materials of Christian history the same standards of authenticity and plausibility that they applied to other historical materials. He had no doubt about the outcome. In his mind the kind but somewhat befuddled Jesus of liberal biblical and theological scholarship was, quite simply, "a Jesus who

[1]Dallas M. Roark, "J. Gresham Machen," *Journal of Presbyterian History* 43 (1965): 124-38, 174-81; Mark A. Noll, ed., *The Princeton Theology* (Grand Rapids MI: Baker Book House, 1983) 11-45; Jack B. Rogers and Donald K. McKim, *The Authority and Interpretation of the Bible* (San Francisco: Harper and Row, 1979) chaps. 5-6, esp. 362-68.

cannot be found in the historical sources." The same was true of plausibility. Hodge demanded to know whether the rise and progress of Christianity is more plausibly explained with the assumption that it is the product of a "myth building fantasy," or whether it is more plausibly explained with the assumption that "the Christ of the New Testament is a reality." In the final analysis, Hodge concluded, "the question of the supernatural origin and character of Christianity, which lies at the basis of its claim to finality, is simply one of evidence."[2]

The Princeton dinosaurs may have had their faults, but timidity was not one of them. Even so, they never had much of an audience outside the Old School constituency. Immeasurably more numerous were the men and women who simply and uncritically presupposed that Christianity originated outside of history and prospered because of nonhistorical influences. Indeed, until the 1930s probably a majority of Protestant ministers, and certainly a majority of church members, fell into this category.[3] Even thoughtful conservatives who defended the supernatural origin of salvation, or the inerrancy of the Bible, or the deity of Jesus Christ, rarely seem to have realized that all claims of this sort logically rest upon a denial of historical process.[4]

A good example of consistent yet uncritical ahistoricism is the 1878 creed of the Niagara Bible Conference, which symbolized the views of countless ordinary Protestants. Except for the articles on eschatology, the creed was a quite traditional declaration of Reformed orthodoxy.

---

[2]Caspar Wistar Hodge, Jr., "The Finality of the Christian Religion," in *Biblical and Theological Studies,* by Members of the Faculty of Princeton Theological Seminary (New York: Charles Scribner's Sons, 1912) 449-55, 491-92.

[3]This generalization is difficult to prove, but historians who have sought to see American religion in the long perspective consistently denote the 1920s and 1930s as a watershed. See, for example, Sydney E. Ahlstrom, *A Religious History of the American People* (New Haven CT: Yale University Press, 1972) 895, 919; Edwin S. Gaustad, *A Religious History of America* (New York: Harper and Row, 1966) 266, 270; Robert T. Handy, *A History of the Churches in the United States and Canada* (New York: Oxford University Press, 1977) 377-78; Winthrop S. Hudson, *American Protestantism* (Chicago: University of Chicago Press, 1961) 149-53.

[4]Henry Nelson Wieman and Bernard E. Meland, *American Philosophies of Religion* (Chicago: Willett, Clark, 1936) 61-70, esp. 62. See also Conal Furay, *The Grass Roots Mind in America* (New York: New Viewpoints, 1977) 19, 26.

What should be noticed is that the writers of the creed revealed, albeit tacitly, how radically ahistorical their premises were: man is "essentially and unchangeably bad"; a "new nature [is] imparted from above"; Christ united "divinity with perfect and sinless humanity"; and so forth. Most revealing is the first article of the creed, which declared that "all Scripture is given by inspiration of God." And to prevent any equivocation about the matter, the word inspiration was explicitly dissociated from that "sense in which it is sometimes foolishly said that works of human genius are inspired." Rather, "the Holy Ghost gave the very words of the sacred writings to holy men of old . . . [extending] equally and fully to all parts of these writings . . . to the smallest word, and inflection of a word."[5]

Lyman Stewart, the millionaire founder and president of Union Oil Company, and chief benefactor of *The Fundamentals* project, provides an even more striking illustration of presupposed ahistoricism. In a letter to the publisher Charles C. Cook, Stewart casually commented that some persons who appear to have died really have not. Stewart noted that, according to James 5:15, the "prayer of faith will save the sick man." Consequently great stalwarts such as George Mueller, who had indubitably exercised the prayer of faith, were "not taken away by sickness" but had simply "fallen asleep." Stewart manifestly was not a crackpot; he was in many ways a shrewd and knowledgeable man of the world. But apparently it never occurred to him, as it never occurred to tens of thousands of conservatives, that abstract doctrine can be modified by human experience, even the experience of death.[6]

II

One way to cope with the agenda set by the modern world was, then, to reject it outright, as Machen did, or to ignore it, as Lyman Stewart and presumably the great majority of orthodox and fundamentalist

[5]"The Fundamentals of the Faith as Expressed in the Articles of Belief of the Niagara Bible Conference" (1878), reprinted in Ernest R. Sandeen, *The Roots of Fundamentalism* (Chicago: University of Chicago Press, 1970) 273-77. For the representativeness and significance of this creed see Sandeen, chap. 6, esp. 141.

[6]Lyman Stewart to Charles C. Cook, 19 April 1907, Stewart Papers, Biola College, LaMirada CA.

Protestants did. But many essentially conservative men and women wanted to address the modern agenda without, at the same time, bartering away the heart of their faith. This second distinct type of response might be described as accommodating ahistoricism. Curtis Lee Laws is a good example. No one was more deeply or personally involved in the struggle to make and keep the Northern Baptist Convention safely evangelical. As the very active editor of the widely read *Watchman-Examiner,* Laws probably exercised more real power than anyone in the denomination. He was not cut from the same intellectual timber as Augustus Strong but he knew precisely what was at stake: "The issue between the liberals and conservatives has to do with the Bible as the authoritative Word of God and the supernatural as a determining factor in human life." Nevertheless, Laws was as far from fundamentalists like William Bell Riley as he was from modernists like Shailer Mathews. He insisted that those who defend the authority of Scripture in terms of a "verbal-mechanical . . . theory of inspiration" are as far from the mark as those who follow Schleiermacher in making "Christian consciousness . . . the seat of authority." Indeed, said Laws, to say that Scripture is infallible is not by any means to say that it is "faultless in every particular." The proper way to view the matter is to regard the Bible as the "record of a progressive revelation made by God to man through the religious experience of his people." This revelation is not designed to tell us about the natural world but it is "sufficient for the purposes of our religious life." Liberals go astray, he suggested, because they fail to see that Scripture really is authoritative, that it really is the external criterion against which Christian consciousness must be judged. Hardline fundamentalists, on the other hand, also fail to see that Scripture is authoritative, not because "any abstract theory of inspiration compels it," but because "it does for us what our souls need." It exercises a "living function in man's religious life."[7]

Whether Laws grasped the full implications of his own remarks is debatable. Nonetheless, the significant point is that the man who "invented" the word fundamentalist perceived that the authority of Scripture in the modern world could not be established by dogmatic

---

[7]Curtis Lee Laws, "The Old and New Theologies," *WE* (1 February 1917) 133-34.

pronouncements. He discerned, in other words, that the status of Scripture was problematic, and that the problem had been created by the modern awareness of history.

Frank Goodchild, the prominent pastor of Central Baptist Church in New York City, is another case in point. He was a prominent and influential presence in the denomination and in the Baptist Fundamentalist Fellowship. Like Laws, Goodchild insisted, without qualification, that Scripture is authoritative for Christians and contains information that human beings never could have acquired on their own. But, also like Laws, Goodchild acknowledged that the manner of divine disclosure is open for discussion; it is a subject on which there is "no room for any one to dogmatize." He admitted that he could live with the view that Scripture is not so much a revelation of God to man as a "record of a revelation." Indeed, people once "accepted the Bible because it claims to be inspired . . . [but now] men accept it because they perceive it to be inspired."[8]

It is difficult to know how widespread the accommodating ahistoricism represented by Laws and Goodchild was among Northern Baptists or among American Protestants in general. But there are several indications that they spoke for a sizable minority of serious, thoughtful conservatives. One is that Goodchild's articulation of the nature of biblical authority was printed in the *Watchman-Examiner* as the official position of the Baptist Fundamentalist Fellowship. Another is the outcome of the so-called Confession Controversy in the Northern Baptist Convention in 1921.[9]

For several months a belief had been growing in the denomination that the only way to stamp out apostasy was to enact a formal confession of faith. This conviction finally boiled to the surface at the fundamentalists' Pre-Convention Conference at Des Moines, where the executive committee of the Fellowship hammered out a short statement that came

---

[8]Frank M. Goodchild, "The Bible—God's Word," *WE* (13 October 1921): 1299-1300.

[9]The best account is Roland Tenus Nelson, "Fundamentalism and the Northern Baptist Convention" (Ph.D. dissertation, University of Chicago, 1964) 149-53, 172-74, 232-40; see also Ernest DeWitt Burton, "Recent Trends in Northern Baptist Churches," *American Journal of Theology* 24 (1920): 333, 338.

to be known as the Goodchild Confession. The preamble of the confession cautiously explained that it was conceived not as a creed, but as a "standard about which our Baptist people may rally." Elsewhere it was described as a light post rather than a hanging post. The birth of Jesus, for example, was defined as "miraculous" rather than virginal. Christ's return to the world was affirmed but without dispensational or millennial stipulations. The ordinances were said to be given for "perpetual observance," but it was not asserted that they were unchangeable in form or meaning. The most revealing article of the creed was the first, which dealt with the nature of Scripture.

> We believe that the Bible is God's word, that it was written by men divinely inspired, and that it has supreme authority in all matters of faith and conduct.

It should be noted that the wonderfully elastic phrase "divinely inspired" was used instead of "inerrant," "infallible," or "unique"—terms that had an exact, purely ahistorical denotation; terms that fundamentalists repeatedly used to exempt the Bible from the grip of historical process. Moreover the Confession located the authority of Scripture in the realm of Christian consciousness, and thus effectively removed it from the court of empirical judgment where consistent ahistoricists such as Caspar Hodge were determined to argue the case. [10]

All in all the Confession was a remarkably delicate formulation for a group of men who claimed that they were prepared to do "battle royal" for the faith delivered unto the fathers. It reflected Goodchild's acute awareness, as he later put it, quoting Richard Baxter, of "how ticklish a business the enumeration of fundamentals is." It also showed that many deeply conservative men and women had come to believe that some accommodation with the prevailing assumptions of the modern world was necessary if orthodoxy was to survive at all. [11]

---

[10]Frank M. Goodchild, "A Confession of Faith," WE (30 June 1921): 805. The hanging post quip was attributed to George Edwin Horr, president of Newton Theological Institution, in Curtis Lee Laws, "Convention Sidelights," WE (7 July 1921): 834.

[11]Goodchild, "The Bible." "Battle royal" is from Curtis Lee Laws, "Convention Sidelights," WE (1 July 1920): 834.

Just as the consistently ahistorical response to historical consciousness took explicit and implicit forms, so too the accommodating response often appeared in more or less unself-conscious forms. The latter was particularly evident in the holiness movement, which had long been influential in the Wesleyan tradition and in the 1880s and 1890s spread into Reformed circles as well. Here we need to be especially careful, for at the level of self-conscious doctrinal reflection holiness leaders could be fiercely ahistorical. Strong's longtime friend A. J. Gordon, for example, could say that "we are to find in the *words* of Scripture the exact substance of what [the Holy Ghost] saith. . . . [Does this theory turn] the writers of Scripture into stenographers, whose office is simply to transcribe the words of the Spirit as they are dictated? . . . There is much in Scripture to support this view of the case." Nonetheless—and it is an important nonetheless—in both the Wesleyan and Reformed wings of the holiness movement there was a persistent inclination to be impatient with questions of confessional regularity and to assume that abstract doctrinal reflection must be anchored in religious experience.[12]

In principle holiness theologians tested the validity of religious experience by criteria they believed to be clearly enunciated in the Bible, but surprisingly often religious experience acquired an independent, if not autonomous, authority of its own. A few leaders, such as the well-known (and well-educated) evangelist B. Fay Mills, virtually discounted the importance of abstract doctrine. To his mind, anyone who "wills to do the will of God, knows the doctrine." In fact, he added, "it is sometimes astonishing to see how little a person need know." More often, though, concern for doctrinal regularity was unintentionally but effectively eclipsed by an overwhelming interest in the Christian "higher life." Typical in this respect was Hannah Whitall Smith, author of the 1870 devotional classic, *The Christian's Secret of a Happy Life*. Near the turn of the century Smith judged that "the trouble with most of the religion of the day is its extreme complexity." But the higher life, she pointed out, avoids "theological difficulties [and] doctrinal dilemmas. . . . No theological training *nor any especial theological views* are needed." Smith recommended the path of the seventeenth-century mystic

---

[12]A. J. Gordon, *The Ministry of the Spirit* (New York: Fleming H. Revell, 1894) 171, 173.

"Brother Lawrence," whose "one single aim was to bring about a conscious personal union between himself and God, and he took the shortest cut he could find to accomplish it." Many otherwise impeccably orthodox Protestants of the period who came to espouse the theology and practice of faith healing similarly admitted that the *experience* of having been healed led them to advocate the *doctrine* of faith healing. A. J. Gordon was astonishingly candid: "Experience is the surest touchstone of truth. It is not always infallible . . . [but] this is a kind of testimony which is not easily ruled out of court." Or, as A. B. Simpson, founder of the Christian and Missionary Alliance—and a man never known to be lax about doctrinal matters—put it, "all caviling criticism [is silenced] before the logic of divine realities and tested facts."[13]

III

In many survey studies of American religion between 1880 and 1920, conservative Protestants are clustered at one end of the theological stage, liberals are clustered at the other end, and a few "moderates" are sprinkled in between. This scenario may be accurate enough for the 1920s, but it obscures the web of social and cultural continuities that linked conservative and liberal Protestants (especially those who shared a Reformed evangelical heritage) up to the eve of the World War. It is often difficult to tell where, or at what point, an essentially ahistorical accommodation to modern thought shaded into an essentially historical accommodation. In theory the line was precise, but in practice many liberals sought to find within the flow of history, and especially within the flow of their own religious experience, a basis for the transcendence of history.

We should not be surprised, therefore, to find that many liberals eventually circled around to quite conventional doctrinal views. In the 1850s, for example, Horace Bushnell was still insisting that contem-

---

[13]B. Fay Mills, *Victory Through Surrender* (Chicago: Fleming H. Revell, 1892) 10, 17; Hannah Whitall Smith, Introduction to *The Practice of the Presence of God,* by Brother Lawrence (New York: Fleming H. Revell, 1895) iii-iv (italics added); A. J. Gordon, *The Ministry of Healing* (Brooklyn NY: Christian Alliance, 1882) 175; A. B. Simpson, ed., *A Cloud of Witnesses for Divine Healing,* 2d ed. (New York: Word, Work and World, 1887) preface.

porary accounts of speaking in tongues and faith healing could be taken at face value as genuine miracles. In the 1870s the liberal orator David Swing was still proclaiming the triune nature of God, the necessity of personal conversion, the innate sinfulness of persons, and the final separation of the righteous and wicked. In the late 1890s Washington Gladden was still advocating foreign missions because "the Light of the World is the only sovereign remedy" for the "vast and overshadowing" woes of unchristianized lands. In the 1900s biblical critic Charles Augustus Briggs was still seeking a scriptural warrant for "future probation" for those who die outside Christian faith. Even in the 1940s Harry Emerson Fosdick was still preaching about human sinfulness and God's grace in rolling phrases any fundamentalists could warmly appreciate (especially if they heard him on the radio and did not know it was Fosdick).[14]

There were, however, less explicit but more profound ways in which many liberals were able to accommodate essentially ahistorical notions into a historically fluid view of culture. Although they tended to make modern culture normative for Christian faith, it was not because they doubted the possibility of knowing the enduring truths of salvation. Rather they esteemed modern culture as a realm God himself had entered and redeemed through the incarnation of Jesus Christ.

To begin with, many liberals were acutely embarrassed by the two-story universe of traditional orthodoxy, but they had no difficulty conceiving God as essentially immanent in history, and God in the modality of immanence, as God the Holy Spirit. Thus the true significance of the Day of Pentecost, said William Newton Clarke, Strong's great rival at Colgate Seminary, was that from that day forward the church had been able "to identify the Holy Spirit as God himself indwelling." Conservatives often complained that liberals such as Clarke tended to

---

[14]Horace Bushnell, *Nature and the Supernatural* (New York: Charles Scribner's Sons, 1858) 464-91; David Johnson et al., eds., *The Trial of the Rev. David Swing* (Chicago: Jansen, McClurg, 1874) 20; Washington Gladden, *The Christian Pastor and the Working Church* (New York: Charles Scribner's Sons, 1916 [1898]) 364-65; Charles Augustus Briggs, *Church Unity* (New York: Charles Scribner's Sons, 1909) 360-63; Harry Emerson Fosdick, *The Living of These Days* (New York: Harper and Brothers, 1956) 221-26. More generally, see Robert T. Handy, "Fundamentalism and Modernism in Perspective," *Religion in Life* 24 (1955) : 381-94.

reduce the Holy Spirit to an impersonal force, or at best, a vaguely divine influence in human affairs. But in his influential survey of *Christian Theology* Clarke insisted otherwise. "The Holy Spirit," he wrote, "is no mere influence, derived, secondary, impersonal, and vanishing, but is no other than God himself, in vital contact and communication with . . . men."[15]

For many liberals the purpose of God's living Spirit in history was the regeneration and sanctification of the whole of creation. Thus Strong's friend Theodore T. Munger, Congregational minister in New Haven and in the 1880s probably the best known spokesman for the New Theology, averred that the Spirit "broods over the 'evil world' " in order to bring about the sanctification of the orders of creation—individuals, families and nations. Munger explained that liberals regarded "Regeneration and Sanctification by the Spirit as the most imperative [of] operations based on the utmost need, and on the actual presence and power of the Spirit in the life of humanity." However valuable the biblical Book of Acts is as a record of the first years of the church, he wrote, it is even "more valuable as introducing the life of the Spirit." Here we have the "full revelation of God evoking the full life of man." Washington Gladden said much the same thing. "The great truth of all Christian experience," he wrote in 1913, is "the constant presence of the divine Spirit in the world . . . shepherding, guiding, teaching his children, renewing them in the spirit of their minds, giving them larger and truer thoughts."[16]

For liberals no less than for conservatives the Spirit's presence was experienced as immediate and personally intimate. Lewis French Stearns of Bangor Seminary was certain that "the reality and present power of things unseen and eternal" is disclosed by "Christ and the Holy Spirit [in whom] God comes near to us and dwells in us." William Newton Clarke similarly judged that one of the Spirit's principal functions is to establish a relation of "filial intimacy with God, by whose influence he

---

[15]William Newton Clarke, *An Outline of Christian Theology* (Cambridge MA: John Wilson, 1894) 147, 331.

[16]Theodore Munger, *The Freedom of Faith* (Boston: Houghton, Mifflin, 1883) 24, 9, 49, 44; Washington Gladden, *Present Day Theology,* 2d ed. (Columbus OH: McClelland, 1913) 20.

should be truly known." Indeed, for many liberals the Spirit's immediate, intimate presence is the very reality that makes salvation possible. The Spirit is the vehicle of grace. Rejecting the Latin view of grace
as an objective quality conveyed through "external channels," A. V. G.
Allen of the Episcopal Theological School urged that grace is better
understood as Christ's "own eternal life . . . [in] contact with human
souls," a contact made possible by the "infinite indwelling Spirit, whose
action is not arbitrary, but uniform as the laws of nature."[17]

While conservative Protestants tended to construe religious experience as a discrete event or succession of discrete events, liberals more
characteristically thought of it as a process, a dynamic appropriation of
the divine life, literally, physically, incarnated in the texture of human
history. Newman Smyth, scholarly minister of the Center Church in
New Haven, cut directly to the epistemic roots of the issue. He argued
that orthodox creedalism was deracinated, and thus artificial, because
its proponents failed to see that there is a "higher power at the fountains
of our moral and religious consciousness," and it is this higher power
that makes rational thought the "outflowing, or development, of the
divine life which is in us." But in Smyth's estimation this higher power
is not, as some romantics had it, reducible to a warm religious sentiment. Rather the divine life that informs human consciousness entered
the course of human experience through the historical person of Christ.
"Therefore we say, we have more than a religion of ideas; ours is a better
confession of faith than that; we have a religion of what God has done
for us; a religion of historical facts."[18]

For liberals who were truly concerned about the fate of orthodoxy
in a historically conscious world, this last point was one they never tired
of reiterating. Munger liked to say that revelation was *of* God, not *from*
God. Clarke insisted that God's self-disclosure is not "in writing at all,
or primarily primarily in speech, but in act and fact." Indeed "revelation is not the giving of information on various themes of religion," but

---

[17]Lewis French Stearns, *Present-Day Theology* (New York: Charles Scribner's Sons,
1893) 541, 536. Clarke, *Christian Theology,* 332-33. Alexander V. G. Allen, *The Continuity of Christian Thought* (Boston: Houghton, Mifflin, 1884) 16-17.

[18]Newman Smyth, *The Orthodox Theology of To-Day* (New York: Charles Scribner's
Sons, 1881) 43, 49-50.

the living expression of God himself in history—and not just the sliver of history seen through the aperture of the Bible, but the totality of history, universal history. In the gracefully fashioned sermons of George A. Gordon, pastor of Boston's Old South, religious experience became the medium of divine revelation. More precisely, revelation is not, he urged, information driven into mundane experience like spikes in a railroad bed, but a special quality or depth of insight disclosed in and through the flux of daily life. Against the orthodox conception of a "wholly non-human" and "bloodless revelation," which he called an abuse of the "mechanism of miracle," Gordon proposed that revelation is better understood as a dialectic between the "Divine appeal" and "man's answer to that appeal."[19]

For many liberals the divine dialectic augured the imminent fulfillment of the historical process. More precisely, God's ever-unfolding truth, richer and fuller than ever before, had rendered the times ripe for the Lord's harvesting. This optimism was well represented in the work of Egbert Smyth of Andover Seminary. "The church of to-day," Smyth wrote in 1885, "has a fuller knowledge of the purpose of God . . . [and] a better conception of the dispensation of the Spirit . . . than it was possible to communicate to the early church." Indeed, "the fulfillments of prophecy" have yielded an ampler knowledge of God's ways than ever before—and to doubt it, Smyth warned, "is a symptom of unbelief." Oberlin College president Henry Churchill King similarly insisted that the time had come for a thorough *Reconstruction in Theology,* as his influential study of 1901 was titled, not because of a "demand from without," but because of a "deepening of the Christian spirit itself . . . [under] the influence of the new intellectual, moral, and spiritual world in which we live."[20]

Added to the belief that they were living in an age throbbing with redemptive power was confidence that the divine guidance of history was leading to the triumph of the literal kingdom of God on earth. Al-

---

[19]Munger, *Freedom,* 10; Clarke, *Christian Theology,* 13, 9; George A. Gordon, *Ultimate Conceptions of Faith* (Boston: Houghton, Mifflin, 1903) 338-39.

[20]Egbert C. Smyth, "Progressive Orthodoxy," in Smyth et al., eds., *Progressive Orthodoxy* (Boston: Houghton, Mifflin, 1892 [1885]) 8-9; Henry Churchill King, *Reconstruction in Theology* (New York: Macmillan, 1901) 29 (italics in original).

though they differed on the details of how it would be accomplished, the famous "Watchword" of the Student Volunteer Movement—"the evangelization of the world in this generation"—reflected the historical aspirations of liberals just as much as it reflected the aspirations of countless evangelicals. The coming kingdom would take into its comprehensive embrace "all human interests," Lewis Stearns declared, "not only in the distinctively religious sphere, but also in . . . the secular."

> The kingdom is to come in the regeneration of society, in all its institutions, in all its corporate interests, in its spirit and tone. . . . In the redemption of the human body from disease and the dominion of death. . . . It is to come in the deliverance of nature from the bondage of corruption and the restoration of the right relations between man and nature.

A more ringing assertion of the sovereignty of the coming Lord is difficult to imagine. Liberals like Stearns were mindful of the grim realities of history, but they were fundamentally confident that ultimately, as George Harris of Andover Seminary put it, "the moral order, as observed in history, is a divine order, for it is above the purpose of this or that individual, above the purpose of any single generation." These words easily could have been Strong's, for until the 1920s—if not later— many liberals and conservatives exhibited a common conviction that God's governance of history is direct and continuous even if implemented through the agency of secondary causes.[21]

IV

When we look at accommodating ahistoricists and historicists in the long perspective it is clear that both groups made significant concessions. The former tended to soften the angularities of orthodoxy in order to make it more compatible with the modern sense of historical process, while the latter found numerous ways to smuggle the timeless assurances of inherited orthodoxy into the flow of the historical process. But just as there were orthodox Protestants who made no, or virtually

---

[21]Stearns, *Present-Day Theology,* 123-24. George Harris, *Moral Evolution* (Boston: Houghton, Mifflin, 1896) 445, 191.

no, compromises with modern thought, so too there were liberals who embraced historicism barehanded and without compromise.

The transition from an accommodating to a consistently historicist position can be seen in the career of the distinguished church historian Arthur Cushman McGiffert, who taught at Union Theological Seminary in New York from 1893 to 1927. In a well-known address given in 1892, he articulated the method of the modern church historian.

> To study an organism in its antecedents and in its genesis, to trace the course of its growth, to examine it in the varied relations which it has sustained to its environment at successive stages of its career . . . is the historic method, and this is the way we study the church today.

Even so, at this stage of his career McGiffert still reflected the views of his teacher, Adolf von Harnack. Harnack maintained (somewhat like Strong) that church history is a record of the church's growing perception of timeless truths. "A sharp distinction must be drawn between divine truth and our conceptions of that truth," said McGiffert, for divine truth "is always and eternally the same, unchanged and unchangeable." To recognize the mutability of doctrinal formulations is necessary if we are to "be true to the truth as it has been revealed unto us."[22]

By 1912 McGiffert had largely outgrown this kernel-and-husk approach. Those who search for a "fixed and unchanging standard" under shifting external forms, he wrote in *The Rise of Modern Religious Ideas,* "still crave external authority for their religious faith as truly as any traditionalist." But the quest for a still point in a turning world is baseless, "a mere chimera." We now know that "authority has everywhere ceased to be, as it once was, absolute. . . . and has become relative, provisional, and fallible." Yet McGiffert still was not as radical as he seemed, for the book concluded with a stirring assurance that the critical study of church history led to appreciation of the Bible's "permanent and incomparable spiritual worth . . . [as] a unique record of

---

[22]Arthur Cushman McGiffert, "The Historical Study of Christianity," reprinted in William R. Hutchison, ed., *American Protestant Thought* (New York: Harper and Row, 1968) 71, 75, 78; see also Henry Warner Bowden, *Church History in the Age of Science* (Chapel Hill: University of North Carolina Press, 1971) chap. 6, esp. 154.

developing religious experience . . . the highest gift of God to man, the gospel of Jesus Christ."[23]

Gradually McGiffert moved toward consistent historicism. "It is a common thing today," he wrote in 1916, "to deal with religion in a wholly naturalistic way, as one of the forces promoting the development of the race, and to estimate it accordingly." In a purely historical analysis of a religious phenomenon such as conversion, he explained, the critical scholar would treat it "not as the immediate and miraculous work of the Spirit of God, but as the natural result of entirely explicable psychical forces." McGiffert sought to distinguish a truly functional and empirical analysis of religious phenomena from the pseudofunctional and pseudoempirical analyses so often found in liberal scholarship. Much if not most of the latter, he complained, is "simply putting into theological form an experience which is itself largely the fruit of the theology which we already have." But if we are to be rigorously historical, "we must be agnostic about all that lies beyond the range of experience."[24]

As McGiffert approached the end of his career, he realized that unflinching historicism entailed more than a willingness to explain the rise and persistence of religious phenomena in terms of their functions. It also entailed a willingness to fashion even the ethical and moral norms of Christian theology from the materials of history. In a way, he had come full circle, insisting, in the end, that the historical and theological tasks cannot be separated. In McGiffert's mature view, peering through the materials of history into some eternal realm is impossible. Rather Christians must distill from those materials, finite and particular as they are, ethical and moral values appropriate for the age. "In the older days," he wrote, "evolution was thought of as the mere unfolding of what was already in the original germ." But no longer. Now we know that "each generation must discover for itself the new truths and the new principles by which it shall live, . . . not simply the old in a changed form, but the new in its own form."[25]

---

[23]Arthur Cushman McGiffert, *The Rise of Modern Religious Ideas* (New York: Macmillan, 1925 [1915] 295, 297, 309. These lectures were originally delivered in 1912.

[24]Arthur Cushman McGiffert, "The Progress of Theological Thought During the Past Fifty Years," *American Journal of Theology* 20 (1916) : 323-25.

[25]Ibid., 327-28.

It may be true, as some have argued, that McGiffert was never as hard-nosed as he seemed; that his monumental studies of the history of doctrine were persistently influenced by unrecognized theological assumptions. Some liberals were, however, consistently and radically historical. Probably the most notable example is the small but influential vanguard of Protestant thinkers who taught at the University of Chicago Divinity School after the turn of the century. Whether these scholars would be, like Walter Lippmann and Charles W. Eliot, more accurately (and more honestly) described as humanists with serious religious interests, is another matter. Here the pertinent point is that they considered themselves Protestant, not in spite of, but precisely because of, their uncompromised allegiance to the premises of modern thought.[26]

Consistent historicism of this sort was well represented by Gerald Birney Smith and Shirley Jackson Case, who taught at Chicago from the turn of the century until 1929 and 1938, respectively. In theory Smith taught systematic theology and Case the history of early Christianity, but in fact both ranged widely over the theological curriculum. More pertinently, both taught a generation of theological students at Chicago and elsewhere exactly how and where to drive the nails into the coffin of orthodox rationalism.

In Smith's mind Augustus Strong and theologians like him were curiosities, harmless fossils in the modern world. He was certain that they represented a historically disembodied—and therefore obsolete—notion of authority. But Smith was considerably less benign toward accommodating liberals who tried to have it both ways. He indicted them for using the "familiar terms and phrases" in order to make new methods and conclusions "seem as much like orthodox doctrine as possible."

---

[26]For McGiffert's residual liberalism see Bowden, *Church History*, 143, 151, 168. For the acute historical consciousness of the University of Chicago Divinity School faculty see the essays in Gerald Birney Smith, ed., *A Guide to the Study of the Christian Religion* (Chicago: University of Chicago Press, 1916) esp. Shailer Mathews's "The Historical Study of Religion," 19-81. There are numerous secondary studies of the school's ideological complexion. Two of the best are Robert W. Funk, "The Watershed of American Biblical Tradition," *Journal of Biblical Literature* 95 (1976) : 4-22, and Bernard E. Meland, "The Empirical Tradition in Theology at Chicago," in Meland, ed., *The Future of Empirical Theology* (Chicago: University of Chicago Press, 1969) 13-40.

As a consequence, "new meanings are thus smuggled in under familiar labels, with a resulting lack of clearness in thinking." Smith admonished his students to recognize at the outset "the dangers involved in serving two masters [at once]."[27]

Against equivocations of that sort, Smith defined theological reflection "as the attempt to think over our religious inheritance in the light of present problems, so as to formulate for today . . . an expression of faith vitally related to our actual life." The presupposition of this approach is that nothing is predetermined; the only touchstone with the past is the "spiritual power" that Christian men and women in the past have known. Smith insisted that this spiritual power cannot be linked with fixed creeds of any kind, however minimal and general they might be. "Christianity is always in the making. Each generation inherits certain beliefs; but these beliefs are brought into relation with new conditions, and are subjected to criticism and reconstruction." Thus the modern theologian must be prepared to alter religious hypotheses "as readily as any science alters the content of its hypotheses in response to more exact knowledge."[28]

Smith particularly hoped to extirpate the half-hearted historicism symbolized in Harry Emerson Fosdick's well-known aphorism, "astronomies change while the stars abide." To recognize the plasticity of doctrine is not enough. Theologians must overcome the assumption that there is in Christianity "some non-historical 'essence' which shall not be subject to the vicissitudes of historical change." Once modern theologians have been freed from encumbering assumptions about what Christianity is or somehow ought to be, they will be able to employ the radically instrumental methods of science. In theological inquiry, as in scientific inquiry, he argued, "a hypothesis is an instrument for exploring the reality of our environment." Consequently a theological hypothesis "works" if it "enables us to establish definite relations with our environment and to receive into our experience the increment which comes from such relationship." The ahistorical methods of the old theology were measured by the *"content of doctrine."* The radically histori-

---

[27]Gerald Birney Smith, "Systematic Theology and Christian Ethics," in Smith, ed., *Guide*, 489-90.

[28]Ibid., 486, 507, 506, 488.

cal, instrumental methods of the new theology are measured by *"accuracy of investigation."* Similarly the aim of the older theology (including, Smith would have said, the theology of accommodating liberalism) was to show that its conclusions were "somehow scriptural." But in the new, consistently historical approach to theological construction, "the all-important matter is to understand how religion functions in human life, rather than to canonize a literature." And once the function of religion in human history is understood, the theologian is free to carry out his constructive task: "To furnish ideas and interpretations which enable men to realize the experience of satisfactory adjustment to the cosmic reality on which they are dependent."[29]

In theory Shirley Jackson Case's conception of the historicity of religious knowledge was no more radical than Gerald Birney Smith's, but Case's application of historicist principles to the study of early Christianity probably had a larger and more enduring impact. In any event, his programmatic essay, "Whither Historicism in Theology," published in 1933, brought historical consciousness to its logical culmination. To say that Case's position was the mirror opposite of Caspar Hodge's would be true but trivial. The more significant point is that Case's historicism was so consistently radical that he was able historically to explain, and therefore genuinely to appreciate, purely ahistorical doctrinal artifacts such as the "vivid apocalyptic teaching of early Christianity." Indeed, Case rebuked "mystics" such as Rudolf Otto and "dialecticians" such as Karl Barth who "assumed the virtual bankruptcy of history as a source for the modern man's doctrinal assurances." "Instead of condemning or ignoring ideas that were later discarded," he shot back, the historically minded theologian should measure the value of doctrine in terms of its "functional significance for a specific situation." And the functional significance of a doctrine is measured not by its congruity with any definable notion of tradition or institution of the past, but by its congruity with the "life-stream of spiritual energy" that animated Christians of the past. "What Christians at any period or

---

[29]Smith, "Systematic Theology," 508, 548, 492; Gerald Birney Smith, "Theological Thinking in America," in Smith, ed., *Religious Thought in the Last Quarter-Century* (Chicago: University of Chicago Press, 1927) 101-102, 105. Smith, "Systematic Theology," 511.

place should believe," Case concluded, "is what they must believe in
accordance with the deepest convictions of their own life and the most
comprehensive range of vision which they can command."[30]

It is not easy to see how the working assumptions of theological
scholars such as McGiffert, Smith, and Case differed from the working
assumptions of the leading scholars in the humanities and the social and
natural sciences. By the end of the 1920s anthropologists such as Ruth
Benedict were arguing that the most universal values of mankind are
not transhistorical but radically historical, "exceedingly old inventions
. . . 'cradle' traits" of the species. Juridical thinkers such as Karl L.
Llewellyn were urging the legal profession to abandon the outworn ideal
that law is a system of timelessly valid principles and to recognize instead that it is nothing but a set of "convenient short hand symbols"
that denote "the actions of the courts." Logicians such as C. I. Lewis
were asserting that the truths of formal logic and mathematics are true
only within a given system, for the "absoluteness of such a priori principles is entirely compatible with . . . historical alteration . . . [and]
subject to considerations of usefulness and to historical change." Even
professional historians, who had resisted historicism longer than any
other group, finally capitulated. By 1930 scholars such as Carl L. Becker
were convinced that for modern scholars the disposition to regard "all
things in their historical setting" had become virtually instinctive. "We
do it without thinking, because we can scarcely think at all without
doing it." Objective historical facts too are largely illusory. "Ideas and
concepts, the truth of things as well as the things themselves," he wrote
in his inimitably elegiac way, are only "points in an endless process,"
a "concurrence, renewed from moment to moment, of forces parting
sooner or later on their way."[31]

---

[30]Shirley Jackson Case, "Whither Historicism in Theology," in Miles H. Krumbine, ed., *The Process of Religion* (New York: Macmillan, 1933) 66-71. See also Case,
"The Historical Study of Religion," *Journal of Religion* 1 (1921) : 1-17.

[31]Ruth Benedict, *Patterns of Culture* (Boston: Houghton, Mifflin, 1961 [1934])
19; Karl Llewellyn, "A Realistic Jurisprudence," *Columbia Law Review* 30 (1930) :
448-49; C. I. Lewis, "Logic and Pragmatism," in George P. Adams and William
Pepperell Montague, eds., *Contemporary American Philosophy* (London: George Allen
and Unwin, 1930) 1:46-48; Carl L. Becker, *The Heavenly City of the Eighteenth-Century
Philosophers* (New Haven CT: Yale University Press, 1965 [1932]) 18-19, 12. The last
remark is apparently a quotation from Sir James H. Jeans.

Not all thoughtful men and women would have agreed with Becker. In this chapter we have seen that historical consciousness took at least four distinct forms—which is to say that among committed Protestants, inherited belief and newly acquired premises jostled and mixed in a variety of ways. But for most scholars in the leading divinity schools, and for virtually all in the universities, there could be little doubt that Becker's words captured the cadence of modernity. And even those who failed or refused to fall in step found that their lives were, willingly or unwillingly, increasingly attuned to history's drummer.

Orthodoxy
and the Modern World

ANTHROPOLOGISTS TELL US that ambiguity is one of life's least tolerable experiences. Indeed, in most cultures purity is linked with the maintenance of clear-cut boundaries, impurity with ambiguity. In daily life, moreover, there is not much difference between experiences of ambiguity and perceptions of paradox. Both are acutely uncomfortable. A certain timelessness echoes through Edmund Gosse's description of his Victorian father's first encounter with Darwinism: "Through my Father's brain . . . rushed two kinds of thought, each absorbing, each convincing, yet totally irreconcilable. There is a peculiar agony in the paradox that truth has two forms, each of them indisputable, yet each antagonistic to the other."[1]

---

[1]Edmund Gosse, *Father and Son* (New York: Oxford University Press, 1974 [1907]) 59. The relation between experiences of ambiguity and paradox on one side and religious rituals and myths on the other is discussed in Catherine L. Albanese, *America: Religions and Religion* (Belmont CA: Wadsworth, 1981) 2-9, and "Exploring Regional Religion: A Case Study of the Eastern Cherokee," *History of Religions* 23 (1984): 344-50.

This is where systematic theology comes into the picture. If one of the functions of myth and ritual is to resolve ambiguity by preserving sharp temporal and spatial distinctions, one of the functions of systematic theological reflection is to resolve conceptual paradox by tinkering with the ingredient categories until an acceptable harmonization is found. Thus it is not surprising that most thoughtful believers who lived through the epistemic revolution of the late nineteenth and early twentieth centuries eventually found satisfactory ways to deal with it, either by giving their hearts to a wholly ahistorical or wholly historical outlook, or by forging a compromise that seemed to do justice to the claims of both. Sooner or later nearly everyone accepted, in one form or another, one of the positions outlined in the previous chapter. And ultimately Strong did too, gradually moving from the first position to the third, and finally coming to rest, for the most part, in the second position, which I have dubbed accommodating ahistoricism.

Even so, to chart the public peregrinations of Strong and of persons like him is to tell only part of the story. What is left out is the private side of the pilgrimage. For many men and women, coming to terms with the conflicting, if not contradictory, demands of orthodoxy and the modern world was a slow, painful process. Admittedly, it is difficult to separate those who achieved a resolution of the tension with little or no soul searching from those who heard the distant rumble of "Faith's melancholy long withdrawing roar" all too clearly. Still, the record leaves little doubt that some felt the tension more persistently than others. The roll call would almost certainly include scientists like George Frederick Wright; biblical scholars like William Rainey Harper; social ethicists like Edgar Gardner Murphy; church historians like Walter Rauschenbusch; missionary leaders like Robert E. Speer; pulpit orators like Henry Van Dyke.[2]

---

[2]For Wright see William James Morison, "George Frederick Wright" (Ph.D. dissertation, Vanderbilt University, 1971) esp. 389. For Harper see Lars Hoffman, "William Rainey Harper and the Chicago Fellowship" (Ph.D. dissertation, University of Iowa, 1978) 68-92. For Edgar Gardner Murphy see Ralph E. Luker, *A Southern Tradition in Theology and Social Criticism* (Lewiston NY: Edwin Mellen Press, 1984) chap. 7. For Walter Rauschenbusch see Winthrop S. Hudson, *The Great Tradition of the American Churches* (New York: Harper and Row, 1953) chap. 10, and "Walter

The tension these persons experienced was felt just as sharply on the other side of the Atlantic. In Western Europe historical consciousness had dawned at least a generation earlier, and its impact on Protestant thinkers may have been even deeper. The radical historicism that took root in German universities should not obscure the struggle of scholars like Isaac Dorner and Adolf Schlatter, who wrestled long and courageously with the problems that historical awareness posed for orthodox belief. What Gerhard Ritter said of the sixteenth century was equally true of the nineteenth: "Even the most passionate and most embittered German criticism of the church could still be called the anger of disillusioned love."[3] In Britain the issues were debated in a manner that resembled the American situation even more closely. This is not surprising; throughout the nineteenth century British and American evangelicalism had been thoroughly intertwined. There were of course differences of style. By and large the attempt to balance ancient doctrine and modern premises was carried off more gracefully by British than by American evangelicals, which may have been because romanticism had deeper roots in Britain and cushioned the blows of Darwinism, higher criticism, and idealist immanentism. Whatever the reason, the relative muting of public stridence in Britain does not mean that

---

Rauschenbusch and the New Evangelism," *Religion in Life* 30 (1961): 412-30. For Robert E. Speer see his articles, "God in Christ the Only Revelation of the Fatherhood of God," and "Foreign Missions or World-Wide Evangelism," in A. C. Dixon et al., eds., *The Fundamentals* (Chicago: Testimony Publishing [1910-1915]) 3:61-75, and 12:64-84, esp. 77, 83. For Henry Van Dyke see his *Gospel for an Age of Doubt* (New York: Macmillan, 1897) esp. vii-x. If the list were extended to include the following generation, scholars such as Herbert Butterfield, C. S. Lewis, and Edward John Carnell would surely need to be added. See Butterfield's essay, "God in History," and Lewis's essay, "Historicism," both in C. T. McIntire, ed., *God, History and Historians: An Anthology of Modern Christian Views of History* (New York: Oxford University Press, 1977) 192-204 and 224-38 respectively. For Carnell see Rudolph L. Nelson, "Fundamentalism at Harvard," *Quarterly Review* 2 (1982): 79-98, esp. 88.

[3]For Isaac Dorner see Claude Welch, *Protestant Thought in the Nineteenth Century* (New Haven: Yale University Press, 1972) 273-82. For Schlatter see his essay, "The Theology of the New Testament and Dogmatics," in Robert Morgan, ed., *The Nature of New Testament Theology* (Napierville IL: Alec R. Allenson, 1973) 117-66. Gerhard Ritter, "Why the Reformation in Germany," *Church History* (1958): 103, as quoted in Sydney E. Ahlstrom, *A Religious History of the American People* (New Haven: Yale University Press, 1972) 23.

for thoughtful individuals the "inner civil war" was less painful. The
Anglican Aubrey Moore, the Presbyterian James Orr, and the Primi-
tive Methodist A. S. Peake readily come to mind as essentially orthodox
men who struggled to live with the historical revolution of the nineteenth century. W. Robertson Smith, another Presbyterian clergyman
and one of the most distinguished Old Testament scholars of the century, also readily comes to mind—but in this case as an essentially
modern man who struggled to preserve the ahistorical uniqueness of
Christianity. Indeed, there is a special poignancy in Smith's lament that
Princeton's Charles Hodge simply had "no conception of the modern
form of the problem."[4]

Hodge perhaps did not, but the British theologian Peter Taylor
Forsyth did. Forsyth, who was Congregational, resembled Strong in
many ways: both were known for erudition leavened with lethal wit;
both were at heart impassioned preachers; both died in 1921. And Forsyth, like Strong, knew that the historical, contextual, and evolutionary understanding of the Christian tradition could not be dismissed with
a dogmatic snort about the infallibility of the Bible. Charging that the
"doctrine of plenary verbal inspiration and inerrancy" was its own best
refutation, he urged the church to "reduce the burden of belief," to ac-

[4]For the basic continuity between British and American evangelicalism see Winthrop S. Hudson, "How American Is Religion in America?" in Jerald C. Brauer, ed.,
Reinterpretation in American Church History (Chicago: University of Chicago Press, 1968)
153-67. For the problems posed for British evangelicals by growing historical con-
sciousness see Willis B. Glover, *Evangelical Nonconformists and Higher Criticism in the
Nineteenth Century* (London: Independent Press, 1954) esp. 80, 106, and Thomas A.
Langford, *In Search of Foundations* (Nashville: Abingdon Press, 1969) 40, 49-53, 88.
For the distinctiveness of the British evangelical response see George M. Marsden,
"Fundamentalism as an American Phenomenon," *Church History* 46 (1977): 217-24.
For Aubrey Moore see James R. Moore, *The Post-Darwinian Controversies* (Cambridge:
Cambridge University Press, 1979) 259-69. For James Orr see Jack B. Rogers and
Donald K. McKim, *The Authority and Interpretation of the Bible* (San Francisco: Harper
and Row, 1979) 385-88. For A. S. Peake, see Glover, *Evangelical Nonconformists,* 261,
270-71, and Marsden, "Fundamentalism," 217. For W. Robertson Smith see T. O.
Beidelman, *W. Robertson Smith and the Sociological Study of Religion* (Chicago: University of Chicago Press, 1974) 33, 38, 40, 52. The Smith quotation is in a letter from
him to J. S. Black, 14 September 1871, quoted in Warner M. Bailey, "William Robertson Smith and American Bible Studies," *Journal of Presbyterian History* 51 (1973):
287; see also 293, 302.

knowledge frankly that some creedal inheritances are more important than others, to see that is is better to have "a few mighty cohesive truths which capture, fire, and mould the whole soul . . . than a correct conspectus of the total area of divine knowledge." The goal of the Christian theologian in the modern world must be, in short, to forge "a minimal creed, an ample science, a maximal faith."[5]

Nonetheless, Forsyth also insisted that the assumptions underlying the modern world view were anything but benign.

> It is all over with truth when man feels himself its creator. . . . Reality gives way under our feet, and standards vanish like stars falling from heaven. . . . Man becomes his own maker, and he has a moral fool for his product. . . . Thought . . . commits suicide, and mankind evolves over an abyss.

Forsyth believed that the New Theology—which he lampooned as "religion of the breezy sort"—had largely capitulated to these assumptions. Liberal churchmen had purchased relevance at the price of a "shallow happiness." They had forgotten that "natural process does not carry with it its own explanation or reveal its own goal." But the fundamental truth about history is God's invasion of history in Christ, who provides us with a "foothold in the Eternal." Even after we have made due concessions to the "historical treatment of [Christ's] religious environment," Forsyth countered, we shall discover that the "connexion between [Christ] and His antecedents is not causal, but teleological." "History, indeed, does not give destiny," Forsyth added, "but in Christ destiny is given in the midst of history, by the way of history, and under historic conditions."[6]

The similarity between Strong and Forsyth suggests that the collision between orthodox and modern epistemologies formed a pattern

---

[5]P. T. Forsyth, *Positive Preaching and the Modern Mind* (New York: Hodder and Stoughton, [1907]) 124-27. For a summary of Forsyth's thought see Samuel J. Mikolaski, "P. T. Forsyth," in Philip Edgecumbe Hughes, ed., *Creative Minds in Contemporary Theology*, 2d ed. rev. (Grand Rapids MI: Eerdmans, 1969) 307-340. See also Rogers and McKim, *Authority,* 393-98; Langford, *Search,* 101-103; and Crerar Douglas, "The Cost of Mediation," *Congregational Quarterly* 3 (1978): 28-35.

[6]P. T. Forsyth, *Christian Aspects of Evolution* (London: Epworth Press, 1950 [1905]) 11, 20, 37-39.

that transcended denominational and, to some extent, national contexts. Even so, each experience was unique; persons affected had to "feel along the edges" of their own lives for the way to "open land." Not everyone was able to encapsulate the conflict, as Strong and Forsyth were, in a sweeping Christological vision. Strong's close friend, E. Y. Mullins, is a good example of one who moved from a rather triumphalist assurance that historic Christianity can be tailored to fit the specifications of modern culture to an increasingly sober recognition, which persisted to the end of his life, that the problem may just be irresolvable.[7]

Mullins was president of Southern Baptist Theological Seminary in Louisville from 1899 until 1928. His eminence among Baptists and other Protestants in the South rivaled Strong's in the North. Although Mullins was an essentially conservative man, he always found it easier to be tolerant toward those on his theological and political left than those on his right. The jaunty mood of Mullins's contribution to the *Fundamentals* in 1910 was characteristic: "Professor [William] James, you know, and other scientific observers concede that religious experience is a witness to the supernatural; only he refuses to admit that Christ is the author." The problem, Mullins added (a bit too easily), is that "these men have not thought through the problem of Christian experience." They have not discerned that "the current on the bosom of the river of thought . . . is religious experience wherein man's upward soaring thought is met by God's descending revelation and love."[8]

In the next dozen years, however, Mullins's mood darkened as unremitting theological controversy riddled the life of the seminary. His

---

[7]"Feel along the edges" is from David Ignatow, *Rescue the Dead,* cited without attribution in Giles Gunn, ed., *New World Metaphysics: Readings on the Religious Meaning of the American Experience* (New York: Oxford University Press, 1981) 405.

[8]E. Y. Mullins, "The Testimony of Christian Experience," in Dixon et al., eds., *Fundamentals* 3:81, 79. More generally see Sydney E. Ahlstrom, "Theology in America," in James Ward Smith and A. Leland Jamison, eds., *The Shaping of American Religion* (Princeton NJ: Princeton University Press, 1961) 303-309, and William E. Ellis, "Edgar Young Mullins and the Crisis of Moderate Southern Baptist Leadership," *Foundations* 19 (1976): 171-85. See also Ellis, *"A Man of Books and a Man of the People": E. Y. Mullins and the Crisis of Moderate Southern Baptist Leadership* (Macon GA: Mercer University Press, 1985) chap. 5.

last major work—significantly titled *Christianity at the Cross Roads*—showed that growing misgivings had cast a shadow over his earlier and quite sanguine perception of the relation between orthodoxy and the modern world. Modern thinkers, Mullins now observed, invariably begin with the assumption that "the universe is not static but dynamic. . . . Nothing is fixed and final. All things are in flux." They then assume that everything that humans do must "always be explained in terms of ordinary cause and effect stated in physical terms. Man is an organism re-acting to stimuli from the world about him." According to this perspective, "religion is a useful function which rises to meet an emergency in man's life. In time he outgrows it." Mullins acknowledged that these assumptions had greatly amplified human understanding of the social and material world, and to this extent he too was undeniably a modern thinker. But he recoiled from the breezy assurance that these notions could adequately explain all dimensions of life. Christianity, he retorted, "protests against dealing with religion on assumptions which destroy religion, and then clamping those assumptions like handcuffs on the wrists of the Christian faith." The nub of the matter is that Christianity "has its own modes of verification, its own constructive principle, its own way of apprehending Reality." It cannot countenance the "forcible imposition of alien standards."[9]

Mullins never admitted that the relation between orthodoxy and modern thought is necessarily contradictory, not logically anyway, but he believed that that is the way it usually works out in practice. The irony of modern historical method, he charged, is that it really is not a method at all, but a world view that makes a priori judgments about the limits of historical process. "The question of . . . the supernatural is determined in advance. No amount of evidence . . . can establish the fact of the resurrection of Christ. This is because such a fact is ruled out before the investigation begins." Still more grievous, in Mullins's estimation, was the inability of those who use only historical method to explain the most pertinacious facts of human existence. "It is in the religious estimate of the two systems that the contrast is manifest," Mullins concluded. The stubborn fact of the sin, guilt, weakness, bondage,

---

[9]E. Y. Mullins, *Christianity at the Cross Roads* (Nashville: Southern Baptist Convention, 1924) 18, 12, 14, 42

of man must be met"—and the simple truth is that Protestant liberalism, "with its beautiful theory of 'realizing the consciousness of Christ,'
never gets into the depths of human religious need."[10]

To this point we have seen that serious, thoughtful, conservative
Protestants like Strong, Forsyth, and Mullins managed, each in his own
way, sooner or later, to strike a truce of sorts with modern thought. But
it would be a distortion to leave the story here, to suggest that everyone
who felt—and fought—the tug of historical consciousness found a way
to hold it at bay. For some, honesty was more costly.

One of the minor ironies of the cultural upheaval described in this
book is that no one perceived the issues more clearly, or registered the
implications more sensitively, than Strong's student George Burman
Foster. After graduating from Rochester Theological Seminary in 1887,
Foster studied in Germany and taught theology at McMaster University. William Rainey Harper brought him to the University of Chicago, where he taught philosophy of religion in the Divinity School,
and later in the department of comparative religion, until his untimely
death in 1918. In very general terms it is quite true that Foster moved
from Reformed orthodoxy to liberalism to functionalism and finally to
frank humanism. But, as Bernard Meland has written, simply to say
this is to miss "all the drama, complexity, and even contradictoriness
that persisted in his thinking, coloring and confounding his thought at
every step." Foster was a "tormented mind and spirit," embroiled in an
"incessant battle with himself as well as with others."[11]

Over the years something like a cottage industry has grown up
seeking to interpret not only Foster's theology, but Foster himself. His
close friend and colleague Gerald Birney Smith, for example, described
him as one of those rare men "who know God and live with God in their
own way." D. C. Macintosh, who had been Foster's student, similarly
said that when Foster talked about "the Christian religious man, one
knew that it was not a case of understanding through mere sympathetic

---

[10]Ibid., 183, 240-41.

[11]For biographical data see Alan Gragg, *George Burman Foster* (Danville VA: Baptist Professors of Religion, 1978). Bernard E. Meland, "The Empirical Tradition in
Theology at Chicago," in Meland, ed., *The Future of Empirical Theology* (Chicago: University of Chicago Press, 1969) 15-17.

imagination; he was speaking out of the depths of his own experience .
. . it was his daily life." Clarence Darrow, in contrast, insisted that Foster's religious evolution had brought him at last to the "Atheistic standpoint—and he was very strongly convinced that all logic led to it." Even Macintosh later changed his mind, judging that Foster tramped around in "the quicksands of modern scepticism and unbelief . . . until at last, apparently, it was too late." No wonder another close friend, William Wallace Fenn, the Unitarian dean of Harvard Divinity School, would remember Foster as a man who died "with pilgrim staff in hand and nobody can tell what would have been the final resting-place of his thought, if, indeed, it had ever found one."[12]

One reason Foster was, and remains, difficult to pin down is because his prose style was richly allusive, frequently dithyrambic, always dense. Moreover, in William R. Hutchison's words, his "driving, probing, somewhat heedless intellectual habits . . . kept him from tidying up the rooms of thought as he swept through them. . . . Foster as often as not let traditional beliefs and slogans lie where they fell, instead of refitting them for use within the newer context." Foster's lack of concern for clarity and consistency would not be so problematic if his spiritual odyssey had been a smooth progression from orthodoxy to humanism. But it was not. The journey was punctuated with numerous backward glances toward the faith of his youth. Though Foster's pilgrimage started where Strong's ended, it is not difficult to see that the demon that troubled Strong tormented Foster.[13]

In his first and most ambitious book, *The Finality of the Christian Religion,* published in 1906, Foster traced the rise and fall of orthodoxy,

---

[12]Gerald Birney Smith, "George Burman Foster," *Biblical World* 53 (1919): 181-83; Douglas Clyde Macintosh, Introduction, *Christianity in Its Modern Expression,* by George Burman Foster (New York: Macmillan, 1921) v; Clarence Darrow to Hjalmar Johnson, 1 February 1931, as quoted by Larry E. Axel, "Conflict and Censure," in Peter Iver Kaufman and Spencer Lavan, eds., *Alone Together* (Boston: Beacon Press, 1978) 101; D. C. Macintosh, *The Problem of Religious Knowledge* (1940) 115, as quoted in William R. Hutchison, *The Modernist Impulse in American Protestantism* (Cambridge MA: Harvard University Press, 1976) 219. William Wallace Fenn, untitled memorial article, *University* [of Chicago] *Record* 5 (1919): 178-79, as quoted in Hutchison, *Modernist Impulse,* 220.

[13]Hutchison, *Modernist Impulse,* 217.

or what he called "authority-religion." In the "old supernaturalistic conception," he wrote, "the divine and the eternal miraculously broke into the time-series at a special point, or points. . . . The divine and eternal, entering thus into time . . . remained unchangeable." But the historicist revolution of the nineteenth century had irrevocably destroyed this possibility. "The modern scientific idea of development, with its ceaseless progress, makes truth a child of its time. . . . To erect evolution into a fundamental law of history is to proclaim the fluidity of all spiritual magnitudes, to relativize truth, and to obliterate all static finalities or absolutes from life." Since this is the case, Foster asked, "Can religion forgo such absoluteness and unchangeability of its truth? Can the Divine partake of the flux and change of time without being belittled? . . . Can man, doomed to absorption in the process of becoming . . . still yearn for a kingdom of eternity?" In 1906 his answer was still yes, albeit a highly qualified yes. "In the mystery of creative personalities," he wrote, "fructified, indeed, by the stream of history, fountains are opened from which higher values, unattainable by us men of ourselves, stream forth from eternity into the human world." For many liberals the notion of a historicized, immanent divinity, who made religion a matter "of spirit and of personality," was a liberating experience. But Foster was not so sure. "A multitude of thoughtful men and women are passing through an experience similar to [my] own," he mused, and "a greater multitude will travel, with bleeding feet, the same *via dolorosa* tomorrow. . . . It is a pathetic and tragic, or inspiring and illuminating, spectacle, according as one looks at it." In his mind the not-so-simple truth was that the "human heart, with its tumultuous experiences . . . [wonders] whether there be, amid the flux, some Eternal Rock whereon it can find strength and stay and rest."[14]

By 1909, when Foster published *The Function of Religion in Man's Struggle for Existence,* he had come to the conclusion that historical criticism of the Bible and of Christian history had made the objective reality of any God, including a radically immanent God, highly problematic. "Subtracting from that which is known what the knower supplies in the process of knowing, what is left as objective reality?" Since the problem "seems to be insoluble," he concluded, "we are wiser

---

[14]George Burman Foster, *The Finality of the Christian Religion* (Chicago: University of Chicago Press, 1906) 173-76, xii-xiii, 8.

today in turning from essence to function." Foster thus defined religion as the conviction that man "is in essence an ideal-achieving being, and that the achievement of his ideals is possible." He acknowledged that a purely functional definition of this sort was a poor substitute for "the full and solid comfort and hope which warmed the hearts and illumined the faces of [our] fathers." But he judged that honest moderns "would rather have a minimum that was sure than a maximum that was not. I have tried to do no more than to cleave to the sunnier side of doubt. And may there be light and warmth enough to keep us from freezing in the dark."[15]

Several times in the remaining decade of his life the grim logic of historical consciousness seemed temporarily to recede. The loss of two children prompted him to pray in 1915 that "our relation to God the Father is the indestructible bond which exalts us above death. . . . We trust that thy Living Love cannot let those that are loved cease to be." And in a study of the vocation of the Christian minister, published the following year, Foster pondered the outcome of the historical under-standing of culture. "If we doubt faith, why not doubt science too? If we doubt the church, the Bible, the state, why not doubt reason, doubt knowledge, doubt morality? . . . Is there no help for lost souls any more?" So long as man is "a *child of God,"* he urged, the ministry cannot be reduced to "so-called 'social service.' " The ministry

> has to do with that deep of man which cries unto the deep of the being of God. There was a lonely hour at the brook Jabbok when Jacob . . . cried: "Tell me, I pray thee, thy name," the Ineffable Name. He wanted to know the eternal mystery and meaning of existence. Not so-called "social service," but the ministry of the interpretation and the satisfaction of this inexpugnable and abysmal need of man, is the supreme and inalienable function of the Christian minister.[16]

---

[15]George Burman Foster, *The Function of Religion in Man's Struggle for Existence* (Chicago: University of Chicago Press, 1909) 279-80; Foster, "The Function of Religion" (1909), reprinted in William R. Hutchison, ed., *American Protestant Thought* (New York: Harper and Row, 1968) 144. Foster, *Function,* xi.

[16]Foster's 1915 prayer was published as *The Function of Death in Human Experience* (Chicago: University of Chicago Press, 1919) 17-18; Foster, "The Contribution of Critical Scholarship to Ministerial Efficiency," in Gerald Birney Smith, ed., *A Guide to the Study of the Christian Religion* (Chicago: University of Chicago Press, 1916) 741, 737.

In the final two years of his life Foster lost a third child—this one a son in the World War—and all remnants of theistic belief. "By and by," he wrote, "when your children have died and your life is almost gone, and you seem to have done almost nothing, is there anything that can give you heart and hope? Or is it the condition of nobility in man that the All should be against him? If there were a foregone assurance of victory, what kind of man would that give?"[17]

II

Brian Gerrish has argued that the effort to relate tradition to the modern world has been the central stimulus underlying creative Protestant theology since the sixteenth century. The attempt by Strong and so many others to erect timeless doctrines upon the shifting sands of historical process was a precarious endeavor, to say the least. Whether Foster's tormented struggle to find a shard of permanence in the process or, for that matter, whether any of the happier and more clear-cut resolutions described in the previous chapter have proved more durable may be debated. But it is clear that Strong did, in any event, gradually come to understand the tragic dimensions of the dilemma in which he was entangled. He was not a Martin Luther who towered above his age, nor a Benjamin Warfield who disdained to be touched by it, and certainly not a William James who lived ahead of it. Rather he was a touchingly human figure: too conservative to discard the nurture of his youth, too honest to discount his own religious experiences, yet too intelligent and well-read to ignore the verdict that the modern understanding of history had rendered on the case for orthodoxy. And it is precisely here that Strong is useful for helping us understand the upheaval that wrenched the foundations of late nineteenth-century Protestant thought.[18]

---

[17]George Burman Foster, review of *The New Orthodoxy* by Edward Scribner Ames in *Christian Century* (24 October 1918): 17-18, as quoted in Hutchison, *Modernist Impulse,* 219.

[18]B. A. Gerrish, *Tradition and the Modern World* (Chicago: University of Chicago Press, 1978) 3, 7, 181-88.

If the incarnational vision in which Strong found—or tried to find—
a resolution of the tension between orthodoxy and the modern world
seems fanciful to the "postmodern," "posthistorical" mind of the late
twentieth century, we might still acknowledge that his instincts were
sound. "At least until recently," Henry May has written, "very few
Americans have gone beyond political, religious and moral skepticism
in the direction of Hume, to distrust the operations of their own minds
and the validity of all general principles. It may be that when real skepticism of this sort becomes widespread, society becomes inoperable as
it did in the France of Louis XVI." And we might grant that Strong's
instincts were sound in another way as well. In this study I have argued
that the key to the riddle of Augustus Strong is that he set out to col-
laborate with God, but found that he first had to reckon with history.
Strong himself would have said that it was the other way around: When
you come to the end of your life, he wrote the morning before he died,
"will you say that you have never seen God? The answer [must] be that
you have never seen anything else." Strong may have seen less than he
thought, but as long as there are serious men and women who seek to
discern the outline of the holy in the midst of the processes of history,
there is reason to believe that an identifiably Christian epistemology will
persist in the modern world.[19]

---

[19]Henry F. May, *The Enlightenment in America* (New York: Oxford University Press,
1976) 360; *WSIB,* 116-17. The epistemic relativism of recent social thought (and
occasional reactions in the direction of "hierarchical objectivism") is described in Edward A. Purcell, Jr. "Social Thought," *American Quarterly* 35 (1983): 80-100.

Historicism:
A Bibliographical Note

THE HISTORICIST TRANSFORMATION that overtook the social disciplines in the United States in the late nineteenth and early twentieth centuries is well attested, but historians differ about when it began—partly because they differ on the criteria for defining it. Morton White, in *Social Thought in America* (Boston: Beacon Press, 1957) 6, and David W. Marcell, in *Progress and Pragmatism* (Westport CT: Greenwood Press, 1974) 37, both see an "antiformalist movement," as they call it, getting well underway in the 1880s. Paul F. Boller, in *American Thought in Transition* (Chicago: Rand McNally, 1969) xii, seems to concur. John Higham, in *Writing American History* (Bloomington: Indiana University Press, 1970) 74-76, ties the movement to broader cultural changes in the 1890s. Henry F. May, in *The End of American Innocence* (Chicago: Quadrangle Paperbacks, 1964) vii-x, 121, focuses on the five-year period between 1912 and 1917, but acknowledges that there were substantial "cracks in the edifice" long before then. Ralph Henry Gabriel, in *The Course of American Democratic Thought,* 2d ed. (New York: Ronald Press, 1956) 407-419, locates the "Great Liberation," as he labels it, in the period between the World Wars. Edward A. Purcell, in *The Crisis of Democratic Theory* (Lexington: University Press of Kentucky, 1973) 17, and Robert H. Wiebe, in *The*

Search for Order: 1877-1920 (New York: Hill and Wang, 1967) 140-49, each argue that there were stages within the historicist transformation. They perceive a semihistoricist stage beginning in the 1880s, which phased into a discernibly more rigorous second stage between 1900 and 1920.

In Europe consistent historicism emerged somewhat earlier than in the United States, and there were differences in tone. But in general European scholars and intellectuals shared the same assumptions; see Higham, *Writing,* 90-93; H. Stuart Hughes, *Consciousness and Society* (New York: Vintage Books, 1961) 10-20; Gerhard Masur, *Prophets of Yesterday* (New York: Macmillan, 1961) vii-viii, 419; W. Warren Wagar, *Good Tidings* (Bloomington: Indiana University Press, 1972) 123-28. Georg G. Iggers, a leading authority on the subject, doubts that truly consistent historicism appeared much before Weber's main work and, in any case, did not take hold generally among the well-educated elite until after World War I; see Iggers, "The Idea of Progress," *American Historical Review* 71 (1965): 8-9.

For the historicist transformation specifically in the empirical social sciences in the United States see Louis Wirth, "The Social Sciences," in Merle Curti, ed., *American Scholarship in the Twentieth Century* (New York: Russell and Russell, 1967 [1953]) 40, 45-68; Thomas C. Cochran, "The Social Scientists," in Robert E. Spiller and Eric Larrabee, eds., *American Perspectives* (Cambridge MA: Harvard University Press, 1961) esp. 101. For a contemporary assessment see *Encyclopedia of the Social Sciences,* s.v. "The Social Sciences as Disciplines—United States," by L. L. Barnard. For assumptional changes in the historical profession see John Higham, *History* (New York: Harper and Row, 1973 [1965]) 87-131; Robert Allen Skotheim, *American Intellectual Histories and Historians* (Princeton: Princeton University Press, 1966) 66-123. For the change in juridical scholarship see Edward A. Purcell, Jr., "American Jurisprudence between the Wars," *American Historical Review* 75 (1969-1970): 424-46; Eugene V. Rostow, "The Realist Tradition in American Law," in Schlesinger and White, eds. *Paths of American Social Thought* (Boston: Houghton, Mifflin, 1970) 203-218. For the reorientation in academic philosophy see Arthur E. Murphy, "Philosophical Scholarship," in Merle Curti, ed., *American Scholarship in the Twentieth Century* (New York: Russell and Russell, 1967) 178-84; Herbert W. Schneider, *A History of American Philosophy,* 2d ed. (New York: Columbia University Press, 1963) 431-92.

On the other hand, Cushing Strout argues that the seminal thinkers in the antiformalist tradition were so enamored with the new dawn of "technocratic rationalism" that they themselves often fell victim to ahistorical assumptions; see Strout, "Twentieth Century Enlightenment," *American Political Science Review* 49 (1955): 321-39. David W. Noble makes a similar charge, with more emphasis on the quasi-religious nature of their faith in humanity, scientific uplift, and inevitable progress; see Noble, "The Religion of Progress in America," *Social Research* 22 (1955): 417-40, and *The Paradox of Progressive Thought* (Minneapolis: University of Minnesota Press). Henry May likewise finds that "most of these thinkers were less radical than they seemed"; see May, *End,* 140-41, 156, 164. Robert H. Wiebe concurs, arguing that the new relativists characteristically thought in terms of "normal and abnormal" (Wiebe, *Search,* 154). The later Morton White similarly contends that the pragmatic philosophers persistently appealed to "sentimental" criteria in the justification of truth claims (*Science and Sentiment in America* [London: Oxford University Press, 1972] chaps. 6-11). These critiques are primarily addressed to the older generation of social thinkers whose main work came before World War I. But the social thinkers of the 1920s and 1930s have not escaped criticism either. In this regard see Robert A. Nisbet, *Social Change and History* (New York: Oxford University Press, 1969) 223-39; Purcell, *Crisis,* 40, 45, 166-71, 179-80, chaps. 8-10; Clinton Rossiter, *Conservatism in America,* 2d rev. ed. (New York: Random House, 1962) 22, 45, 128-62.

Bibliography

I. PRIMARY SOURCES
BY OR PERTAINING TO AUGUSTUS H. STRONG

A. Published works by Strong

Strong, Augustus H. *American Poets and Their Theology*. Philadelphia: Griffith and Rowland Press, 1916.

_____. [Annual Alumni Dinner Address (title varies)]. *Rochester Theological Seminary Record* 1 (1906)-7 (1912).

_____. *Annual Report of the New York Baptist Union for Ministerial Education*. "Report of the President." Rochester NY: 1895-1912.

_____. Appreciation [of William Rainey Harper]. *Biblical World* 27 (1916): 235-36.

_____. *Autobiography of Augustus Hopkins Strong* [1896, 1906, 1908, 1917]. Edited by Crerar Douglas. Valley Forge PA: Judson Press, 1981. (Handwritten and typed versions are on deposit at the American Baptist Historical Society, Rochester NY.)

_____. *Christ in Creation and Ethical Monism*. Philadelphia: Roger Williams Press, 1899.

_____. "Confessions of Our Faith." *Watchman-Examiner* 9 (9 July 1921): 910.

_____. *The Great Poets and Their Theology*. Philadelphia: American Baptist Publication Society, 1897.

_____. Introduction to *Control in Evolution: A Discussion of the Fundamental Principles of Social Order and Progress,* by George F. Wilkins. New York: A. C. Armstrong and Son, 1903.

_____. *Lectures on Theology.* Rochester NY: Press of E. R. Andrews, 1876.

_____. "Man a Living Soul." *Rochester Theological Seminary Record* 7 (May 1912): 12-16.

_____. *Miscellanies.* 2 vols. Philadelphia: Griffith and Rowland Press, 1912.

_____. "Modifications in the Theological Curriculum." *American Journal of Theology* 3 (1899): 326-30.

_____. "My Views of the Universe in General." *Baptist* 1 (29 May 1920): 625-26.

_____. *One Hundred Chapel-Talks to Theological Students Together with Two Autobiographical Addresses.* Philadelphia: Griffith and Rowland Press, 1913.

_____. *Philosophy and Religion: A Series of Addresses, Essays, and Sermons Designed to Set Forth Great Truths in Popular Form.* New York: A. C. Armstrong and Son, 1888.

_____. *Philosophy and Religion.* 2d ed. New York: Griffith and Rowland Press, 1912.

_____. *Popular Lectures on the Books of the New Testament.* Philadelphia: Griffith and Rowland Press, 1914.

_____. Review of *Theories of the Will in the History of Philosophy* by Archibald Alexander. *American Journal of Theology* 3 (1899): 344-46.

_____. *Systematic Theology: A Compendium and Commonplace Book Designed for the Use of Theological Students.* Rochester NY: Press of E. R. Andrews, 1886.

_____. *Systematic Theology.* 5th ed., rev. and enl. New York: A. C. Armstrong and Son, 1896.

_____. *Systematic Theology,* 6th ed., rev. and enl. New York: A. C. Armstrong and Son, 1899.

_____. *Systematic Theology.* 7th ed., rev. and enl. New York: A. C. Armstrong and Son, 1902.

_____. *Systematic Theology.* 3 vols. 8th ed., rev. and enl. Philadelphia: Griffith and Rowland Press, 1907-1909. Reprint (3 vols. in 1). Old Tappan, NJ: Fleming H. Revell, 1970.

_____. *A Tour of the Missions: Observations and Conclusions.* Philadelphia: Griffith and Rowland Press, 1918.

_____. *The Uncertainty of Life: A Sermon Preached in the First Baptist Church, Cleveland* [OH], *January 28, 1866*. N.p.: n.d.

_____. *Union with Christ: A Chapter of Systematic Theology*. Philadelphia: American Baptist Publication Society, 1913.

_____. [Wilkinson Lectures.] "Five Lectures Delivered in 1921 on the Foundation of the William Cleaver Wilkinson Lectureship." Oak Brook IL: Northern Baptist Theological Seminary, n.d.

_____. *What Shall I Believe? A Primer of Christian Theology*. New York: Fleming H. Revell, 1922.

B. *Manuscript materials*

In one of his *Annual Reports,* Strong indicated that he often wrote one hundred or more letters each week. Nearly all have been lost, along with most of his personal papers. A few items of marginal value are, however, housed in the archival collections listed here.

Chicago IL. University Library. Approximately thirty letters to William Rainey Harper, in President's Papers, 1889-1925, Box 54, folder 26, and Box 62, folder 10.

Louisville KY. Southern Baptist Theological Seminary Library. President E. Y. Mullins Papers. Thirty-five letters to Mullins.

Rochester NY. American Baptist Historical Society. Letters to Clarence Barbour and Walter Rauschenbusch. Personal letters to family members. 1918 diary. 1920 travelogue of Europe. Notes for unpublished sermons and lectures. Manuscript of *Autobiography,* plus a typescript version emended, apparently, by Strong and John Henry Strong.

At the time the research for this study was carried out all of Strong's surviving grandchildren were contacted. None owned any of his papers except for miscellaneous personal letters and photographs. I especially wish to thank Ms. Margaret Crosman, Ms. Macauley Smith, and Mr. R. B. Sewall for their assistance.

C. *Memorials*

"Augustus H. Strong Memorial Number." *Northern Baptist Theological Seminary Bulletin* 9 (December 1921): 6.

"Augustus Hopkins Strong Memorial Number." *Rochester Theological Seminary Bulletin* (supplement, May 1922).

Calvert, John B. "Dr. Strong, the Scholar and Friend." *Watchman-Examiner* 9 (22 December 1921): 1623.

Carman, Augustine S. "The Legacy of a Life." *Baptist* 2 (10 December 1921): 1420.

Cleaves, Arthur W. [?] "A Great Leader Has Passed." *Baptist* 2 (10 December 1921): 1422.

"Dr. Strong Called Home." *Baptist Banner: The West Virginia State Paper* 32 (15 December 1921): 6.

"Dr. Strong's Last Work." *Watchman-Examiner* 9 (8 December 1921): 1551.

Heinrichs, Jacob. "Dr. Strong and Foreign Missions." *Watchman-Examiner* 9 (22 December 1921): 1622.

"Immortality of Influence." *Baptist Observer: Official Paper of Indiana Baptists* 20 (22 December 1921): 2.

Laws, Curtis Lee [?]. "Dr. Augustus Hopkins Strong." *Watchman-Examiner* 9 (8 December 1921): 1549.

"Rev. Dr. A. H. Strong Dead." *New York Times,* 3 December 1921, 13.

[Obituary]. *Democrat and Chronicle* (Rochester NY), 30 November 1921.

Taft, George W. "Augustus H. Strong." *Baptist* 2 (10 December 1921): 1420.

II. OTHER PRIMARY SOURCES

Abbott, Lyman. Review of *Christ in Creation and Ethical Monism* by Augustus H. Strong. *Outlook* 66 (1900): 129-30.

Allen, A. V. G. *The Continuity of Christian Thought: A Study of Theology in the Light of Its History.* Boston: Houghton, Mifflin, 1884.

Anderson, Willis A. Review of *Systematic Theology* by Augustus H. Strong. *Andover Review* 8 (1887): 96-99.

Baptist. Chicago. 1920-1922.

Baptist Doctrines: Addresses Delivered at the North American Pre-Convention Conference, Des Moines, Iowa, June 21, 1921. N.p., 1921.

Baptist Fundamentals: Being Addresses Delivered at the Pre-Convention Conference at Buffalo, June 21 and 22, 1920. Philadelphia: Judson Press, 1920.

Becker, Carl L. *The Heavenly City of the Eighteenth-Century Philosophers.* New Haven CT: Yale University Press, 1965. Originally published in 1932.

Beckwith, Clarence Augustine. Review of *Systematic Theology* (1907, vol. 2) by Augustus H. Strong. *American Journal of Theology* 12 (1908): 502-505.

Behrends, A. J. F. "Ethical Monism." *Methodist Review* 77 (1895): 357-70.

Benedict, Ruth. *Patterns of Culture.* Boston: Houghton, Mifflin, Sentry Edition, 1961. Originally published in 1934.

Briggs, Charles Augustus. *Church Unity: Studies of Its Most Important Problems.* New York: Charles Scribner's Sons, 1909.

Brown, William Adams. "Recent Treatises on Systematic Theology." *American Journal of Theology* 12 (1908): 150-55.

Burton, Ernest DeWitt. "Recent Tendencies in the Northern Baptist Churches." *American Journal of Theology* 24 (1920): 321-38.

Bushnell, Horace. *Nature and the Supernatural, as Together Constituting the One System of God.* New York: Charles Scribner's Sons, 1858.

Carman, Augustine S. "A Great Theological Quintet." *Rochester Theological Seminary Record* 7 (May 1912): 26-27.

Case, Shirley Jackson. "The Historical Study of Religion." *Journal of Religion* 1 (1921): 1-17.

_____. "Whither Historicism in Theology." In *The Process of Religion: Essays in Honor of Dean Shailer Mathews,* edited by Miles H. Krumbine. New York: Macmillan, 1933.

Clarke, William Newton. *An Outline of Christian Theology.* Cambridge MA: John Wilson and Son, 1894.

Dewey, John. *Reconstruction in Philosophy.* Boston: Beacon Press, 1957. Originally published in 1920.

Dixon, A. C. et al., eds. *The Fundamentals: A Testimony to the Truth.* 12 vols. Chicago: Testimony Publishing, [1910-1915].

"Dr. Strong's Theology." *Journal and Messenger* 76 (31 January 1907): 6-7.

Eliot, Charles W. *The Religion of the Future.* Boston: Ball Publishing, 1909.

Fosdick, Harry Emerson. *The Living of These Days: An Autobiography.* New York: Harper and Brothers, 1956.

Forsyth, Peter Taylor. *Christian Aspects of Evolution.* London: Epworth Press, 1950. Originally published in 1905.

_____. *Positive Preaching and the Modern Mind.* New York: Hodder and Stoughton/George H. Doran, n.d. Originally published in 1907.

Foster, George Burman. "The Contribution of Critical Scholarship to Ministerial Efficiency." In *A Guide to the Study of the Christian Religion,* edited by Gerald Birney Smith. Chicago: University of Chicago Press, 1916.

_____. *The Finality of the Christian Religion.* Chicago: University of Chicago Press, 1906.

_____. *The Function of Death in Human Experience.* Chicago: University of Chicago Press, 1919. Originally published in 1915.

_____. "The Function of Religion." In *American Protestant Thought: The Liberal Era,* edited by William R. Hutchison. New York: Harper and Row, 1968. Originally published in 1909.

_____. *The Function of Religion in Man's Struggle for Existence.* Chicago: University of Chicago Press, 1909.

Fountain, Charles Hillman. *The Denominational Situation: Should Our Schools Be Investigated?* Plainfield, NJ: privately printed, 1920.

Gladden, Washington. *The Christian Pastor and the Working Church.* New York: Charles Scribner's Sons, 1916. Originally published in 1898.

_____. *Present Day Theology.* 2d ed. Columbus OH: McClelland, 1913.

Goodspeed, Calvin. Review of *Systematic Theology* (1907, vols. 1-2) by Augustus H. Strong. *Review and Expositor* 5 (1908): 242-53.

Gordon, A. J. *The Ministry of Healing: Miracles of Cure in All Ages.* Brooklyn NY: Christian Alliance Publishing, 1882.

_____. *The Ministry of the Spirit.* New York: Fleming H. Revell, 1894.

Gordon, Ernest. *The Leaven of the Sadducees.* Chicago: Bible Institute Colportage Association, 1926.

Gordon, George A. *Ultimate Conceptions of Faith.* Boston: Houghton, Mifflin, 1903.

Harris, George. *Moral Evolution.* Boston: Houghton, Mifflin, 1900.

Hastings, James. Review of *Christ in Creation and Ethical Monism* by Augustus H. Strong. *Expository Times* 11 (1899-1900): 315-16.

_____. Review of *Systematic Theology* (1907, vol. 1) by Augustus H. Strong. *Expository Times* 19 (1907-1908): 29-30.

_____. Review of *Systematic Theology* (1907, vol. 2) by Augustus H. Strong. *Expository Times* 20 (1907-1908): 317-18.

_____. Review of *Systematic Theology* (1909, vol. 3) by Augustus H. Strong. *Expository Times* 20 (1908-1909): 466.

Henry, Carl F. H. *God, Revelation and Authority.* 5 vols. Waco TX: Word Books, 1976-1983.

Hodge, Caspar Wistar, Jr. "The Finality of the Christian Religion." In *Biblical and Theological Studies by the Members of the Faculty of Princeton Theological Seminary.* New York: Charles Scribner's Sons, 1912.

_____. Review of *Systematic Theology* (1907, vols. 1-2) by Augustus H. Strong. *Princeton Theological Review* 6 (1908): 335-41.

_____. Review of *Systematic Theology* (1909, vol. 3) by Augustus H. Strong. *Princeton Theological Review* 8 (1910): 333-35.

_____. Review of *What Shall I Believe? A Primer of Christian Theology,* by Augustus H. Strong. *Princeton Theological Review* 20 (1922): 681-82.

Hovey, Alvah. "Dr. Strong's Ethical Monism." *Watchman* 75 (13 December 1894): 10-11; (20 December 1894): 10-11; (27 December 1894): 11-12.

_____. Review of *Systematic Theology,* by Augustus H. Strong. *Baptist Quarterly Review* 8 (1886): 567-69.

Johnson, David et al., eds. *The Trial of the Rev. David Swing.* Chicago: Jansen, McClurg, 1874.

Johnson, Elias H. "Dr. Strong's Theology." *Baptist Quarterly Review* 12 (1890): 395-406.

_____. *Ethical Monism, in Two Series of Three Articles Each, and Christ in Creation, with a Review by Professor Elias H. Johnson.* New York: Examiner, 1896.

Johnson, John W. "Prerequisites to an Understanding of the System of Theology of Augustus Hopkins Strong." *Review and Expositor* 19 (1922): 333-41.

King, Henry Churchill. *Reconstruction in Theology.* New York: Macmillan, 1901.

Knox, George William. "Some Recent Works on Systematic Theology." *Harvard Theological Review* 1 (1908): 189-206.

Krutch, Joseph Wood. *The Modern Temper: A Study and a Confession.* New York: Harcourt, Brace and World, Harvest Book, 1956. Originally published in 1929.

Lake, Kirsopp. *The Religion of Yesterday and Tomorrow.* Boston: Houghton, Mifflin, 1926.

Langford, S. Fraser. "The Gospel of Augustus H. Strong and Walter Rauschenbusch." *Chronicle* 14 (1951): 3-18.

Lewis, Clarence Irving. "Logic and Pragmatism." In *Contemporary American Philosophy: Personal Statements.* Edited by George P. Adams and William Pepperell Montague. 2 vols. London: George Allen and Unwin, 1930.

Lippmann, Walter. *A Preface to Morals.* Boston: Beacon Press, 1960. Originally published in 1929.

Llewellyn, Karl. "A Realistic Jurisprudence—the Next Step." *Columbia Law Review* 30 (1930): 431-65.

Lutheran Quarterly. Review of *Systematic Theology* by Augustus H. Strong 17 (1887): 133.

Machen, J. Gresham. *The Christian Faith in the Modern World*. Grand Rapids MI: William B. Eerdmans, 1965. Originally published in 1936.

_____. "Christianity in Conflict." In *Contemporary American Theology*, edited by Vergilius Ferm, 1:245-74. New York: Round Table Press, 1932.

MacKenzie, W. Douglas. Review of *Christ in Creation and Ethical Monism*, by Augustus H. Strong. *American Journal of Theology* 4 (1900): 648-50.

Masters, Victor I. "Dr. A. H. Strong's Terrible Arraignment of Destructive Criticism." *Western Recorder* 100 (21 October 1926): 11-12.

McGiffert, Arthur Cushman. "The Historical Study of Christianity." In *American Protestant Thought: The Liberal Era*, edited by William R. Hutchison. New York: Harper and Row, 1968.

_____. "The Progress of Theological Thought During the Past Fifty Years." *American Journal of Theology* 20 (1916): 321-32.

_____. *The Rise of Modern Religious Ideas*. New York: Macmillan, 1925. Originally published in 1915.

Merriam, Edmund F.[?] "President Strong's Theology." *Watchman* 89 (29 August 1907): 7.

_____. Review of *Christ in Creation and Ethical Monism*, by Augustus H. Strong. *Watchman* 89 (19 September 1907): 7.

Methodist Review. Review of *Systematic Theology*, by Augustus H. Strong. 5th series 68 (1886): 939-941.

Mills, B. Fay. *Victory Through Surrender: Plain Suggestions Concerning Entire Consecration*. Chicago: Fleming H. Revell, 1892.

Mullins, E. Y. *The Christian Religion in Its Doctrinal Expression*. Philadelphia: Judson Press, 1917.

_____. *Christianity at the Cross Roads*. Nashville: Southern Baptist Convention, 1924.

_____. "The Testimony of Christian Experience." In *The Fundamentals: A Testimony to the Truth*. Edited by A. C. Dixon et al. Chicago: Testimony Publishing, [1910-1915].

Munger, Theodore. *The Freedom of Faith*. Boston: Houghton, Mifflin, 1883.

Newman, Albert Henry. *A Century of Baptist Achievement*. Philadelphia: American Baptist Publication Society. 1901.

_____. "Strong's Systematic Theology." *Review and Expositor* 2 (1905): 41-66.

Northern Baptist Convention. *Annual*. 1920, 1921.

Patton, Francis L. Review of *Systematic Theology* by Augustus H. Strong. *Presbyterian Review* 8 (1887): 365-67.

Pepper, G. D. B. "Strong's Systematic Theology." *Watchman* 67 (18 November 1886): 1.

Pollard, Edward B. "Baptists and Fundamentalism." *Homiletic Review* 87 (1924): 265-67.

"Rochester Seminary Anniversary." *Watchman* 94 (16 May 1912): 3-13.

Rochester Theological Seminary Bulletin: Rauschenbusch Number. Sixty-ninth Year (November 1918).

Rochester Theological Seminary Bulletin: The Seventy-Fifth Anniversary Volume of the "Record." Seventy-fifth year (May 1925).

Schlatter, Adolf. "The Theology of the New Testament and Dogmatics." In *Nature of New Testament Theology,* edited and translated by Robert Morgan. Napierville IL: Alec R. Allenson, 1973.

Simpson, A. B., ed. *A Cloud of Witnesses for Divine Healing.* 2d ed. New York: Word, Work and World Publishing, 1887.

Smith, Gerald Birney. "Systematic Theology and Christian Ethics." In *A Guide to the Study of the Christian Religion,* edited by Gerald Birney Smith. Chicago: University of Chicago, 1916.

_____. "Theological Thinking in America." In *Religious Thought in the Last Quarter-Century.* Chicago: University of Chicago Press, 1927.

Smith, Hannah Whitall. Introduction. *The Practice of the Presence of God: The Best Rule of A Holy Life* by Brother Lawrence. New York: Fleming H. Revell, 1895.

Smith, W. Robertson. *The Religion of the Semites: The Fundamental Institutions.* London: Adam and Charles Black, 1907.

Smyth, Egbert. "Progressive Orthodoxy." In *Progressive Orthodoxy: A Contribution to the Christian Interpretation of Christian Doctrines,* edited by Smyth et al. Boston: Houghton, Mifflin, 1892. Originally published in 1885.

Smyth, Newman. *The Orthodox Theology of To-Day.* New York: Charles Scribner's Sons, 1881.

Standard [Chicago]. Review of *Systematic Theology* by Augustus H. Strong. 55 (25 April 1908): 980.

Stearns, Lewis French. *Present-Day Theology: A Popular Discussion of Leading Doctrines of the Christian Faith.* New York: Charles Scribner's Sons, 1893.

Stevens, George B. Review of *Philosophy and Religion* by Augustus H. Strong. *New Englander and Yale Review* new series 12 (1888): 421-31.

_____. Review of *Systematic Theology* by Augustus H. Strong. *New Englander and Yale Review* new series 10 (1887): 31-47.

Stewart, Lyman. Papers. Biola College, LaMirada, California.

Strong, Charles Augustus. "Nature and Mind." In *Contemporary American Philosophy: Personal Statements,* edited by George P. Adams and William Pepperell Montague. 2 vols. London: George Allen and Unwin, 1930.

Taft, George W. "Two Remarkable Men and Their Books: Augustus Hopkins Strong and William Newton Clarke." *Standard* (18 January 1913): 576-78, and (25 January 1913): 607-608.

Thomas, Jesse B. "Dr. Strong's Last Work." *Watchman* 81 (9 August 1900): 11-12.

Valentine, M. Review of *Christ in Creation and Ethical Monism,* by Augustus H. Strong. *Lutheran Quarterly* 30 (1900): 279-84.

Van Dyke, Henry. *The Gospel for an Age of Doubt.* New York: Macmillan 1897.

Warfield, Benjamin B. Review of *Christ in Creation and Ethical Monism* by Augustus H. Strong. *Presbyterian and Reformed Review* 12 (1901): 325-26.

_____. Review of *Philosophy and Religion* by Augustus H. Strong. *Presbyterian Review* 9 (1888): 679.

_____. Review of *Systematic Theology* (1896) by Augustus H. Strong. *Presbyterian and Reformed Review* 8 (1897): 356-58.

_____. "'The Victorious Life.'" *Princeton Theological Review* 16 (1918): 321-73. Reprinted in *Perfectionism,* edited by Samuel G. Craig. Philadelphia: Presbyterian and Reformed Publishing, 1974.

Watchman-Examiner: A National Baptist Newspaper. New York. 1917-1922. (edited by Curtis Lee Laws.)

Wright, George Frederick. Review of *Systematic Theology* (vol. 1, 1907) by Augustus H. Strong. *Bibliotheca Sacra* 64 (1907): 773-76.

_____. Review of *Systematic Theology* (vol. 2, 1907) by Augustus H. Strong. *Bibliotheca Sacra* 65 (1908): 591.

_____. "Strong's Systematic Theology." *Bibliotheca Sacra* 44 (1887): 300-334.

Youtz, Herbert Alden. Review of *Systematic Theology* (vol. 3, 1909) by Augustus H. Strong. *American Journal of Theology* 13 (1909): 468-70.

III. SECONDARY SOURCES

Ahlstrom, Sydney E. *A Religious History of the American People.* New Haven CT: Yale University Press, 1972.

_____. "The Scottish Philosophy and American Theology." *Church History* 24 (1955): 257-72.

_____. "Theology in America: A Historical Survey." In *The Shaping of American Religion,* edited by James Ward Smith and A. Leland Jamison. Princeton: Princeton University Press, 1961.

_____, ed. *Theology in America: The Major Protestant Voices from Puritanism to Neo-Orthodoxy.* Indianapolis: Bobbs-Merrill, 1967.

Altholz, Josef L. "The Mind of Victorian Orthodoxy: Anglican Responses to *Essays and Reviews,* 1860-1864." *Church History* 51 (1982): 186-97.

Arnold, Charles Harvey. *God Before You and Behind You.* Chicago: Hyde Park Union Church, 1974.

Ashworth, Robert A. "The Fundamentalist Movement among the Baptists." *Journal of Religion* 4 (1924): 611-31.

Axel, Larry E. "Conflict and Censure: The Religious Odyssey of George Burman Foster." In *Alone Together: Studies in the History of Liberal Religion,* edited by Peter Iver Kaufman and Spencer Lavan. Boston: Beacon Press, 1978.

Bailey, Warner M. "William Robertson Smith and American Bible Studies." *Journal of Presbyterian History* 51 (1973): 285-308.

Baptist Advance: The Achievements of the Baptists of North America for a Century and a Half. Nashville: Broadman Press, 1964.

Baumer, Franklin L. *Modern European Thought: Continuity and Change in Ideas, 1600-1950.* New York: Macmillan, 1977.

Beidelman, T. O. W. *Robertson Smith and the Sociological Study of Religion.* Chicago: University of Chicago Press, 1974.

Berlin, Isaiah. *Karl Marx: His Life and Environment.* 3d ed. New York: Oxford University Press, 1963. Originally published in 1939.

Blau, Joseph L. "John Dewey's Theory of History." *Journal of Philosophy* 57 (1960): 89-100.

Boller, Paul F., Jr. *American Thought in Transition: The Impact of Evolutionary Naturalism, 1865-1900.* Chicago: Rand McNally, 1969.

_____. *American Transcendentalism, 1830-1860: An Intellectual Inquiry.* New York: G. P. Putnam's Sons, 1974.

Boorstin, Daniel J. *The Lost World of Thomas Jefferson.* Boston: Beacon Press, 1960. Originally published in 1948.

Bowden, Henry Warner. *Church History in the Age of Science: Historiographical Patterns in the United States, 1876-1918.* Chapel Hill: University of North Carolina Press, 1971.

_____. *Dictionary of American Religious Biography.* Westport CT: Greenwood Press, 1977.

Bozeman, Theodore Dwight. *Protestants in an Age of Science: The Baconian Ideal and Antebellum Religious Thought.* Chapel Hill: University of North Carolina Press, 1977.

Bradbury, John W. "Curtis Lee Laws and the Fundamentalist Movement." *Foundations* 5 (1962): 52-58.

Brereton, Virginia Lieson. "Protestant Fundamentalist Bible Schools, 1882-1940." Ph.D. dissertation, Columbia University, 1981.

Brown, Ira V. "The Higher Criticism Comes to America, 1880-1900." *Journal of the Presbyterian Historical Society* 38 (1960): 193-212.

Butterfield, Herbert. *Man on His Past: The Study of the History of Historical Scholarship.* Cambridge: Cambridge University Press, 1969.

Carter, Paul A. *The Spiritual Crisis of the Gilded Age.* Dekalb: Northern Illinois University Press, 1971.

Cassirer, Ernst. *The Philosophy of the Enlightenment.* Princeton: Princeton University Press, 1951.

Cauthen, Kenneth. *The Impact of American Religious Liberalism.* New York: Harper and Row, 1962.

Chiles, Robert E. *Theological Transition in American Methodism: 1790-1935.* New York: Abingdon Press, 1965.

Cobban, Alfred. *In Search of Humanity: The Role of the Enlightenment in Modern History.* New York: George Braziller, 1960.

Coben, Stanley. "The Assault on Victorianism in the Twentieth Century." *American Quarterly* 27 (1975): 604-628.

Cole, Stewart G. *The History of Fundamentalism.* Westport CT: Greenwood Press, 1971. Originally published in 1931.

Coleman, Richard J. *Issues of Theological Warfare: Evangelicals and Liberals.* Grand Rapids MI: William B. Eerdmans, 1972.

Collingwood, R. G. *The Idea of History.* London: Oxford University Press, 1956. Originally published in 1946.

Crismon, Leo. "The Literature of the Baptists." *Religion in Life* 25 (1955-1956): 117-31.

Curti, Merle, ed. *American Scholarship in the Twentieth Century.* New York: Russell and Russell, 1967. Originally published in 1953.

Demarest, Bruce A. *General Revelation: Historical Views and Contemporary Issues.* Grand Rapids MI: Zondervan Publishing House, 1982.

Dictionary of American Biography. S.v. "Strong, Augustus Hopkins," "Strong, Charles Augustus."

Dictionary of the History of Ideas: Studies of Selected Pivotal Ideas. S.v. "Darwinism," "Determinism in History," "Historicism," "Positivism in Europe to 1900," and "Romanticism."

Dollar, George W. *A History of Fundamentalism in America.* Greenville SC: Bob Jones University Press, 1973.

Douglas, Crerar. "The Cost of Mediation: A Study of Augustus Hopkins Strong and P. T. Forsyth." *Congregational Journal* 3 (1978): 28-35.

_____. "The Hermeneutics of Augustus Hopkins Strong: God and Shakespeare in Rochester." *Foundations* 21 (1978): 71-76.

Ellis, Walter Edmund Warren. "Social and Religious Factors in the Fundamentalist-Modernist Schisms among Baptists in North America, 1895-1934." Ph.D. dissertation, University of Pittsburgh, 1974.

Ellis, William E. "Edgar Young Mullins and the Crisis of Moderate Southern Baptist Leadership." *Foundations* 19 (1976): 171-85.

_____. "Edgar Young Mullins: Southern Baptist Theologian, Administrator, and Denominational Leader." Ph.D. dissertation, University of Kentucky, 1974.

_____. "A Man of Books and a Man of the People": E. Y. Mullins and the Crisis of Moderate Southern Baptist Leadership." Macon GA: Mercer University Press, 1985.

Encyclopedia of Philosophy. S.v. "Bowne, Borden Parker," "Common Sense," "Hamilton, William," "Historicism," "Lotze, Rudolf Hermann," "Personalism," and "Reid, Thomas."

Encyclopedia of the Social Sciences. S.v. "Fundamentalism," "The Social Sciences as Disciplines in the United States."

Ernst, Eldon G. "American Baptists and the New World Movement, 1918-1924." *Foundations* 8 (1965): 161-71.

Flower, Elizabeth, and Murphey, Murray G. *A History of Philosophy in America.* 2 vols. New York: G.P. Putnam's Sons, Capricorn Books, 1977.

Funk, Robert W. "The Watershed of American Biblical Tradition: The Chicago School, First Phase, 1892-1920." *Journal of Biblical Literature* 95 (1976): 4-22.

Furay, Conal. *The Grass-Roots Mind in America: The American Sense of Absolutes.* New York: New Viewpoints/Franklin Watts, 1977.

Furniss, Norman F. *The Fundamentalist Controversy, 1918-1931.* Hamden CT: Archon Books, 1963. Originally published in 1954.

Gabriel, Ralph Henry. *The Course of American Democratic Thought.* New York: Ronald Press, 1940. Also 2d edition, 1956.

Gay, Peter. *The Enlightenment: An Interpretation; The Rise of Modern Paganism.* New York: Random House, Vintage Books, 1968. Originally published in 1966.

Gerrish, B. A. *Tradition and the Modern World: Reformed Theology in the Nineteenth Century.* Chicago: University of Chicago Press, 1978.

Gilkey, Langdon. "Social and Intellectual Sources of Contemporary Protestant Theology." In *Religion in America,* edited by William G. McLoughlin and Robert N. Bellah. Boston: Beacon Press, 1968. Originally published in 1966.

Glover, Willis B. *Evangelical Nonconformists and Higher Criticism in the Nineteenth Century.* London: Independent Press, 1964.

Gosse, Edmund. *Father and Son: A Study of Two Temperaments.* Edited by James Hepburn. New York: Oxford University Press, 1974. Originally published in 1907.

Gragg, Alan. *George Burman Foster: Religious Humanist.* Danville VA: Association of Baptist Professors of Religion, 1978.

Grave, S. A. "The Able and Fair Reasoning of Butler's Analogy." *Church History* 47 (1978): 308-24.

Greene, John C. *Darwin and the Modern World View.* Baton Rouge: Louisiana State University Press, 1961.

Handy, Robert T. "Fundamentalism and Modernism in Perspective." *Religion in Life* 24 (1954-1955): 381-94.

_____. *A History of the Churches in the United States and Canada.* New York: Oxford University Press, 1977.

Hays, Samuel P. *The Response to Industrialism: 1885-1914.* Chicago: University of Chicago Press, 1957.

Henry, Carl F. H. *Personal Idealism and Strong's Theology.* Wheaton IL: Van Kampen Press, 1951.

Higham, John. *History: Professional Scholarship in America.* New York: Harper and Row, Harper Torchbooks, 1973. Originally published in 1965.

_____. *Strangers in the Land: Patterns of American Nativism, 1860-1925.* New York: Atheneum, 1973. Originally published in 1955.

_____. *Writing American History: Essays on Modern Scholarship.* Bloomington: Indiana University Press, 1970.

Hill, Samuel S. "A Typology of American Restitutionism, From Frontier Revivalism and Mormonism to the Jesus Movement." *Journal of the American Academy of Religion* 44 (1976): 65-76.

Hoeveler, J. David, Jr. *James McCosh and the Scottish Intellectual Tradition: From Glasgow to Princeton.* Princeton: Princeton University Press, 1981.

Hoffecker, W. Andrew. *Piety and the Princeton Theologians: Archibald Alexander, Charles Hodge, and Benjamin Warfield.* Grand Rapids MI: Baker Book House, 1981.

Hofstadter, Richard. *The Age of Reform: From Bryan to F. D. R.* New York: Random House, Vintage Books, 1955.

_____. *Social Darwinism in American Thought.* Rev. ed. Boston: Beacon Press, 1955. Originally published in 1944.

Hoffman, Lars. "William Rainey Harper and the Chicago Fellowship." Ph.D. dissertation, University of Iowa, 1978.

Holifield, E. Brooks. *The Gentleman Theologians: American Theology in Southern Culture, 1795-1860.* Durham NC: Duke University Press, 1978.

Howe, Daniel Walker. "American Victorianism as a Culture." *American Quarterly* 27 (1975): 507-32.

Hudson, Winthrop S. *Baptists in Transition: Individualism and Christian Responsibility.* Valley Forge PA: Judson Press, 1979.

_____. "How American is Religion in America?" In *Reinterpretation in American Church History,* edited by Jerald C. Brauer. Chicago: University of Chicago Press. 1968.

_____. *The Great Tradition of the American Churches* (New York: Harper and Row, 1953).

_____. *Religion in America.* 3d ed. rev., New York: Charles Scribner's Sons, 1981. Originally published in 1965.

_____. Review of *Autobiography of Augustus Hopkins Strong,* edited by Crerar Douglas. *Christian Scholar's Review* 12 (1983): 264-65.

_____. "Walter Rauschenbusch and the New Evangelism." *Religion in Life* 30 (1961): 412-30.

Hughes, H. Stuart. *Consciousness and Society: The Reorientation of European Social Thought, 1890-1930.* New York: Random House, Vintage Books, 1961. Originally published in 1958.

Hutchison, William R., ed. *American Protestant Thought: The Liberal Era.* New York: Harper and Row, 1968.

_____. "Cultural Strain and Protestant Liberalism." *American Historical Review* 76 (1971): 386-411.

_____. "Modernism and Missions: The Liberal Search for an Exportable Christianity, 1875-1935." In *The Missionary Enterprise in China and America,* edited by John F. Fairbank. Cambridge MA: Harvard University Press, 1974.

_____. *The Modernist Impulse in American Protestantism.* Cambridge MA: Harvard University Press, 1976.

_____. "The Moral Equivalent for Imperialism." In *Missionary Ideologies in the Imperialist Era,* edited by Torben Christensen and Hutchison. Aarhus, Denmark: Aros Publishers, 1982.

Iggers, Georg G. *The German Conception of History.* Middletown CT: Wesleyan University Press, 1968.

_____. "The Idea of Progress: A Critical Reassessment." *American Historical Review* 71 (1965): 1-17.

Jahrer, Frederic Cople. *Doubters and Dissenters: Cataclysmic Thought in America, 1865-1918.* London: Free Press of Glencoe, 1964.

Johnson, Paul E. *A Shopkeeper's Millennium: Society and Revivals in Rochester, New York, 1815-1837.* New York: Hill and Wang, 1978.

Jones, Howard Mumford. "The Influence of European Ideas in Nineteenth-Century America." *American Literature* 7 (1935-1936): 241-73.

Jones, Maldwyn Allen. *American Immigration.* Chicago: University of Chicago Press, 1960.

Jordy, William H. *Henry Adams: Scientific Historian.* New Haven: Yale University Press, 1952.

Kantzer, Kenneth S. "Unity and Diversity in Evangelical Faith." In *The Evangelicals: What They Believe, Who They Are, Where They Are Changing,* edited by David F. Wells and John D. Woodbridge. Nashville: Abingdon Press, 1975.

Langford, Thomas A. *In Search of Foundations: English Theology, 1900-1920.* Nashville: Abingdon Press, 1969.

_____. *Practical Divinity: Theology in the Wesleyan Tradition*. Nashville: Abingdon Press, 1983.

Lee, Dwight E., and Beck, Robert N. "The Meaning of Historicism." *American Historical Review* 59 (1954): 568-77.

Lewis, R. W. B. *The American Adam: Innocence, Tragedy, and Tradition in the Nineteenth Century*. Chicago: University of Chicago Press, 1955.

Lichtheim, George. "The Concept of Ideology." In *Studies in the Philosophy of History*, edited by George H. Nadel. New York: Harper and Row, Harper Torchbooks 1965.

Link, Arthur S., and Catton, William B. *American Epoch: A History of the United States Since 1900*. 2 vols. 4th ed. New York: Alfred A. Knopf, 1973. Originally published in 3 vols. in 1955.

Loewenberg, Bert James. *Darwinism Comes to America, 1859-1900*. Philadelphia: Fortress Press, 1969. Originally published in 1941.

Louthan, Henry Thompson, ed. *The American Baptist Pulpit at the Beginning of the Twentieth Century*. Williamsburg VA: privately printed, 1903.

Lovejoy, Arthur O. *Essays in the History of Ideas*. New York: G. P. Putnam's Sons, 1960. Originally published in 1948.

_____. *The Great Chain of Being: A Study of the History of an Idea*. New York: Harper and Row, Harper Torchbooks, 1960. Originally published in 1936.

Luker, Ralph E. *A Southern Tradition in Theology and Social Criticism, 1830-1930: The Religious Liberalism and Social Conservatism of James Warley Miles, William Porcher Dubose, and Edgar Gardner Murphy*. Lewiston NY: Edwin Mellen Press, 1984.

McDonald, Hugh Dermot. *Theories of Revelation: An Historical Study, 1860-1960*. London: G. Allen and Unwin, 1963.

MacHaffie, Barbara Zink. " 'Monument Facts and Higher Critical Fancies': Archaeology and the Popularization of Old Testament Criticism in Nineteenth-Century Britain." *Church History* 50 (1981): 319-28.

Macintosh, Douglas Clyde, ed. Introduction. *Christianity in Its Modern Expression*. New York: Macmillan, 1921.

Mandelbaum, Maurice. *History, Man, and Reason: A Study in Nineteenth-Century Thought*. Baltimore: Johns Hopkins University Press, 1971.

Mannheim, Karl. *Ideology and Utopia: An Introduction to the Sociology of Knowledge*. Translated by Louis Wirth and Edward Shils. New York: Harcourt, Brace and World, 1936.

Manuel, Frank E. *The Eighteenth Century Confronts the Gods.* New York: Atheneum, 1967. Originally published in 1959.

_____. *Shapes of Philosophical History.* Stanford CA: Stanford University Press, 1965.

Marcell, David W. *Progress and Pragmatism: James, Dewey, Beard, and the American Idea of Progress.* Westport CT: Greenwood Press, 1974.

Maring, Norman H. "Baptists and Changing Views of the Bible, 1865-1918." *Foundations* 1 (July 1958): 52-75; 1(October 1958): 30-61.

_____. "Conservative But Progressive." In *What God Hath Wrought: Eastern's First Thirty-Five Years,* edited by Gilbert L. Guffin. Chicago: Judson Press, 1960.

Marsden, George M. "The Collapse of American Evangelical Academia." In *Faith and Rationality: Reason and Belief in God,* edited by Alvin Plantinga and Nicholas Wolterstorff. Notre Dame IN: University of Notre Dame Press, 1983.

_____. "Everyone One's Own Interpreter? The Bible, Science, and Authority in Mid-Nineteenth-Century America." In *The Bible in America: Essays in Cultural History,* edited by Nathan O. Hatch and Mark A. Noll. New York: Oxford University Press, 1982.

_____. *Fundamentalism and American Culture: The Shaping of Twentieth-Century Evangelicalism, 1870-1925.* New York: Oxford University Press, 1980.

_____. "Fundamentalism as an American Phenomenon: A Comparison with English Evangelicalism." *Church History* 46 (1977): 215-32.

_____. "J. Gresham Machen, History, and Truth." *Westminster Theological Journal* 42 (1979): 157-75.

Marty, Martin E. "America's Iconic Book." In *Humanizing America's Iconic Book; Society of Biblical Literature Centennial Addresses 1980,* edited by Gene M. Tucker and Douglas A. Knight. Chico CA: Scholars Press, 1983.

Masur, Gerhard. *Prophets of Yesterday: Studies in European Culture, 1890-1914.* New York: Macmillan, 1961.

May, Henry F. *The End of American Innocence: A Study of the First Years of Our Own Time, 1912-1917.* Chicago: Quadrangle Paperbacks, 1964. Originally published in 1959.

_____. *The Enlightenment in America.* Oxford: Oxford University Press, 1976.

May, Mark A. *The Education of American Ministers.* 4 vols. New York: Institute of Social and Religious Research, 1934.

Mead, Sidney E. *The Lively Experiment: The Shaping of Christianity in America*. New York: Harper and Row, 1963.

Meland, Bernard E. "The Empirical Tradition in Theology at Chicago." In *The Future of Empirical Theology*, edited by Bernard E. Meland. Chicago: University of Chicago Press, 1969.

Meyer, D. H. "American Intellectuals and the Victorian Crisis of Faith." *American Quarterly* 27 (1975): 585-603.

_____. *The Instructed Conscience: The Shaping of the American National Ethic*. Philadelphia: University of Pennsylvania Press, 1972.

Meyer, Donald H. *The Democratic Enlightenment*. New York: G. P. Putnam's Sons, 1976.

Meyerhoff, Hans, ed. *The Philosophy of History in Our Time: An Anthology*. Garden City: Doubleday Anchor Books, 1959.

Mikolaski, Samuel J. "P. T. Forsyth." In *Creative Minds in Contemporary Theology*, edited by Philip Edgecumbe Hughes. Grand Rapids MI: William B. Eerdmans, 1966.

Miller, Perry, ed. *American Thought: Civil War to World War I*. San Francisco: Rinehart Press, 1954.

Moehlman, Conrad Henry. "How the Baptist Super-University Planned for New York City Was Built in Chicago." *Colgate Rochester Divinity School Bulletin* 11 (1938-1939): 119-34.

_____. "Walter Rauschenbusch and His Interpreters." *Crozer Quarterly* 23 (1946): 34-50.

Moore, James R. *The Post-Darwinian Controversies: A Study of the Protestant Struggle to Come to Terms with Darwin in Great Britain and America, 1870-1900*. Cambridge: Cambridge University Press, 1979.

Moore, LeRoy, Jr. "Academic Freedom: A Chapter in the History of Colgate Rochester Divinity School." *Foundations* 10 (1967): 64-79.

_____. "Another Look at Fundamentalism: A Response to Ernest R. Sandeen." *Church History* 37 (1968): 195-202.

_____. "The Rise of American Religious Liberalism at the Rochester Theological Seminary, 1872-1928." Ph.D. dissertation, Claremont Graduate School, 1966.

Morison, William James. "George Frederick Wright: In Defense of Darwinism and Fundamentalism, 1838-1921." Ph.D. dissertation, Vanderbilt University, 1971.

National Cyclopedia of American Biography. S. v. "Strong, Augustus Hopkins."

Nelson, Roland Tenus. "Fundamentalism and the Northern Baptist Convention." Ph.D. dissertation, University of Chicago, 1964.

Nelson, Rudolph L. "Fundamentalism at Harvard: The Case of Edward John Carnell." *Quarterly Review* 2 (1982): 79-98.

Nevins, Allan. *John D. Rockefeller: The Heroic Age of American Enterprise.* 2 vols. New York: Charles Scribner's Sons, 1940.

Nisbet, Robert A. *Social Change and History: Aspects of the Western Theory of Development.* New York: Oxford University Press, 1969.

Noble, David W. *The Paradox of Progressive Thought.* Minneapolis: University of Minnesota Press, 1958.

_____. "The Religion of Progress in America, 1890-1914." *Social Research* 22 (1955): 417-40.

Noll, Mark A. "Christian Thinking and the Rise of the American University." *Christian Scholar's Review* 9 (1979): 3-16.

_____. *The Princeton Theology, 1812-1921: Scripture, Science, and Theological Method from Archibald Alexander to B. B. Warfield.* Grand Rapids MI: Baker Book House, 1983.

Persons, Stow. *American Minds: A History of Ideas.* New York: Holt, Rinehart and Winston, 1958.

_____. *Evolutionary Thought in America.* New Haven: Yale University Press, 1950.

_____. "Religion and Modernity, 1865-1914." In *The Shaping of American Religion,* edited by James Ward Smith and A. Leland Jamison. Princeton: Princeton University Press, 1964.

Pinnock, Clark H. "The Modernist Impulse at McMaster University, 1887-1927." In *Baptists in Canada: Search for Identity Amidst Diversity,* edited by Jarold K. Zeman. Burlington, Ontario: G. R. Welch, 1980.

Pointer, Steven Roy. "The Perils of History: The Meteoric Career of Joseph Cook (1838-1901)." Ph.D. dissertation, Duke University, 1981.

Purcell, Edward A. "American Jurisprudence Between the Wars." *American Historical Review* 75 (1969-1970): 424-46.

_____. *The Crisis of Democratic Theory: Scientific Naturalism and the Problem of Value.* Lexington: University Press of Kentucky, 1973.

_____. "Social Thought." *American Quarterly* 35 (1983): 80-100.

Reist, Irwin. "Augustus Hopkins Strong and William Newton Clarke: A Study in Nineteenth Century Evolutionary and Eschatological Thought." *Foundations* 13 (1970): 26-43.

Rice, Daniel F. "An Attempt at Systematic Reconstruction in the Theology of Thomas Chalmers." *Church History* 48 (1979): 174-88.

Roark, Dallas M. "J. Gresham Machen: The Doctrinally True Presbyterian Church." *Journal of Presbyterian History* 43 (1965): 124-38, 174-81.

Robins, Henry Burke. "Dr. Strong's 'Theology': An Appreciation." *Rochester Theological Seminary Record* 2 (1907): 9.

Rogers, Jack B., and McKim, Donald K. *The Authority and Interpretation of the Bible: An Historical Approach.* San Francisco: Harper and Row, 1979.

Rossiter, Clinton. *Conservatism in America: The Thankless Persuasion.* 2d ed., rev. New York: Random House, Vintage Books, 1962. Originally published in 1955.

Russell, C. Allyn. *Voices of American Fundamentalism: Seven Biographical Studies.* Philadelphia: Westminster Press, 1976.

Russett, Cynthia Eagle. *Darwin in America: The Intellectual Response, 1865-1912.* San Francisco: W. H. Freeman, 1976.

Sandeen, Ernest R. "The Baptists and Millenarianism." *Foundations* 13 (1970): 18-25.

_____. *The Roots of Fundamentalism: British and American Millenarianism, 1800-1900.* Chicago: University of Chicago Press, 1970.

Sandon, Leo, Jr. "Boston University Personalism and Southern Baptist Theology." *Foundations* 20 (1979): 101-108.

Schlesinger, Arthur M., Jr., and White, Morton, eds. *Paths of American Thought.* Boston: Houghton, Mifflin, 1970. Originally published in 1963.

Schlesinger, Arthur Meier, Sr. *The Rise of the City, 1878-1898.* Chicago: Quadrangle Books, 1971. Originally published in 1933.

Schneider, Herbert W. *A History of American Philosophy.* 2d ed. New York: Columbia University Press, 1963. Originally published in 1946.

_____. *Religion in Twentieth Century America.* Cambridge MA: Harvard University Press, 1952.

Skotheim, Robert Allen. *American Intellectual Histories and Historians.* Princeton: Princeton University Press, 1966.

Smith, Gary S. "Calvinists and Evolution, 1870-1920." *Journal of Presbyterian History* 61 (1983): 335-53.

Smith, Gerald Birney. "George Burman Foster." *Biblical World* 53 (1919): 181-83.

Spiller, Robert E., and Larrabee, Eric, eds. *American Perspectives: The National Self-Image in the Twentieth Century.* Cambridge MA: Harvard University Press, 1961.

Stonehouse, Ned B. *J. Gresham Machen: A Biographical Memoir.* Grand Rapids MI: William B. Eerdmans, 1955.

Strout, Cushing. "The Twentieth-Century Enlightenment." *American Political Science Review* 49 (1955): 321-39.

_____. "The Unfinished Arch: William James and the Idea of History." *American Quarterly* 13 (1961): 505-515.

Sweet, Leonard I. Review of *Autobiography of Augustus Hopkins Strong,* edited by Crerar Douglas. [Colgate-Rochester Divinity School] *Bulletin from the Hill* 54 (1982): 4.

_____. "The University of Chicago Revisited: The Modernization of Theology, 1890-1940." *Foundations* 22 (1979): 324-51.

Symington, Thomas A. *Religious Liberals and Conservatives: A Comparison.* New York: Teachers College, Columbia University, 1935.

Szasz, Ferenc Morton. *The Divided Mind of Protestant America, 1880-1930.* University AL: University of Alabama Press, 1982.

Thelen, David P. "Social Tensions and the Origins of Progressivism." *Journal of American History* 56 (1969): 323-41.

Tinder, Donald. "Fundamentalist Baptists in the Northern and Western United States, 1920-1950." Ph.D. dissertation, Yale University, 1969.

Torbet, Robert G. *A History of the Baptists.* Valley Forge PA: Judson Press, 1963. Originally published in 1950.

_____. *Venture of Faith: The Story of the American Baptist Foreign Mission Society.* Philadelphia: Judson Press, 1955.

Towne, Edgar A. "A 'Singleminded' Theologian: George Burman Foster at Chicago." *Foundations* 20 (1977): 36-59, 163-80.

Trachtenberg, Alan. *The Incorporation of America: Culture and Society in the Gilded Age.* New York: Hill and Wang, 1982.

Tuveson, Ernest Lee. *Millennium and Utopia: A Study in the Background of the Idea of Progress.* New York: Harper and Row, 1964. Originally published in 1949.

Vedder, Henry Clay. "Fifty Years of Baptist History." *Bibliotheca Sacra* 57 (1900): 660-79.

Veysey, Laurence R. *The Emergence of the American University.* Chicago: University of Chicago Press, 1965.

Wagar, W. Warren. *Good Tidings: The Belief in Progress from Darwin to Marcuse.* Bloomington: Indiana University Press, 1972.

Warner, Sam Bass, Jr. *The Urban Wilderness: A History of the American City.* New York: Harper and Row, 1972.

Welch, Claude. *Protestant Thought in the Nineteenth Century: Volume 1, 1799-1870.* New Haven: Yale University Press, 1972.

West, William Beryl. "Theistic Evolution in the Writings of A. H. Strong and Bernard Ramm." Th.M. thesis, Southwestern Baptist Theological Seminary, Fort Worth, Texas, 1962.

White, Morton. *Science and Sentiment in America: Philosophical Thought from Jonathan Edwards to John Dewey.* London: Oxford University Press, 1972.

_____. *Social Thought in America: The Revolt Against Formalism.* Boston: Beacon Press, 1957. Originally published in 1947.

Wiebe, Robert H. "The Progressive Years, 1900-1917." In *The Reinterpretation of American History and Culture,* edited by William H. Cartwright and Richard L. Watson. Washington DC: National Council for the Social Studies, 1973.

_____. *The Search for Order: 1877-1920.* New York: Hill and Wang, 1967.

_____. *The Segmented Society: An Introduction to the Meaning of America.* New York: Oxford University Press, 1975.

Wieman, Henry Nelson, and Meland, Bernard Eugene. *American Philosophies of Religion.* Chicago: Willett, Clark, 1936.

Willey, Basil. *The Eighteenth Century Background: Studies on the Idea of Nature.* Boston: Beacon Press, 1961. Originally published in 1946.

_____. *Nineteenth Century Studies: Coleridge to Matthew Arnold.* New York: Columbia University Press, 1949.

Williams, Daniel Day. "Tradition and Experience in American Theology." In *The Shaping of American Religion,* edited by James Ward Smith and A. Leland Jamison. Princeton: Princeton University Press, 1961.

Wills, Garry. *Inventing America: Jefferson's Declaration of Independence.* New York: Random House, Vintage Books, 1979. Originally published in 1978.

Wish, Harvey. *The American Historian: A Social-Intellectual History of the Writing of the American Past.* New York: Oxford University Press, 1960.

Witmer, S. A. *The Bible College Story.* Manhasset NY: Channel Press, 1962.

Woodbridge, John D. et al., eds. *The Gospel in America: Themes in the Story of America's Evangelicals*. Grand Rapids MI: Zondervan Publishing House, 1979.

Index